WHAT IS MORALITY?

Donal Harrington

What is Morality?

the columba press

First published in 1996 by
the columba press
93 The Rise, Mount Merrion, Blackrock, Co Dublin

Cover by Bill Bolger
Origination by The Columba Press
Printed in Ireland by Colour Books Ltd, Dublin

ISBN 1 85607 149 9

Acknowledgements
I would like to acknowledge with gratitude the friends and col-
leagues who generously read the manuscript. Their observations
have been a great help and encouragement.

Contents

Introduction

The topic of this book is the way we think about morality – not so much *what* we think, but *how* we think. There is no extended consideration of the ethics of war or divorce or euthanasia or any of the other specific issues that concern us as a society and as a Church. The book is written a step back from the details of such topics, in order to focus on the ways in which we approach moral issues.

The background for this is the pluralism in society and the tension in the Church concerning morality. In our society we are still learning to contend with widespread and often fundamental disagreement about very important moral issues. As a Church, we are still coming to terms with the gaps that exist between what is proposed by the teaching authority and what is the thinking and practice of God's people on a range of moral questions.

The basic idea of this book is that part of what is involved in these tensions and disagreements is that people think about morality in different ways. Besides differences on particular issues, there is the diversity in how people approach the issues in the first place. Mutual incomprehension is sometimes due to people having differing conceptions of what morality itself is all about.

This book seeks to bring some of these differences to light. The presumption throughout is that diversity is enriching. It is presumed that there is truth on all sides and that a rounded or comprehensive perspective on morality may be attained through an appreciation of the various ways in which people think about the nature of morality itself.

The first chapter presents an outline sketch of five ways of looking at morality. The five ways are presented under the headings of morality as law, morality as inner conviction, morality as personal growth, morality as love, and morality as social transformation. Each approach yields a valuable and indispensable perspective on

morality. Any of them on its own is only partial and is in fact impoverished if there is no reference to the other four. All together make
for a rich and rounded appreciation of the meaning of morality.

Chapters two, three and four take three important themes in morality
and consider each from the perspective of all five approaches, so as to
illustrate the need for, and the value of, a comprehensive viewpoint.
The three themes are the ten commandments, God and morality, and
the sense of sin. Chapter five reflects on how Jesus understood morality, and relates his understanding to the five approaches.

The remainder of the book goes into a more detailed exploration of
the different perspectives. The five approaches are categorised into
three groups, namely, those with an objective or act-centred focus
(morality as law), those with a subjective or person-centred focus
(morality as inner conviction, morality as personal growth, morality
as love), and those with a social focus (morality as love again, and
morality as social transformation).

Under the heading of an objective style of moral theology, we consider
the themes of the natural law and the 'small print' in moral theology
(chapters six and seven). Under the heading of a person-centred style
of moral theology, we reflect on the themes of freedom, love, conversion, and conscience (chapters eight, nine and ten). Under the heading of a socially-oriented style of moral theology, we reflect on the
theme of justice, on the theme of sexuality, and on the image of the
Church as 'home' (chapters eleven, twelve and thirteen).

Divisions of this kind are somewhat artificial, as can be seen in the
way that morality as love straddles different categories. Indeed it
will be found that the categories link into each other in different
ways. This may be seen as an indication both of the value of the different approaches and of the desirability of a comprehensive viewpoint.

While much of what is discussed might be new to people, much
more of the discussion might be seen as confirming and putting
shape on what people are already thinking for themselves. For, in
the context of our daily decisions and our experience of life, we all
reflect on morality and we all have our own wisdom on how to go
about living well. I hope that this book succeeds in giving expression to some of that wisdom.

CHAPTER 1

Five ways of looking at morality

The main concern of this chapter is to present in outline five different but inter-related ways of looking at morality. This is the foundation on which the rest of the book will be built.

From What to How

People differ in their views on moral issues both in the Church and
in society generally today. Such difference may well be the most
striking aspect of the contemporary experience of morality, though
some would find it confusing while others find it enriching. But
underneath the different views people have on particular issues,
there are different ideas as to what morality itself is.

These underlying differences are reflected in the language people
use. One person says: 'If you do what you feel is right, then you are
right.' Another says: 'Young people don't know the ten commandments anymore.' Yet another says: 'All that really matters is love.'
Such differences themselves raise further questions. Should we do
as we feel or as we are told? Is there an objective right and wrong? Is
love enough?

For the moment, though, let us stay with the statement that people
differ in their ideas as to what morality means. Frequently these
ideas are more implicit than explicit. People may be quite clear in
their own minds as to their views on the rights and wrongs of lying
or violence or divorce or euthanasia. But their differences on such
issues may conceal underlying differences about the nature of
morality of which the individuals themselves are not fully aware.

In order to get in touch with these underlying ideas, we would need
to stand back a little from the firmness of our convictions and the
heat of debate. We would need to turn the spotlight from *what* we
think to *how* we think. We might then find that there is a range of

factors that come into play in moral discussions, such as feeling and principles and love and consequences. We might find that our own personal style or method of thinking represents a good balance of these factors, or that it emphasises some more than others, or even that it concentrates on one to the neglect of others.

Some may have already worked out these matters for themselves. Many of us, however, will not have done so. Many of us have simply fallen into a particular way of thinking. That style of thinking may have come from our parents or it may have come from reacting against our parents. It may have come from the culture or it may be counter-cultural. But the point is that it is more like something that has happened to us than something we have really sorted out for ourselves. As a result we may be less free than we suppose in our ethical thinking.

The concern of this chapter is to make explicit some of these underlying ways of thinking about morality. We will identify and outline five different ways of thinking about morality. These are: morality understood as law; morality as inner conviction; morality as personal growth; morality as love; and morality as social transformation. But these will only be sketched in at this point. Many themes deserving of greater elaboration will be taken up in greater detail later in the book.

It may well be that the reader will think of other approaches, or will prefer to put these ones differently, but these five seem to be fairly representative of the range of ways we see morality. While it will be easy to recognise all five, we may be able to recognise only some of them in the way we ourselves think. All five are right in the sense that each stands for some important aspect of morality. One might, however, feel that some present a fuller picture than others.

Somebody once used the phrase: 'the truth looks different from here'. The phrase suggests both a sense that there is something objective and a sense that there are different perspectives. There is something that we call morality, but it looks different from different perspectives. It is like looking into a room through its different windows; each view is real and true and still it is only one view. Somewhat similarly, each of these five ways of looking at morality is a valid view, but only the five together yield a complete picture.[1]

Morality as Law

The first way of looking at morality is to see it in terms of law. This is probably the one that will be most familiar to us, both from our experience of living in society and from our experience in the Church. But it is also one that is often dismissed too hastily because of the negative connotations it can have.

In this view morality is something external, in the sense that it is not something of our own creation but rather something that imposes itself upon us. It is given to us, not made by us; something we discover and not something we create. One thinks of the famous lines in Sophocles' play *Antigone* where the eponymous heroine resists the unjust laws of King Creon:

> 'Nor did I think that your orders were so strong that you, a mortal man, could over-run the gods' unwritten and unfailing laws.'

To speak of morality as law is to speak of it as being bigger than any of us. While society can make and change its laws, the moral law is different. It is beyond our determination and to it we must submit.

Because morality is understood as coming from outside of us, it is often associated with an authority figure. Morality is seen to come from our parents, or the parish priest, or the Pope. If this aspect is strongly emphasised, it can appear that a particular action is wrong or right because this figure says so, rather than on the grounds of rational arguments. Some people who see morality this way, when asked why a particular action is wrong, cannot give any reasons other than 'because the Pope (or some other authority figure) says so.'

The truth, however, is that not alone does morality come from outside of us, but it also comes from outside such authority figures. In other words, morality is founded on the nature of things and not on any individual will; it is *objective*. What morality understood as law emphasises is that there is a moral order to the universe and that it is not within any human being's power to decide what that order is. At the same time we can work it out, through reflection and discussion. To help us work it out, authority figures interpret this order to us or for us; but they do not create it.

Because this view of morality is so closely associated in our minds with authority, our own role has often been cast in terms of duty or obedience. It is probably no exaggeration to say that, a generation or two ago, such words seemed to sum up what for most people morality was all about. Obedience was the fundamental virtue. One thinks of the words of Jesus: 'Do you thank the servant because he did what was commanded? So you also, when you have done all that was commanded you, say, "We are unworthy servants; we have only done what was our duty"' (Luke 17:9-10).

We could easily slip into caricature when reflecting on the language of authority and obedience in morals, and so these words of Jesus are salutary. Of course obedience may and often does become blind subservience, particularly in a culture of hierarchy and uniformity, but in the present context what the word entails primarily is the recognition that the moral order is something greater than ourselves, not of our own making, and therefore demanding our profound respect.

The words *reward* and *punishment* are also very much a part of this way of looking at morality. They stand for the outcomes of moral behaviour. If morality comes to me as a demand from without, as law, and if the response called for is a sense of duty and an attitude of obedience, then reward is what follows on such a response, punishment on its opposite. The sanctions themselves may be anything from a sweet or a spanking for a child, to the eternal sanctions we know as heaven and hell.

Sometimes it is felt that this language betrays a selfish moral attitude. The morality of Christians is compared with that of others who have no religious affiliation. It is said that, for the latter, morality is purer because done for its own sake, whereas the religious motivation may be far from other-centred and more a matter of 'saving my soul'. No doubt this is sometimes the case and it is another instance of how the view of morality as law may become distorted.

In the chapter about God and morality, we shall ask what it means to say that God rewards and punishes. But in the present context we might just remark that the language of reward and punishment is often extrinsic language, in that it usually refers to another conferring some benefit or burden on me because of what I have done. But it sometimes has a different sense; for instance, when we say that virtue is its own reward, we are speaking of an outcome that is intrinsic to the action itself.

Morality as Inner Conviction

The term 'inner conviction' not alone describes the second way of looking at morality, but also captures the contrast between it and the first way. Whereas in the first way morality came from without, here it arises from within. This too can be caricatured, as if morality were simply something we make up for ourselves as we go along. Rather, what is meant is that morality has been internalised. It is not simply an imposition by some authority, demanding our obedience, but it is a requirement arising from an inner conviction.

As a psychological experience, inner conviction comes later in life than obedience. A child can obey without knowing why; it is only later that we grow in the capacity to think for ourselves. But when we can think out right and wrong for ourselves, then we make the law our own. Now we can see for ourselves why the law commends this and forbids that. It is now an inner law, where values are personal convictions and not arbitrary impositions. In exceptional cases we may even come to the conviction that a particular formulation of the moral law is wrong or inapplicable or in conflict with moral value.

This inner law goes by the name of conscience and thus conscience is a key word within this second perspective on morality. Vatican II's document *The Church in the Modern World* put it that 'deep within our conscience we discover a law which we have not laid upon ourselves but which we must obey' (paragraph 16). This is the inner law, the law which has become part of a person, a person's own conscientious conviction. We come to the stage, for instance, when we no longer need another to tell us not to steal because we have come to see and feel its injustice for ourselves.

But at this stage, the language of law and obedience, which is used in the quotation from Vatican II, begins to appear inadequate because of its external focus. To describe what is meant by being moral or not being moral, words like *integrity* and *authenticity* are now more appropriate. If values are internalised and if conviction comes from within, then morality is a matter of being faithful to our inner voice or inner wisdom. This is what is meant by speaking of a person of integrity, one who does not betray deeply held convictions on what is felt to be right because of some temptation of gain or some pressure of the moment.

Likewise, the language of reward and punishment yields to something less extrinsic. If morality comes from within it hardly makes sense to think in terms of an external authority conferring reward or punishment. Instead, reward and punishment are seen as self-bestowed or self-inflicted. This is where we speak of the alternatives of inner peace *versus* inner disquiet.

The inner peace of a good conscience attends the knowledge that I have been true to my principles. The reward is all the greater if this integrity has been achieved at some price, if it has cost some sacrifice along the way. On the other hand, an inner disquiet accompanies the realisation that I have failed myself by going against what I know to be right. I feel guilty, my conscience is pained. To the conscientious person, no externally imposed punishment could be more painful than this disappointment with self.

Morality as Personal Growth

With this third way of looking at morality we achieve a very valuable expansion of our understanding. What sets it off from the first two ways is that, whereas they focus mainly on our moral behaviour in itself, what we do and what we shun, now the focus is shifted onto ourselves. We move, in other words, from the action being done to the person doing it. Our attention shifts to what is happening the person as a result of the action.

Take, for example, the telling of lies. We can speak in terms of a commandment that prohibits telling lies, and we can even inquire what exceptions there might be to this command. In terms of morality as inner conviction, we can speak of a conscientious conviction as to the wrongfulness of deceit and the harmfulness of deceiving. But this third view of morality adds a further perspective by asking: what happens the person? It suggests that the real tragedy in deceit lies not in the infringement of a law but in a person's becoming dishonest, or in a relationship becoming false thereby.

In the moral tradition this way of seeing things is represented by the language of *virtue* and *vice*. While this language has lost much of its richness today (think of phrases such a person of 'easy virtue' or 'the vice squad'), within the moral tradition it refers to a way of thinking about morality that emphasises the personal qualities that are the outcome of behaving consistently in determinate ways. Virtues and vices are the good and bad dispositions or qualities that result from and then inspire our actions.

If I repeatedly lie, I become more of a deceitful person, and the more I do so, the more am I inclined by this vicious quality to behave thus on future occasions. And the same is true of the converse. Thomas Aquinas remarked that it is very hard for people in the state of grace to commit sin, because their whole inclination goes against it. Thus virtues and vices might be called moral habits. They are dispositions which arise out of patterns of behaviour and which then dispose the person to act in certain ways in the future.

It is worth noting that this way of thinking is of great antiquity, just as is the language of law. While the Old Testament was setting forth what we know as the ten commandments, the Greek philosophers Plato and Aristotle were articulating a view of morality in terms of virtue. Their influence is reflected in the fact that the great thirteenth century theologian Thomas Aquinas, in composing the moral section of his compendium of theology, the *Summa Theologiae*, chose virtue rather than commandment as his framework – the theological virtues of faith, hope and charity, and the cardinal virtues of prudence, justice, courage and temperance. It is only in more recent centuries that the language of law has dominated to the extent of almost eclipsing from our horizon the language of virtue.

In shifting the focus to what is happening the person, we also move from a more static to a more dynamic view of morality. The first and second views tend to be concerned in their different ways with the rights and wrongs of particular actions. But if the focus is on what is happening the person, then that allows us to speak of change in the person, be it development or regression. This is the language of moral conversion. It gives us access to the dynamics of challenge and change, of what it is like for people to try to change for the better.

Finally there are the outcomes of morality as understood within this view. Previously we had spoken of reward and punishment and of a good or uneasy conscience. In this third view we would speak of the contrast of wholeness *versus* fragmentation. The personal qualities that we call virtues are many, such as truthfulness, courage, humility, non-violence, compassion. Each might be seen as a partial realisation of self. So growth in virtue is a many-sided challenge and as growth proceeds on different fronts, albeit unevenly, we are becoming whole, the fully-rounded persons that God envisaged in our creation. Conversely, when virtue is mingled with vice, to that extent the thrust towards wholeness is frustrated and our moral being is becoming fragmented.

Morality as Love

For all that we have referred to already, there are still vast areas of morality that we have not touched on. This is because the first three perspectives all concentrate on the moral agent as an individual person. The remaining two perspectives add to this considerably by seeing morality in terms of relationship and by seeing the moral agent as fundamentally social. This, of course, is a welcome corrective to individualistic tendencies in moral thinking.

In speaking of morality as love, we have in mind the idea that we are primarily relational beings. To explain this we might think of the analogy of the pieces in a chess game. Apart from their place on the board the pieces are incomprehensible, shorn of their essential meaning. Likewise, people are social. They exist in relation to one another as do the pieces on the board. Apart from others we are cut off from essential aspects of what we are. Even hermits have spoken of their 'leaving' the world as a way of coming closer to the world.

Contemporary philosophy highlights the category of 'the other'. This suggests that the primary moral experience is an experience of other persons. Or, to use an image popular in moral theology, the structure of moral reality is one of 'invitation and response'. Because we all inhabit the same space, each of us, simply by virtue of our common humanity, exerts a call or invitation on each other. My presence before you is implicitly a call on you for your kindness and courtesy, a call on your sense of fairness and your sense of sympathy.

Within this perspective, being moral is a matter of being faithful to the fact of our interrelatedness and to the demands of relationship.

It is about becoming alive to that fact, and being responsive to the demands that it entails. It is about going beyond ourselves, transcending our own egoism and egoistic horizons, and in the process realising our existence as love – realising that what we are and can be is simply 'love'.

The alternative to this is betrayal. Betrayal means any stance or act or omission that amounts to a denial of our common humanity. Because morality is cast in terms of interrelatedness, what wrongdoing amounts to is basically a matter of betrayal of others or another, rather than a private matter. However, it should also be said that in failing others we are also failing ourselves. In not responding to the demands of relationship we are also betraying ourselves and missing out on our own self-realisation.

When morality is seen as love, the outcomes of being moral might be expressed in terms of communion *versus* isolation. Whereas reward and punishment refer to what happens people as a consequence of their actions, these terms speak of what happens to a relationship. Insofar as people assent to the invitation-response structure of existence, they grow in communion; insofar as they do not respond to the demands of relationship, they betray, and the outcome is isolation.

The words *communion* and *isolation* give a deeper insight into the meaning of reward and punishment. If morality is about responding in relationship, then communion is clearly the 'reward', though reward is no longer a serviceable term, as it suggests something extrinsicly added, whereas communion is the intrinsic outcome of being faithful to each other. Likewise, isolation is punishment in this intrinsic sense rather than an externally imposed sanction. When we recall that without relationship there is no flourishing, we can appreciate how great a punishment it is.

Morality as Social Transformation
The fifth and final way of looking at morality opens on to yet a further horizon. It continues to see morality as relationship but it goes beyond the small world of interpersonal relationships to the larger world that is society. And just as the view of morality as love was seen as a corrective to individualism in morality, so this broader view is to be welcomed for transcending the tendency to live within

our own small circle without any great advertence to the moral issues affecting society or the world as a whole. It also transcends the tendency to tribalism, the attitude that sees moral obligation extending only to our own – the attitude Jesus had in mind when he said: 'For if you love those who love you, what reward do you have? Do not even the tax collectors do the same?' (Matthew 5:46).

So moral obligation, like the ripples in the water, keeps reaching outwards. There is nobody who is not our neighbour; all humanity in some real way calls for our response. The word that stands for this perspective is 'justice' – a word that has come dramatically to the centre of moral consciousness in contemporary society. This is not to say that justice had hitherto been neglected; rather it has emerged with new meaning.

The classical definition was that justice is the constant determination to give to every person what is due to that person. However, it is fair to say that we have tended to think about this largely with reference to one-to-one relationships. What is new about today's sense of justice is its sense of responsibility, not just to the individual other, but also for the 'whole state of affairs'. This is captured by the now widely used term 'social justice'.

In this fifth way of looking at morality, being moral is about being personally affected by suffering and injustice and being motivated to do what one can in response. It is about a sense of solidarity with victims, all who lose out or are discriminated against or suffer, be they as near as next door or far across the globe. And responding is not just a matter of providing immediate aid; it also involves asking why the wrongs are happening and questioning the way things are structured in society.

The opposite of such solidarity is individualism. The pressure of competition encourages the individualistic mentality that it is everyone for himself or herself. When this mentality pervades, justice is reduced to keeping within the law, and any sense of solidarity is numbed by the pressure to get on and to succeed. It is not that getting on and succeeding are anything but good, but that something serious is wrong when their pressure is such as to numb the sense of solidarity, or even to rationalise it away in phrases such as 'a rising tide lifts all boats' and 'it's their own fault if they're poor'.

The possible outcomes of morality on this view could be described in terms of social peace *versus* division. When there is a lively sense of solidarity there is the possibility of transforming society into a place where the humanity of each is cherished and where nobody's suffering is tolerated. In the Christian tradition this is what is known as peace. To quote again from *The Church in the Modern World* (paragraph 78): 'Peace is more than the absence of war... A firm determination to respect the dignity of other persons and other peoples, along with the deliberate practice of fraternal love, are absolutely necessary for the achievement of peace.' Whereas if the individualistic ethic prevails, to that extent the divisions that are already there are only deepened and, as the saying goes, the rich get richer and the poor get poorer.

Finally, a further dimension of this view of morality should be acknowledged. It is that, as the concept of justice has broadened in recent times in the way described, it has also come to embrace the issue of humanity's relationship to the environment and to proclaim this to be a moral question of immense proportions. In some real sense, our 'solidarity' is to be with all of creation. We are to understand all creation as one great community or partnership of being and we, the conscious or reflective level in the whole of creation, are called to learn respect and to repent abuse.

Morality as Law	
Duty, Obedience	Reward *versus* Punishment
Morality as Inner Conviction	
Conscience, Integrity	Inner Peace *versus* Disquiet
Morality as Personal Growth	
Virtue, Conversion	Wholeness *versus* Fragmentation
Morality as Love	
Faithfulness, Response	Communion *versus* Isolation
Morality as Social Transformation	
Justice, Solidarity	Social Peace *versus* Division

Integrating the Five Approaches

As we said at the start, we have each of us our own way of seeing morality and this fivefold schematisation may help clarify or make explicit for each of us the way we have been seeing things. But if it transpires that one of these ways has taken precedence in our thinking, the question arises as to how we can take account of, and incorporate, the other four.

For a start it might be remarked that the five are not so self-contained as to have no relationship to each other. There are certain points of contact and we could even regard each of the five as seeing the same truth through a different 'window', so that we can translate from one to another. For example, where the law says 'thou shalt not kill', the language of personal growth would speak of the call to become a non-violent person. Again, it is not so much that 'inner peace' and 'communion', or 'duty' and 'integrity', are different realities, as that they are different ways of talking about a single reality.

So we can say that all five perspectives are right. Each offers some indispensable truth about and insight into morality, yet each on its own is incomplete. Each possesses a piece of the truth so that, on its own, it is both valuable and partial. Even as we moved from one to the next, we saw new horizons on morality opening up, challenging us to achieve a comprehensive viewpoint. Each of us is still entitled to our preference, in the sense of being attracted to either law or inner conviction or personal growth or love or social transformation as the motif of our moral sensibility. But we are also obliged to take account of the other four and to integrate them into our perspective.

Failure to integrate one with the rest leaves us with an impoverished and possibly distorted perspective. This failure accounts for many aberrations in moral theory and practice. For instance, what is 'legalism' but a focus on the first approach which neglects the other four? Surely moral law is an articulation of what justice in society is all about, of what love means, of the direction in which personal growth is to be pursued, of how inner conviction is to be formed. If our appreciation of moral law is not informed and inspired by these further perspectives, then it becomes just law, absorbed in itself, missing the wood for the trees – so that people are burdened with demands that make no sense because there is no meaningful reference frame.

Likewise, what is 'subjectivism' but an adoption of the second approach that ignores the rest? Inner conviction is a valid base from which to talk about morality, but subjectivism in its pejorative sense means an emphasis on 'following my conscience' that is oblivious to the truth that conscience itself is nothing other than the capacity to appreciate the underlying meaning of moral law, of the dynamics of moral growth, and of the complex demands of love and justice.

If morality as personal growth is taken on its own, it may be reduced to a search for personal fulfilment that has little reference to others. What the moral law reveals is that personal growth is a matter of love and justice, and without this understanding we may be left with a much impoverished idea of growth as pursuit of fulfilment in a very self-centred sense.

In relation to the fourth approach taken on its own, we might refer to the term 'situation ethics'. This stands for the theory which holds that morality has only one absolute, namely, to do the loving thing. After that, it depends on the situation what the loving thing may be. Here love comes to mean nothing because it can mean anything. It lacks any of the definition it would have if it were to be interpreted in the light of the other ways of seeing morality.

Lastly, commitment to justice is distorted if seen in isolation. It must be subject to the demands of love and integrity if it is not to justify the use of any means in achieving its ends. One thinks of the utilitarian theory of 'the greatest good of the greatest number', whereby the individual might be sacrificed for the sake of the greater good. The desirability of what is striven after does not give a *carte blanche* to achieve it by any means.

All the same, such absolutising of a single perspective is understandable. Those who ask where have the ten commandments gone may feel that the only way to preserve the sense of right and wrong in society is to keep insisting on the need for law. But others feel equally strongly that we need to celebrate and cherish inner conviction because for too long people have been slaves to moral authority, unable to think for themselves, crippled by guilt. Others again say that all this is futile theorising and is taking our attention away from the real issues of injustice and violence in the world.

We can readily see the legitimacy of each concern, but we can also note the blindspot in each. Ultimately the absolutising of any one approach distorts our whole understanding of morality. If each approach could appreciate the insight contained in the other perspectives, a fuller truth would become available.

It is worth applying all this to the 'generation gap' as it affects morality and moral consciousness. The generations formed prior to Vatican II were formed very much along the lines of morality as law, while it is largely the younger generations that toast the language of freedom and conscience. The word 'largely' is used because there are many older people who have experienced the release of escaping from the painful constraints of law-become-legalism.

If we listen to the older generation we often hear, besides genuine admiration for the young, a bemoaning of 'the youth' and their (supposed) loss of moral standards, of their being captives to subjectivism and relativism. There is much truth in this, especially in thinking of it as a captivity. But there is also the shining truth that it is among the young that commitment to the fifth perspective, that of social solidarity and transformation, is most vibrant. Among young people, sexual morality is nowhere as black-and-white as among their parents; but they can be very absolute and unyielding in their moral principles concerning injustice, war and ecological destruction. Seen in this light, morality seen as law is alive and well, just that it has to be looked for somewhere else than hitherto.

The Five Approaches and Christian Morality

Up to this point, reference to God or to religion has been incidental, as we have been concentrating on morality in itself and on the different ways in which it can be understood. But if we now turn our attention to religion and morality, the question arises: does one or other of these perspectives do better justice than the others to the meaning of Christian morality? If each were imagined to be a kind of key, is there one which unlocks more of what Christian morality is all about? Or if each were seen as a language for speaking about morality, are some better able than others to articulate the full dimensions of Christian morality?

We might begin answering this question by noting that all five can be found represented in the Bible. The language of law is found throughout the Bible, in the Old Testament particularly. Many would think immediately of the ten commandments. If morality is approached in terms of inner conviction, we might think of the theme of the biblical theme of the 'heart' as the source of moral decisions, or of Jesus' emphasis on the significance of the intention behind the action. When it comes to the language of personal growth, Paul's three great virtues of faith, hope and charity come to mind. Morality as love is familiar all through the pages of the gospels. And when one thinks of morality as social transformation, the concern of the prophets for right relationships in society, as well as Jesus' love for the poor, come to mind.

All five are there in the pages of scripture, but it is perhaps fair to say that the language of law is the one that has preoccupied us. The tendency has been to view biblical morality through the lens of law. However, this is not so much because law is the dominant biblical perspective, as that it is what has dominated our approach to the Bible. And even though the language of law figures very prominently throughout the Bible, it can be argued both that it is not the crucial perspective in the Bible and that, as a key, it is limited in what it can unlock of the riches of biblical and Christian morality.

Indeed, if we confine ourselves to this approach we will quickly run into paradox. There is the paradox that to love simply in obedience to a commandment is not really to love. There is the paradox that Christians must be obedient as 'slaves of Christ' even though the same Christ has set them free (Galatians 5). Such paradoxes do not make the language of law invalid; they just reveal its limitations.

When Paul speaks of 'the law of the Spirit of life in Christ Jesus' (Romans 8:2), and when Thomas Aquinas speaks of the 'New Law' which is 'chiefly the grace itself of the Holy Spirit' (*Summa Theologiae*, II-I, 106, 1), it is clear that the idea of law cannot contain what they are talking about unless its meaning be transformed. They indicate to us that the language of law is inadequate for unlocking the deep meaning of Christian morality.

We might go on to suggest that the language of the second and third ways of looking at morality are incomplete also. For one thing, they are too much focused on the individual, whereas the Bible is more properly focused on the salvation of a people. They also concentrate on what the person is doing, whereas the Bible concentrates on the action of God as primary.

All this leads us to the fourth and fifth perspectives, with their language of invitation-response and of social transformation. These are perhaps the most promising approaches to the Bible. The covenant that lies at the heart of both testaments is presented as God's invitation calling on our response. And responding as a people to God's invitation is seen as the way towards right relationships throughout society.

However, we will leave further elaboration to the following three chapters where we will consider three important themes in biblical and Christian morality, namely, the ten commandments, God and morality, and sin, in terms of the five approaches. That will give us a fuller insight into the relevance of each of the five approaches in appreciating Christian morality.

Five Approaches: Three Styles

The final concern of this chapter will be to comment on the five approaches as they have manifested themselves in the recent history of moral theology. We would suggest that, when viewed in this historical context, they can be distilled down to three groups, representing what might be called an 'objective', a 'subjective' and a 'social' style of moral reflection, and that these appear as successive emphases in the recent history.[2] It is this threefold division that supplies the structure for the second part of the book (chapters six to thirteen), where each of the three (and thereby all five ways of seeing morality) will come in for more extended discussion.

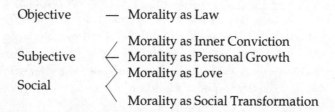

Objective	—	Morality as Law
Subjective		Morality as Inner Conviction
		Morality as Personal Growth
		Morality as Love
Social		Morality as Social Transformation

The style of moral theology up to the middle of the present century was very objective, very much a morality in terms of law. By objective is meant an approach to morality that concentrates on the action that is done or omitted. It works out whether a given line of action is right or wrong and it does this by considering, not so much the consequences of the act, but the principles and values that should guide moral behaviour, and the conformity, or lack of it, of the particular action to such principles or values.

As we shall see later, this style allows for the consideration of possible exceptions to the rule and the justification, if any, for such exceptions. It also includes consideration of factors such as fear or ignorance, which may diminish the person's freedom and responsibility. But what is notable is the brevity of the discussion of such factors, no more than a few pages in most texts, which effectively constituted no more than a footnote. What this means is that the more subjective aspects of morality lose out in the concentration on the objective.

In the years leading up to Vatican II, there emerged a new emphasis on morality from a subjective or personalist perspective, that is, with the focus on the person acting and not just on the act being done. Originally this was inspired by the renewed scriptural scholarship of the previous decades. That scholarship brought out the centrality in the Bible of themes such as conversion, discipleship and love. While at the heart of the gospels, these were strangely subdued and often absent in moral theology; in effect moral theology was often no more than moral philosophy. Books appeared in the 1950s with titles such as *The Primacy of Charity in the Moral Life*, *The Master Calls* and, best known, Bernard Häring's *The Law of Christ*. Häring's foreword announced that moral theology was to be focused on Christ and that it could not be viewed solely from the point of view of law.

The word *personalist* well describes this enrichment to moral theology. Without any depreciation of objectivity in morals, it brings the person to centre stage. It considers morality as a personal calling; it reflects on what that calling is and on what it entails. We can readily see how the perspectives on morality as inner conviction and as personal growth correspond with this. Seeing morality as love also belongs here, in that the personal calling that is at the heart of Christian morality is fundamentally a call to love.

In more recent years there has been taking place a further development in moral theology, which might be described as a move from the personal to the social. Of course, to see morality as love is already to see it as social, but this is social only in a modified sense. This is because, despite the personalist enrichment of a hitherto objectivist moral theology, much of the thrust was still in terms of an individual person making a moral decision and on the demands of interpersonal relationships. Much of the focus had now shifted from the decision and action to the person deciding, but the frame was still largely individualist.

The shift to the social in moral theology has to do with its experiencing the fruits of the 'liberation theology' that swept into western thinking from Latin America in the 1970s. Here, theology starts with reflecting on the inequalities and injustices in society. This contrasts with the previous style, which discussed mainly the rights and wrongs of an individual's actions. It corresponds to the shift that begins in our fourth way of looking at morality (morality as love) and which emerges fully in the perspective that sees morality in terms of justice and social transformation.

With this scheme of objective-personalist-social in mind, we can ask how different people in the Church think about morality today. We can ask: how do members of Christ's faithful actually think about and think through their Christian morality? How do moral theologians think about morality? How do Church leaders think about morality?

Take moral theologians first. It is quite surprising how many textbooks presenting themselves as introductions to moral theology, many of them regarded as 'state of the art' works, contain little or no reference to the themes of justice and social transformation. These are left to 'applied' moral theology. In their methodology moral theologians are still very much involved in the transition from an objective to a personalist way of seeing morality. This may explain why themes such as freedom, conscience and authority are such major preoccupations in their writings.

If the discipline of moral theology is still thus engaged in the debate on the relationship between objective and subjective morality, Church teaching about morality appears even less attentive to subjective or personalist aspects. This would seem to be because of its concern to protect an objective moral order against the perceived threat of relativism. However, it must be said that many Church documents are much more alive to morality in the socio-political mode, as is witnessed by a now century-long tradition of social teaching. This is a point that will be developed in a later chapter.

What then of the individual disciple? How does he or she think about morality? There is hardly a single answer. Some think very much in the language of conscience and feel great tensions in relation to the morality of law and authority. Others are firmly rooted in the language of law. Others again find themselves uncomfortably between the two. Others still have been taken up by the cries for justice in the world and see morality very much through the prism of this passion. At the end of this chapter the question that is left for each of us is: where do you stand yourself?

CHAPTER 2

The Ten Commandments

Reference has already been made to the sentiment expressed in such words as, 'where have the ten commandments gone?' This chapter will propose an answer to that question, but will do so in the light of the first chapter. We want to see what happens when the schema of five ways of looking at morality is applied to this central theme within Christian morality.

More than Guidelines

From the *Catechism of the Council of Trent* (1566) to the recent *Catechism of the Catholic Church* (1992), the ten commandments have funct-ioned as the framework for setting forth the Church's moral teach-ings. Because the commandments have such an important place in scripture and because they articulate fundamental moral and reli-gious values, they provide a good basis also for presenting moral teachings that are not actually envisaged within the command-ments themselves. Thus, for example, euthanasia can be considered in relation to the commandment not to kill, or media ethics in rela-tion to the commandment not to bear false witness. As a result, the ten commandments have come to be seen as a summary statement of the main principles of Christian morality.

This is valid as far as it goes, but it conceals a couple of problems. One problem has to do with the word 'Christian'. It seems odd at first sight that an Old Testament formulation should provide the framework for New Testament morality. It has to be asked whether what is distinctive about a specifically Christian morality will be adequately expressed within such a framework. And indeed, when we survey the moral section of the recent *Catechism*, this concern is made more acute; witness, for example, the absence from it of such key themes of New Testament morality as conversion and disciple-ship. This warns us to be alive to the danger of considering the ten commandments simply as a moral code, in a vacuum, with no reference to context.

An even more basic problem is that presentations of the commandments may not even express what is distinctive about Old Testament morality. If we take the commandments simply as commandments, there is little that is remarkable about them, certainly about the last seven of them. Common sense would tell us that these are the kinds of laws that would inform any civilised society – laws about life and property, about truthful witness, about marriage and family values – even if the details were to differ in different societies. Indeed, scholarship has unearthed for us laws that are very similar to the ten commandments of Exodus 20 and Deuteronomy 5 in the codes of neighbouring societies of the time.

What we are hinting at is best expressed by Paul in the first and second chapters of the letter to the Romans. In condemning some of the moral practices of the Romans, he realises that these 'Gentiles' do not possess the law in the way that the Jews do (that is, the law of Moses). Nevertheless they are still to be held responsible because, as he puts it, they have the law 'written on their hearts' (Romans 2: 14-15). We might paraphrase by saying that the content of the ten commandments is not the sole preserve of the Old Testament. There is some universal moral instinct, by virtue of our common humanity, which we would expect to find expressed across the moral codes of all societies in ways that are broadly similar.

Very often, talk of 'bringing back the commandments' conceals this problem. What is being sought may be simply a renewed sense of right and wrong, a sense of moral order – which is perfectly valid and extremely important, but about which there is nothing specifically Christian or religious. This is the limitation of seeing the ten commandments as 'law'. Of course they are 'law', but they are also much more. To speak of them as principles of social order or as guidelines for behaviour captures only a fraction of the rich meaning they possess in their biblical context.

The reader might be forgiven for feeling some confusion at this point. We have a mental picture from the Bible of God giving Moses the ten commandments on Mount Sinai, and so we call the commandments 'the law of God'. Yet we know that most of these com-

mandments were already current before Sinai, enshrined in the
legal codes of neighbouring societies. So how can we speak of them
as the revealed law of God? This is the problem we are confronted
with if we see the commandments only as law, but which ceases to
be such a problem once there is an appreciation of their proper context.[1]

Gift and Promise

There is both a 'what' and a 'why' in morality. The 'what' refers to
what we do and what we should do, the rights and wrongs of
behaviour. The 'why' concerns the underlying meanings and values that inform our action. It refers to the meaning we live by, the
philosophy of where things are going, that gives our living its sense
and direction.

In fact, it could probably be argued that there is no such thing as a
pure moral code, a content detached from any vision or philosophy
of life, a 'what' without any 'why'. Morality is always rooted in
some context, so that we speak, for example, of Islamic morality or
Victorian morality or liberal morality. This does not mean that
morality is relative, or that right and wrong are no more than what
is normative in a particular culture. Rather, it is to highlight the
manner in which the context contributes a highly significant dimension of the meaning of moral codes and precepts.

Thus in the Bible we find a 'what' that is represented by the ten
commandments. But it is the underlying 'why', the vision about
life's meaning, the hope about its direction, that gives the 'what' its
distinctive tone or flavour. We begin to sense this 'why' in the language which the *Catechism* uses in introducing the ten commandments (paragraphs 2056 to 2063). It says that they are a 'gift', 'the
gift of God himself'. It says that they are 'a path of life'. It talks of
their 'liberating power'. It says that the commandments 'must first
be understood in the context of the exodus, that they themselves
'come in the second place' and only 'take on their full meaning
within the covenant'. They are about 'the implications of belonging
to God'; they present moral existence as 'a *response* to the Lord's
loving initiative'. This is not the language of law.

The key words are *exodus* and *covenant*, because they refer to the
context from which the commandments, as presented in the Bible,

derive their significance. Exodus (meaning a 'going out') refers to God's bringing the people of Israel up out of Egypt, liberating them from slavery. But this liberation was itself for the sake of covenant. Because of this, the purpose of exodus was not simply that the people be politically liberated, but that they might be God's own people. What was happening was essentially spiritual.

The word *covenant* refers to some form of agreement or contract. In the Bible it often referred to a treaty between unequal parties, where the more powerful party offered protection to the weaker and the weaker would then be expected in some way to serve the former. Likewise, the covenant of Sinai between God and Israel contained elements of both sovereignty and reciprocity. Its simple definition is: 'They shall be my people and I shall be their God' (Jeremiah 32:38). It is a pledge of mutual fidelity.

The ten commandments are what summarises Israel's part in the relationship. Thus they are more than simply law; we are taken beyond the contractual. The decisive fact is that the commandments are set within a story of liberation and hope. The liberation is the pure gift of God and, as consequence of it, the commandments too assume the nature of gift and are experienced as gift. They are not so much legal, contractual obligations as the putting in concrete terms of the divine offer of new life.

Teasing this out, let us begin with the decisive reality at the heart of the experience of exodus, which is that of gift or grace. The exodus was the experience of a people who were nothing and nobodies, their experience of being approached in absolute gratuitousness by the God of infinite mystery. The graciousness is well expressed in a text from the book of Deuteronomy (7:6-8):

> 'For you are a people holy to the Lord your God; the Lord your God has chosen you out of all the peoples on earth to be his people, his treasured possession. It was not because you were more numerous than any other people that the Lord set his heart on you and chose you – for you were the fewest of all peoples. It was because the Lord loved you…'

Graciousness here is total and pure. There is no reason whereby it is earned or necessitated. It is simply love bestowing itself in the miracle of generosity. This theme is at the heart of the New Testament also: 'But when the goodness and loving kindness of God our Saviour appeared, he saved us, not because of any works of right-eousness that we had done, but according to his mercy' (Titus 3:4-5).

God's graciousness is put more vividly in Ezekiel's symbolic render-ing of the story of exodus and covenant. There, Israel is likened to a new-born baby that is radically uncared for: 'On the day you were born your navel cord was not cut, nor were you washed with water... No eye pitied you... but you were thrown out in the open field' (Ezekiel 16:4-5). On this abhorred child the Lord's mercy shines:

> 'I passed by you, and saw you flailing about in your blood. As you lay in your blood I said to you: "Live! and grow up like a plant in the field"... I passed by you again and looked on you; you were at the age for love. I spread the edge of my cloak over you, and covered your nakedness. I pledged myself to you and entered into a Covenant with you, says the Lord God, and you became mine.' (16:6-8)

Besides the pure giftedness, there is also a strong theme of promise in this basic experience of the people of Israel. The covenant experi-ence of grace initiates a relationship and thereby establishes a future. Just as lovers have plans and hopes for their future together, so God's covenant is full of promise, giving life meaning and direc-tion.

This is captured in the biblical symbol of the promised land. While the symbol obviously has a geographical and political reference, it refers more deeply to a state of being that is promised by God. In this state all will be right among the people who live under the presence of God. Thus, exodus-covenant is the experience of those who had no future now being established in a future imagined for them by God.

This is the background against which the notions of the plan of God and the will of God are perhaps best explained. In ordinary usage people usually intend these ideas to refer to God's providence, but the way they are sometimes used can convey the picture of a God who manipulates us as a puppeteer would puppets, and even the picture of a God who foresees tragedy yet looks on unaffected as it unfolds 'according to his will'. When these images are to the fore, the idea of promise seems inappropriate.

But what the plan of God and the will of God mean is simply that which God wants. What the covenant tells us is that God passionately desires all that is right for God's people. This is God's will and plan and it is the spirit of the exodus story from the very start. 'I have observed the misery of my people who are in Egypt; I have heard their cry... I know their sufferings, and I have come down to deliver them' (Exodus 3:7-8). Passion and compassion are at the core of the will of God. Promise is the very spirit of God's plan for us.

Invitation and Response

We are saying that the first step in understanding the commandments is to appreciate the covenant, an appreciation which highlights the themes of grace and promise. But this relationship between covenant and commandments has important implications for our understanding of Christian morality. These implications have to do with how we balance our own role in our moral lives with the role of God. The idea of 'invitation and response' – part of our fourth way of looking at morality – captures the balance that the themes imply.

First of all, the very inequality of the relationship of grace holds an indispensable truth. We tend to think of morality in an 'if... then...' mode. If I do good, then I will receive (or earn or merit) grace; if I do wrong I will be punished as I deserve. There is obvious truth in this view of things, in its affirmation of the link between actions and consequences. But from the perspective of what we have been saying about the grace and promise of the covenant, the whole thing in fact appears to be the wrong way around.

It is not that if I do good I gain grace, but rather that I first experience grace, experience myself as graced, and am therefore enabled or inspired to do good. What comes first is God's gratuitous love – in the words of John: 'In this is love, not that we loved God but that he loved us...' (1 John 4:10). Only then comes our action in response to what God is doing in our lives. It is not that we earn grace so much as that, by our response, we accept or reject the love that is already bestowed.

The *Catechism* makes this point clearly when considering the idea of merit. Any merit on our part arises only from the fact that God has freely chosen to associate us with the work of grace. 'Since the initiative belongs to God in the order of grace, no one can merit the initial grace of forgiveness and justification, at the beginning of conversion' (paragraph 2010). In this precise sense, absolutely everything depends on grace, on what God does.

The language of invitation-response handles this fundamental truth far better than does the language of law. The latter is structured to think in terms of 'if... then...', of actions and consequences, of behaviour and sanctions. Everything hinges on what we do. But invitation-response sees our action as a consequence of something more fundamental. There is simply no response without an invitation and, while the response may be free, absolutely everything depends on the invitation. To talk about response without reference to the invitation that makes it possible in the first place makes no sense.

Yet our constant temptation is to think that it all depends on us, that the most decisive factor in determining our destiny is what we do, all a matter of earning. This is what comes of speaking of the commandments without the covenant. Of course, what we do is determinative, but Christian morality is not about trying frantically to earn God's love or to secure our salvation through our own powers. It is about responding joyfully to a love that is simply given. This can only be appreciated if attention is diverted from the response itself and focused on the significance of the invitation.

Turning to the theme of promise, the same balance is implied. The theme tells us that Christian morality is about entering into the future of God's promise. Moral existence hinges on the future imagined for us by God, rather than on our carving out our own future unaided. Again, our sense of autonomy leads us to think that everything depends on us. It is hard to accept that, in a very real sense, everything has been worked out for us. Our future is offered to us and what we must learn to do is to accept.

The analogy of teaching a baby to walk might be helpful. The parent envisages a future where the baby will walk, a future the baby cannot see, though he or she strives towards it. Likewise, for all our autonomy and insight, we do not press forward on our own, but rather are called to co-operate with what God has imagined for us as our deepest fulfilment. Morality is meant to be a joyful matter of doing everything we can to discern and to collaborate with what God has envisaged, so that the promise may come true. This again is the language of invitation and response.

Laws of Relationship

Much of what we are saying is implied in the way in which the ten commandments themselves are presented. The texts in question do not begin with the first commandment but with the words, 'I am the Lord your God who brought you out of the land of Egypt, out of the house of slavery' (Exodus 20:2; Deuteronomy 5:6). And the commandments follow, just as response follows invitation. They follow, that is, as the statement of what response in the covenant relationship looks like. Thus they are laws, but they are much more. They are about what we must do, but they are about much more besides.

The commandments are perhaps best described as the laws of a relationship, making concrete what the relationship is to be like between God and God's people. They express the mutuality of covenant. They are the 'today' of covenant; in their observation covenant is realised in the present and God's people in the present come up out of Egypt. Conversely, not to observe them means much more than infringement of law. It means rejection of the covenant and the reversal of exodus. Thus Hosea can say of an unfaithful people: 'They shall not remain in the land of the Lord; but Ephraim shall return to Egypt'; 'for you are not my people and I am not your God' (Hosea 9:3; 1:9). To break commandment is to break covenant; it is spiritually to return to exile.

The inseparability of the commandments from the covenant cannot be emphasised enough. To speak of the commandments on their own is to miss the wood for the trees. Again the Book of Deuteronomy captures this, with great conciseness: 'He declared to you his covenant, which he charged you to observe, that is, the ten commandments' (4:13). The two words verge on being interchangeable.

We can even say that the covenant context of invitation and response means that law is not the right kind of word to be using at all. In fact, the Old Testament knows the commandments as 'the ten words'. They are not laws in the familiar sense of 'if you steal, you will receive such a punishment'. They are more like teaching than

law. As teaching they are future-focused directions for living, setting out what is to be the basic moral substance of the people.
Familiar to others as a code of social order, their meaning here is
deeper. Within the context of covenant they appear as a path to life,
the promise of happiness. 'They are a sign of divine care; they set
forth that pattern of human existence which leads to blessedness.'[2]

If we refer here to the five ways of looking at morality, it is clear that
the foregoing discussion has been in terms of morality as love. To
see morality only in terms of law will bring us to the ten commandments, but will not bring us to the covenant. We will not be able to
speak of 'response' because we will have no sense of 'invitation'.
This gives a primacy to the language of love. Yet it does not mean
neglect of the language of law, for the commandments are still laws.
It is just that they have their sense as law only in unfolding or speci-
fying what love is about, what are the dimensions of responding to
God's gracious invitation.

An Internal Affair

Let us now move on to consider the ten commandments in relation
to the remaining ways of looking at morality. If we take morality as
inner conviction and morality as personal growth together, as the
person-centred approaches to morality, we can readily come to
appreciate their potential for further unfolding the meaning of the
commandments.

Take the words of Moses, after the presentation of the commandments to the people, where he is exhorting them to follow in the
path that has been given:

'Hear, O Israel: the Lord is our God, the Lord alone. You shall
love the Lord your God with all your heart, and with all your
soul, and with all your might. Keep these words that I am commanding you today in your heart. Recite them to your children
and talk about them when you are at home and when your are
away, when you lie down and when you rise. Bind them as a
sign on your hand, fix them as an emblem on your forehead, and
write them on the doorposts of your house and on your gates.'
(Deuteronomy 6:4-9)

This is the language of interiority. This is clear, not just from the references to heart and soul and might, but from the sense that we carry these words everywhere, because they have become part of ourselves. It is very much the point we made in describing morality as inner conviction: when the moral law is internalised, its demands arise from within as a part of ourselves.

A second passage, from Ezekiel, can also be read as a restatement of the ten commandments in a language that is closer to the view of morality as internal than to the view of morality as law:

> 'If a man is righteous and does what is lawful and right – if he does not eat upon the mountains or lift up his eyes to the idols of the house of Israel, does not defile his neighbour's wife... does not oppress anyone, but restores to the debtor his pledge, commits no robbery, gives his bread to the hungry and covers the naked with a garment... withholds his hand from iniquity, executes true justice between contending parties, follows my statutes, and is careful to observe my ordinances, acting faithfully – such a one is righteous; he shall surely live, says the Lord God.' (18:5-9)

The passage paints a portrait of the kind of person who obeys the commandments, highlighting the interior qualities that underlie their observance. It is a picture of somebody dedicated to God's ways, committed and faithful, a person of integrity, with a deep respect for others and a passion for rightness in all relationships.

Notably, the verses just preceding the passage quoted are often referred to as marking the emergence in Israel, around the time of Ezekiel, of a fully fledged sense of personal responsibility, in contrast to the sense up to then that responsibility was corporate and guilt inherited.[3] In other words, at a time when a truly interior sense of morality was being articulated, it is no surprise to see the commandments being re-expressed from within this new consciousness.

The mentality of the third way of looking at morality, that of the growth of personal moral qualities, is also implicit in the text of the commandments themselves. For example, the sixth commandment says not to commit adultery, and the ninth not to covet one's neighbour's wife. Also in parallel, the seventh says not to steal, and the tenth not to covet one's neighbour's goods. In each pair there is the

external action, adultery or theft, and the interior disposition or vice
of covetousness. It is like two sides of a coin, action being the external aspect of an interior attitude. Again, it would seem that the fifth
commandment refers, not simply to the action of killing, but also to
the underlying attitudes of jealousy and vindictiveness that can set
off a trail of killings.

The *Catechism* confirms this interior aspect of the commandments
when, speaking of the last two commandments, it says: 'The tenth
commandment concerns the intentions of the heart; with the ninth
it summarises all the precepts of the Law' (paragraph 2534). In a
way, the commandments happen inside the person, in the heart.
This is what Jesus meant when he said: 'For out of the heart come
evil intentions, murder, adultery, fornication, theft, false witness,
slander' (Matthew 15:19).

We might add that, even though there is this personal, interior
aspect, there is nothing individualistic about the commandments.
While keeping them is a response to God's gracious initiative, they
are essentially the response of a people rather than the private acts
of individuals. For it was a people rather than just individuals that
was called out of Egypt. In our age of privatisation, there is a useful
lesson for us in seeing that an ethic of deep interiority and an ethic
that is strongly communitarian can be one and the same.

The Commandments and Justice

In order to reveal the potential of the view of morality as social
transformation for unlocking the meaning of the commandments,
we will begin with two stories from the Old Testament. Coincid-
entally, both have quite a similar structure. More importantly, both
have a very strong sense of right and wrong that will quickly
engage the sensibility of any moral being.

One is the story of King David and Bathsheba (2 Samuel 11-12).
Walking on the roof of the king's house, David sees Bathsheba
bathing and is attracted by her beauty. He sends for her and ends
up lying with her. Subsequently, she sends to David to tell him that
she is pregnant. Her husband, Uriah, is away with the army at war,
so David sends for him and encourages him to relax at home. But
Uriah will not, as long as his fellow soldiers are out in the field; nor
can plenty of food and drink entice him to lie with his wife. David is

forced to take extreme measures. He arranges with the army commander to have Uriah put in the front line of battle and then to draw back from him when the fighting is heaviest. And so he is killed. After the period of mourning is over, David takes Bathsheba as his wife and in due course a son is born to the king.

The other (1 Kings 21) is the story of King Ahab and Naboth, whose vineyard borders on the palace of the king. Anxious to acquire the vineyard as a vegetable garden, Ahab offers Naboth a fair deal, either a better vineyard elsewhere or its value in money. But Naboth feels constrained not to sell off his ancestral heritage. Ahab goes home sulking, takes to the bed and will not eat. Enter his wife, Jezebel who, on hearing the story, takes command of the situation. She arranges to have two scoundrels falsely accuse Naboth of cursing both God and king. The penalty of death by stoning is duly administered and, shortly afterwards, Ahab takes possession of the vineyard.

There is more to each story, but let us first reflect on this much. There is, as remarked above, a similarity of structure. Each story tells of a desire awakened. Desire as such is quite ordinary – Ahab's desire to have a vegetable garden is quite legitimate, and even David's desire to cover his tracks is at least understandable. The problem arises when desire comes up against an obstacle. Both Naboth and Uriah are acting out of a sense of moral principle and at this stage one would expect that desire should yield to the higher values at stake. But instead, desire become covetous and expansive; it oversteps the bounds and higher principles are annulled. Desire becomes a law onto itself.

The outcomes in each case are breath-taking. With no law supervening upon desire, the other person becomes no more than an obstacle, dispensable, a means to an end. This is all the more stark when the other is as weak and defenceless as are Uriah and Naboth before the might of the king. And as the powerless individual is eventually dispensed with, others are drawn into the evil – the army commander, the accusers. When evil takes hold, it spreads like a rot. The irony, though, is that the whole scene is disguised as justice. What seems to be the case is that a brave soldier dies for his country and that a blasphemer is punished for his sins. Something terribly wrong is presented as utterly right, yet nobody is any the wiser.

If on reading these stories we did not feel outraged by the evil, we would surely be lacking a moral sense. The two stories convey to us the 'guts' of what morality in the Bible is about. But ask yourself: how many of the commandments have been broken? You shall not kill... You shall not commit adultery... You shall not steal... You shall not bear false witness... You shall not covet your neighbour's wife... You shall not covet your neighbour's goods.

It is quite impressive! But the point is that it is all part of two very real human situations. Clearly, the commandments are not dry dusty rules or authoritarian impositions. They go to the heart of what social living is all about. They are shorthand for how people are meant to be with each other; if they are disregarded life together becomes impossible. They are focused very sharply on justice and right relationships in society.

But there is more to each story, and more to the commandments. In each case, a new figure enters the story, the prophet Nathan in the case of David, the prophet Elijah in the case of Ahab. Nathan says to David: 'Why have you despised the Word of the Lord, to do what is evil in his sight?' Elijah says to Ahab: 'You have sold yourself to do what is evil in the sight of the Lord.' Both men then undergo punishment for their evil, but the point is the extra dimension, the new context into which their actions have been set. In doing what they did, they despised the Lord. In breaking the commandments they have broken covenant.

At this point we should attend to the structure of the commandments. They divide into two groups, the first three and the remaining seven. The first three concern right relationship with God – you shall have no other gods before me; do not take the Lord's name in vain; keep holy the Sabbath. The last seven all concern right relationships in society and, apart from the command to honour one's father and mother, all seven were disregarded between the two stories.

The significance of what the prophets say to David and Ahab, and a key to the activity of the prophets generally, is the link they make between the two sets of commandments. They bring into the clear light of day the truth that, for a covenant people, the deepest significance and tragedy of rupturing right relationship in society is the concomitant rupturing of relationship with the God of the covenant.

Put another way, it is not so much that the commandments divide
into two groups as that they bring together two concerns, perhaps
the two great concerns of the Old Testament. One of these is faith in
God, and this includes the monotheism of the people of Israel and
the value they placed on worship of the true God. The other is the
concern for right relationships throughout society, with a particular
regard for the defenceless (witnessed by the relative benevolence of
Israel's legislation regarding the treatment of widows and orphans,
aliens, casual workers and slaves). The prophets' insight was that,
in the words of the song, 'you can't have one without the other'.
Worship and the practice of justice belong together. Worship without the practice of justice is a sham; but to practise justice is to co-
operate with God's plan for God's people.

Thus the prophet Amos speaks on behalf of the Lord: 'I hate, I
despise your festivals, and I take no delight in your solemn assem-
blies' – because those whom he addresses try to worship God while
practising injustice (Amos 5:21). Likewise Isaiah: 'Is not this the fast
that I choose: to loose the bonds of injustice… to share your bread
with the hungry and bring the homeless poor into your house…'
(Isaiah 58:6-7). Even more pointedly Jeremiah, talking about those
who practise justice, concludes by saying: 'Is this not to know me?
says the Lord' (Jeremiah 22:16). 'Knowing' God comes of the practice of justice. The idea that God could be known within a worship
that is not accompanied by the practice of justice is strenuously
rejected.

Throughout their writing, it is the style or method of the prophets
to keep relating injustice back to faith. They repeatedly lament all
the sins of their society and they do so in the language of the ten
commandments. For instance, Hosea says: 'There is no faithfulness
or loyalty, and no knowledge of God in the land. Swearing, lying,
and murder, and stealing and adultery break out…' (Hosea 4:1-2).
The commandments are like a grid against which can be defined
the quality of relationships in society.

But the prophets' writings are far more than such litanies of commandments broken. The heart of what they say is to be found in
their imagery. In breaking the commandments Israel is like a child
turning from its parents (Hosea 11); like the adopted orphan leaving ungratefully to become a whore (Ezekiel 16); like the rupturing

of a marriage bond in betrayal and adultery (Jeremiah 3). This is covenant imagery and it recurs again and again as the prophets seek to bring home to the people the deep spiritual significance of how they are living.

The Spirit of the Commandments

Seeing the commandments as a summary statement concerning right relationships in society breathes new life into the idea of law, for it is the anticipation of a just society that gives law its urgency and dignity. However, to see the ten commandments simply as being about justice and the transformation of society would be a narrowing of vision, just as it would be to see them only as law. The point of the prophets is that justice is to be understood in a spiritual setting.

The fuller perspective, then, is one that joins together the emphasis on covenant relationship between God and God's people and the emphasis on right relationships in society. We might conclude that the view of morality as invitation-response and the view of morality as justice together (and without neglecting the other three views) unlock the essential and deepest meanings of the ten commandments.

This brings us to what is one of the Old Testament's most pithy statements of the relationship between justice and faith, of what we might call the spirit behind the ten commandments. This statement is to be found for instance in the detailed injunctions that follow on the presentation of the ten commandments, where it says: 'You shall not wrong or oppress a resident alien, for you were aliens in the land of Egypt' (Exodus 22:21). Observing the ten commandments is inspired by the memory of exodus: 'for you were aliens in the land of Egypt'.

The same idea is found in texts outlining the way in which the people of God marked off times that were to be dedicated in a special way to God. Every seventh (or 'sabbatical') year was to be a special year of favour. In this year (described in Leviticus 25 and Deuteronomy 15) the earth was to be left fallow; there was to be a freeing of slaves and a cancelling of debts. Besides these sabbatical years, every fiftieth year was to be a year of 'jubilee' when, in addition to the customs of the sabbatical year, there was to be a general emancipation whereby all would return to their property and to their families and where all who had lost their ancestral land could regain it.

Although what is described may have been more the ideal than the reality, the ideal contains within it the spirit or essence of morality in the Old Testament and perhaps in the whole Bible. This is to be seen in the motivation behind the institution. In the text of Deuteronomy (15:15) it reads simply: 'Remember that you were a slave in the land of Egypt and the Lord your God redeemed you; for this reason I lay this command upon you today.'

Behind the commandments is this outlook, this fundamental attitude about life in society, that is inspired by the memory of exodus. It is a mentality of remembering exodus-covenant, when the people were nothing and the Lord was their liberation, and of living out of that memory. As a moral principle it might be defined as: treat others the way God has treated you; treat them the way God would treat them. This is the kernel of Old Testament morality, to do unto others as God would, by practising in social relationships the very gratuitousness of God.

'Doing unto others as God would' brings to mind the golden rule, 'Do to others as you would have them do to you' (Matthew 7:12). That rule could simply mean enlightened self-interest – treat others as you yourself would like to be treated and they will probably treat you well also. Such would be an 'if... then...' mentality. But we have already seen that the covenant mentality is one of 'because... therefore...' – because you have been graciously loved, therefore you can love graciously in turn and in return.

According to this mentality, treating others well is not done in order to achieve certain outcomes. Rather, treating others well is itself an outcome, namely, the outcome of how the people have themselves been treated by God. It is a carrying forth into relationships with others of the experience of gift and graciousness and generosity. 'Treat others as God has treated you; treat them as God would treat them.'

In this sense, the meaning of the ten commandments lies beyond all our ways of looking at morality, whether it be law or inner conviction or personal growth or love or social transformation. These approaches, in particular the last two, help us enter into the biblical perspective. But in the end they point to something beyond their own horizon, to a morality that is divine in origin and inspiration. Morality begins with what God does. It begins with the gift of exodus-covenant, the gift of being invited into the experience of God's liberating love. Moral living is a joyful response to this gift and invitation, whereby we live out of the spirit, or mindset, of gift, and seek to allow God's way with God's people to inform and transform our own ways with each other.

CHAPTER 3

God and Morality

Who is the God of our morality? Drawing on the five ways of understanding morality, we will explore the picture of God conveyed by the way we understand morality, and the idea of morality conveyed by the way we understand God. We will be especially concerned with talking about morality in a way that does justice to who God is.

God the Lawgiver

When we think of God in relation to morality, the view of morality as law is often to the fore. The image of God as lawgiver is possibly the picture of God most familiar to us. If there is a moral law, and if it is in some way founded in God, then the most concrete way of grasping this (but not the only way) is to think of God as lawgiver. God determines the moral law, requires obedience, judges behaviour, and rewards or punishes us accordingly.

There is much in the Bible that might be taken as supporting this view of God. Indeed, we already remarked in chapter one on the presence in scripture of the language of law, though we also remarked on our tendency to be preoccupied with this particular language. Now we would simply add that this language presents or implies a corresponding image of God.

For instance, the Old Testament tells us that God 'gave [Moses] the two tablets of the covenant, tablets of stone, written with the finger of God' (Exodus 31:18). Again, St Paul says: 'For all of us must appear before the judgment seat of Christ, so that each may receive recompense for what has been done in the body, whether good or evil' (2 Corinthians 5:10). And of course Jesus speaks of a judgment 'where there will be weeping and gnashing of teeth', when the evil 'will go away into eternal punishment, but the righteous into eternal life' (Matthew 24:51; 25:46). Within the language of law the Bible

presents God as the one who gives the law and judges our observance of it with reward or punishment.

These images go very deep in us, forming our sense both of God
and of morality. But if, as we have already seen, morality is more
than law, might the same not be true of God also? Might not God be
more than a God of law? Is it not the case that this language, on its
own, presents a deceptive understanding of God? Certainly it must
be acknowledged that this picture contains a sense of fairness and
of justice being done. Nevertheless it presents a stern and austere
God. At its worst, it has even suggested to many that God is not on
our side at all, not basically sympathetic to our struggle but, rather,
impersonal and unfeeling and cruelly impartial.

What is happening is that the language and the imagery are domi-
nating to such an extent that they are actually determining the reality rather than the other way around. The language of law is so
rooted in us as the way to talk about morality that it creates a
groove, to which our thinking about God tends to conform

The language comes from the courtroom and has God in the place
of the judge. Now, while the law court is a most valuable and cherished institution, the image imprinted on us is frequently of something cold and unfeeling, more cruel than kind. Think, for instance,
of how, within the legal system, it is a very complex matter to incorporate considerations of motivation – intentions are hard to prove.
It is a system focused on what is objective, out there. This aspect
tends to be exaggerated in our minds, and nowhere more so than
when the imagery is applied to God.

The language and imagery bring to mind another context also, that
of the relationship between a parent (usually the father) and a child.
We have only to think of phrases such as 'you just wait till your
father gets home' to get in touch with another world of authority
and obedience, of fear and punishment. As with the courtroom,
much of this is perfectly normal and necessary. But again there is
the extreme. We can all conjure up easily a picture of a cowering,
fearful child and a disciplinarian father. How often does this represent the link between God and morality in adult consciousness?

Many will be familiar with Lawrence Kohlberg's theory of six
stages in the process of moral development from childhood to

adulthood.[1] The earliest stage is that of the young child and it is very much a matter of thinking in terms of rewards and punishments. For the child, morality is extrinsic to actions, goodness and badness are determined by the consequences rather than by any human meaning residing in the action itself. Avoiding punishment is fundamental; the child quickly learns the difference between a sweet and a slap, and learns to act accordingly. In later stages we move on to thinking in terms of social approval, or of the need for law and order, before arriving at a stage when we think and behave out of internalised and freely chosen moral values or principles.

The significant point for our purposes is that, from this psychological viewpoint, reward-and-punishment language belongs to a very primitive stage of moral thinking. It is the language of a child. One might object that society also has its systems of punishment for adults who break the law. But this could be answered by saying that if all that is motivating adults in their doing of what is right is the fear of punishment, then they are less than mature in their thinking. Insofar as adults behave as responsible adults, reward and punishment are not the motivation. Adults, as adults, should have left that kind of thing behind them.

Yet it is striking how large reward and punishment can loom in adult consciousness of the link between God and morality. Psychologists tell us that we progress in our moral thinking towards something more rational, more internalised, than reward and punishment and blind obedience. Yet in reality childish forms of moral thinking and of moral thinking about God abound. They are deeply embedded and are often predominant well into adult life. For many adults, their relationship to God is comparable to that between a cowering child and a disciplinarian father.

One could ask why this is so, whether for instance the Church's style of moral teaching has contributed to it. Whatever the answer, our concern here is to point out what an offence this mentality is to the nature of God. Think of the language in which it is sometimes reflected. We say, for instance, that God sends trials to test us, that God gives us crosses to bear. We speak of tragedies being the will of God. We speak of punishing as one of the main things God does to us.

Theologically, this language says something very important about

the providence of God in the midst of adversity, what St Paul meant
when he said that in everything God works for the good (Romans
8:28). The theological meaning is that everything can be transformed 'in Christ'. But when this language is used loosely, the
impression can be formed that God is actively doing these things. It
is as if God, after setting out the law for our observance, then sets
obstacles along the way to test us out, like some form of continuous
assessment that feeds into a final grading where the marking will
be strict.

It requires only a little reflection to see the poverty of this line of
thinking. Are these things that human beings do to each other? Do
we put trials or crosses in each other's way? Do we test each other?
Do we, in our ordinary relationships, punish one another? Are we
hard on each other? What would life be like if we regularly did
these things? And yet we tend to presume that they are done regularly by God.

It should be emphasised at this point that we are not in any way
belittling the language of law as an approach to morality. Rather we
are sketching a quite widespread sense of how God and morality
are linked. This sense arises from a combination of two factors. One
is that the language of law is being used to the neglect of the other
languages. The second, probably a consequence of this, is that law
itself is being thought of in an extrinsic way, with little or no reference to inner conviction. If we move on to consider other ways of
thinking about God and morality, we might then be able to appreciate better where the language of law fits into the picture.

God as Lover

If we look more closely at the Bible we will find that it is not so neat
and tidy as some of the above ideas about God would suggest. In
the Bible, in fact, there is a struggle to find the true face of God. In
one way, that struggle is what the whole story of the Bible is all
about. This resonates very much with our own experience. For so
many of us, understanding God involves struggle and a perhaps
painful journey, as we leave behind inadequate notions and come
to a perspective that does better justice to both God and morality. It
is often described as the journey from the God of fear to the God of
love.

Two examples will illustrate this struggle. In Exodus chapter 32 the people have just formed and have been worshipping the golden calf, while Moses is up the mountain with the Lord. The Lord vents his anger before Moses: 'Now let me alone, so that my wrath may burn hot against them and I may consume them.' Moses is presented as trying to placate God. Reminding God of the exodus itself, he asks what will the Egyptians think but that it was with evil intent that God liberated the Israelites, and concludes: 'Turn from your fierce wrath; change your mind and do not bring disaster on your people.' The scene ends as Moses had hoped: 'And the Lord changed his mind about the disaster that he planned to bring on his people.'

Now to speak of God 'changing his mind' is to ascribe a human characteristic to God. It certainly brings the story to life, but it should not be taken literally. One suspects that the one who was really changing his mind was Moses, as he tried to figure God out. What kind of God is the Lord? More specifically, what kind of God is the Lord in the face of human infidelity? Is God a God of fear and punishment, or some other kind of God?

The Book of Amos provides a second illustration. Amos proclaims a 'Day of the Lord' when the Lord's wrath will burn against the sins of the people. But it emerges that it is not quite so clearcut. As the Lord shows Amos the terrible punishments that are about to befall, Amos cries: 'O Lord God, forgive, I beg you! How can Jacob stand? He is so small.' The passage continues: 'The Lord relented concerning this. "It shall not be", said the Lord' (Amos 7:2-3). And more succintly still in another context: 'The eyes of the Lord are upon the sinful kingdom, and I will destroy it from the face of the earth – except that I will not utterly destroy the house of Jacob, says the Lord' (Amos 9:8).

The 'except' says it all. But again, it is not God who is vascillating and indecisive. It is God's people trying to come to some definition about their God. And as both passages indicate, the struggle is being resolved in the direction of a merciful God. The people's infidelity may well merit destruction, except that there is something more to God than wrath and punishment.

At this point we might reflect for a moment on the variety of images that the Old Testament brings into play when talking about God. The images of lawgiver and judge represent but one strain. God is also quite frequently called a 'rock' or a 'fortress'. This language stands for the faithfulness or constancy of God. God is called a 'shepherd' or a 'vinedresser', language that stands for care and providence. Such language has to be put beside the language of judgment and punishment and be allowed to interact with it.

But the most predominant Old Testament imagery in talking about God, which is particularly evident in the prophets, is the imagery of marriage, of the love and faithfulness between a husband and wife. This love provides the best analogy that can be found when talking about God, the closest approximation to what God is like. Even though the covenant is between two infinitely unequal partners, it is nevertheless more intimate than unequal. Intimacy and faithfulness are the basic currency. 'O Israel, you will not be forgotten by me' (Isaiah 44:21).

All these reflections are drawing us away from the first way of seeing morality and pointing us towards the fourth way, that of invitation and response, of morality as love. Here we speak in terms of fidelity conquering betrayal and creating communion, where betrayal only makes for isolation. The whole thrust of the Bible, of the spiritual struggle of Moses and the prophets, seems to be telling us to start here in our search to understand God and morality, and not with the language of command and obedience.

Thus we would speak of God as lover rather than as lawgiver. The idea of love that is intended here is that one who loves another participates in the existence of that other by acknowledging the other's goodness and affirming what has yet to be realised in the other's goodness. Such language best captures God's stance in relation to our moral existence. It says that God is fundamentally on our side, wishing for our well-being, committed to our future. It says that God has invested Godself in us.

In this context the language of law is not so much relegated as properly appreciated. If we start here, we will be better able to grasp the significance of words like command and obedience. Within the language of love, *command* will appear more like benevolent and providential guidance, *obedience* more like a persevering attentive-ness to the one whom we know loves us (the spirit of 'listening' that is emphasised so much in Deuteronomy and Jeremiah). We shall see later in the chapter what happens the language of reward and punishment when set within this context.

Jesus, The True Face of God

The gospels bring out fully that this is the proper starting point for understanding the relationship between God and morality. There we are presented with Jesus, the true face of God, in whom it is revealed to us how God relates to our moral endeavours. Obviously, nothing resembling a comprehensive elaboration of this is possible within this chapter (chapter five will discuss further aspects of the picture of morality that comes across from the ministry of Jesus). What we will do here is reflect on one particular theme, that of for- giveness, as a way of illustrating how God's stance with regard to morality is definitively clarified in the ministry of Jesus.

Few themes pervade the pages of the gospel in the way forgiveness does. There are the stories of Zacchaeus and of the prodigal son, of the woman taken in adultery and of the woman who washes the feet of Jesus. There is Jesus' table fellowship with sinners and his forgiving the sins of the paralytic. There is the teaching of the Our Father about forgiveness, the teaching about forgiving seventy- seven times and the story of the unmerciful steward. There is the story of the two sons and there is the contrast between the fate of Judas and the reconciliation of Peter. Clearly, the thinking and prac- tice of Jesus about forgiveness is going to tell us something very fundamental about the question of God and morality.

In fact it tells us something at odds with the picture of judging and punishing described above. The mentality of Jesus is perhaps best portrayed in the story of the woman taken in adultery (John 8:2-11). The Pharisees wanted her stoned, as this was the punishment which the law lay down for adultery. But Jesus, by making them aware of their own share of sinfulness, caused them to retreat and, left with the woman, he assured her that she was not condemned, while making it clear that the sin was not thereby condoned.

The difference between Jesus and the Pharisees could be described as follows. They defined the woman in terms of her past and thus she was an adulteress. But Jesus thought of her in terms of her

future and saw that the adultery, while it was wrong and could not
be undone, could assume a different significance as part of a larger
story of repentance and reconciliation. He was fully alive to the
wrongness of what she had done; but he was also fully alive to what
she could yet be.

We do not hear how the woman's life turned out subsequently but
other gospel stories lead us to presume that it was transformed. For
instance, the stories of the sinner woman (Luke 7:36-50) and of
Zacchaeus (Luke 19:1-10) both tell us what happened after the experience of forgiveness. Zacchaeus' life is transformed by generosity,
while the sinner woman's washing and kissing and anointing the
feet of Jesus' are expressive of the newly-released love that was
pouring forth from her heart.

This is what Jesus points to when he says to his Pharisee host: 'Her
sins, which were many, have been forgiven; hence she has shown
great love.' Being forgiven is a release. It opens up the heart blocked
by sin, so that the person can start loving again. The love that was
blocked up can flow freely again and a new future becomes possible, a future that transforms the incident of the sin into a chapter in
a larger and more hopeful story. If it was Jesus' 'policy' always and
unconditionally to forgive, perhaps it was because he knew that
this was what being forgiven could effect in a person's life.

These stories show us that Jesus was able to think about people, to
think in terms of people, in a way that the Pharisees around him
were not. As they come across, the law is something quite unfeeling, simply to be applied. The same impression is formed by their
conflict with Jesus over the observance of the Sabbath. Perhaps it is
this kind of legalistic attitude to morality on the part of religious
leaders that leads to God being misrepresented. It is not that God is
such a God in relation to our morality, but that God *appears* thus
when this is the stance of those who act in God's name.

In the above stories, it is not Jesus himself who is wronged by the
particular sin, but in another case it is, and in that case the meaning
of forgiveness reaches full clarity. On the cross Jesus says the
words: 'Father, forgive them; for they do not know what they are
doing' (Luke 23:34). God's power in the face of human sinfulness,
even in the face of the ultimate sin which is the putting to death of

the Saviour, is not the power of punishment, but what might be called the powerfulness of defencelessness. This means that there is no end to this forgiving love. The relationship will never be terminated by the one who initiated it. It will be always full of promise.

We can now bring together the implications of the discussion thus far. The discussion would point to the conclusion that the fundamental reality of our moral existence in relation to God is the reality of being accepted. The Bible seems to suggest, on the one hand, that Jesus' teaching on God's enduring love and fidelity is the definitive revelation of the character of God. On the other hand, it seems to be saying that judgment, punishment and condemnation reflect God's true nature. Our discussion points clearly to the former of these two as the truer impression. God's relationship to morality is grasped in the statement that we are accepted by God in a way that is constant and unwavering and full of hope for us.

Context and Content

To develop further this fundamental point regarding God and morality, we would recall the distinction between the 'what' and the 'why' of morality. This distinction tells us that, besides the content of what we do and the attendant articulation of principles and norms, there is the context of what we do, the underlying values and vision and motivation. In speaking about the ten commandments we were presenting the view that it is the context that is central in biblical ethics. What is distinctive about Christian morality lies more in the vision of life that inspires it than in its prescriptions concerning right and wrong.

Linking this to the theme of the present chapter, we can distinguish between God in some way giving us the content (the 'what') of our morality and God providing a context (a 'why') for our moral living. To see God as lawgiver puts the emphasis on God giving us the content of morality. But to see God as lover is to focus on the context for moral living. It tells us that the context for the moral life is one of being accepted. Our Christian existence begins in a God who cares, who is not distant or harsh, but who reaches out to God's people with infinite compassion.

Thus it was with compassion that God 'observed the misery' and 'heard the cry' of the people in exile (Exodus 3:7). It was with compassion that God continued to hold out before a sinful people the possibility of new life: 'How can I give you up, Ephraim? How can I hand you over, O Israel? (Hosea 11:8). This compassion of God finally became incarnate in the person of Jesus. The story of salvation is thus a story where moral living is embraced or surrounded by God's compassion.

The Christian doctrine that gives expression to this context of being accepted is the doctrine of the Trinity. This doctrine speaks of God as a community of love, Father, Son and Spirit, reaching out to embrace all of humanity and to invite all of humanity to share in its own divine life. This good news is what gives shape and meaning and direction to our lives. It reveals to us the context of our moral living.

It took a few centuries of theological reflection before the doctrine of the Trinity came to precise definition. But the doctrine is there in embryo in the earliest New Testament writings. As the early Christians reflected on the significance of the resurrection of Jesus, they found themselves using trinitarian language. They spoke of Jesus as 'Son of God' and of God as 'the God and Father of our Lord Jesus Christ'. Further, they experienced the resurrection as the outpouring of the 'Spirit', an outpouring which links us to the divine life of Jesus. Thus we find passages such as the following:

> 'But when the fulness of time had come, God sent his Son, born of a woman, born under the law, in order to redeem those who were under the law, so that we might receive adoption as children. And because you are children, God has sent the Spirit of his Son into our hearts, crying, 'Abba! Father! So you are no longer a slave but a child, and if a child then also an heir, through God.' (Galatians 4:4-7)

Where St Paul uses the metaphor of adoption, St John is even more radical in speaking of a new birth: 'Everyone who believes that Jesus is the Christ has been born of God' (1 John 5:1); 'no one can enter the kingdom of God without being born of water and Spirit' (John 3:5). But whether adoption or new birth, what is being spoken about throughout is 'context'. For Christians, the context of all their living is this trinitarian structure of existence, whereby we are drawn by the Spirit to share with Jesus as children of the Father. This is our dignity and this is our destiny.

It is often remarked how both Christians and non-Christians can exhibit the same high moral values. As a consequence it is asked: what then sets off Christian morality as distinctive? The answer surely lies here, in the 'why' rather than the 'what'. The difference is that Christian morality, being rooted in the gospel, has a sense of the whole shape of things, of where it all is ultimately going. This is what is articulated as the trinitarian structure of existence in the passage from St Paul.

Thus God can be said to relate to our morality firstly in terms of context. God's compassionate invitation, the full dimensions of which are revealed in the life, death and resurrection of Jesus, is no less than the invitation to participate in God's own trinitarian life, and to participate with the status of son or daughter 'in the Son'. This gives our lives meaning and direction. It gives all that we do its tone and texture.

So, while Christian and non-Christian may lead outwardly similar moral lives, there is this underlying difference. It has to do with the ultimate significance which each sees in living the moral life. It is about the motivation that this perspective inspires. Both Christian and non-Christian might lead similar lives, embodying similar values. But they would give different accounts of what they are doing. It is not unlike the way in which people who fall in love continue to do many of the things they did before, and yet do them in a new way, motivated by their new vision and hope.

However, there is a sense in which the content of Christian morality is unique to Christians, because of its intimate relationship to the trinitarian context of life. For both content and context are characterised by love. On the one hand, love is at the heart of God as Trinity. In the celebrated image of St Augustine, God the Father is the lover, God the Son is the beloved, and God the Holy Spirit is the bond of their love. More pithily, in the words of St John, 'God is love' (1 John 4:8). To speak of God as Trinity is to speak of God as the mystery of love and loving communion. This is such a contrast to the image of 'the old man in the sky', so alone and so unlike love.

On the other hand, love is our being too, we who are made in the image and likeness of God: 'So God created humankind in his image, in the image of God he created them; male and female he created them' (Genesis 1:27). The difference is that, whereas God *is* love, we must *become* love. And this is morality or the moral call, to recognise that our inner being is love and to realise this, to bring this forth. Insofar as we fulfil our vocation to become love, to that extent we are becoming sons and daughters in the Trinity. Thus for Paul, our 'adoption' is both present and future, both achieved and outstanding:

> 'For the creation waits with eager longing for the revealing of the children of God... We know that the whole creation has been groaning in labour pains until now; and not only the creation, but we ourselves, who have the first fruits of the Spirit, groan inwardly while we wait for adoption, the redemption of our bodies.' (Romans 8:19, 22-23)

Love is the link between God and morality. God is love and our being is a reflection of God. Morality is the call to become love and to become thereby daughters and sons in the very life of the Trinity. In love, the 'what' and the 'why' of morality come together. In the words of John: 'We know that we have passed from death to life because we love one another' (1 John 3:14).

Personal and Social Aspects

If we draw now on the other three ways of looking at morality, we find that they fill out the above. The idea of morality as personal growth relates readily to what we have been saying. It would suggest that morality is a matter of discovering the image of God within ourselves and bringing it to birth. This is the law of our growth, and the different virtues that grow in us can be seen as different aspects of the becoming of love itself.

Because love is the image of God in us, the context for personal growth is trinitarian. This transforms the significance of our growing morally. We can now say, with some of the early Church Fathers, that as we grow in love, we are entering into our divinity. We are not merely human, for there is this spark of the divine in us. Our moral growth is ultimately a divine affair, for divinity is the deepest dimension of what we are.

The approach to morality as inner conviction would internalise the link between God and morality. We have already referred to how both Paul and Aquinas regard the new 'law' of the gospels as the law of the Spirit. From this perspective, morality is about following this inner law that is the prompting of the Spirit leading us to become sons and daughters in Christ. Thus Paul speaks of morality as following the law of the Spirit, as being led by the Spirit, as living by the Spirit, as walking in the Spirit (Romans 8:2; Galatians 5:18, 25).

From this perspective also, conscience can be seen as a matter of listening to this inner voice, attending to this inner law or dynamism. It is not simply the individual deliberating about what to do, but is more an internal dialogue between our spirit and the Spirit of God. It is about prayer and discernment. This is how we should understand the image of conscience as a voice, as it is used for instance in *The Church in the Modern World* (paragraph 16): 'Conscience is the most secret core and sanctuary of the person. There the person is alone with God whose voice echoes in the depths.'

Finally, the language of justice and social transformation would broaden our discussion to include the social and the global. It opens up the picture of God's love embracing the whole of human society and human history. In one passage, John Paul II links this line of thinking explicitly to the doctrine of the Trinity:

> '... awareness of the common fatherhood of God, of the brotherhood of all in Christ... and of the presence and life-giving action of the Holy Spirit, will bring to our vision of the world a new criterion for interpreting it. Beyond human and natural bonds, already so close and strong, there is discerned in the light of faith a new model of the unity of the human race, which must ultimately inspire our solidarity. This supreme model of unity, which is a reflection of the intimate life of God, one God in three Persons, is what we Christians mean by the word 'communion'.'[2]

Here again context and content are one. Morality is envisaged as the endeavour to build communion on earth according to the model of the Trinitarian communion. It will include a struggle against all forms of human relationship that contradict this. In this way, the practice of justice and entry into our divinity are one in the mind of the Christian.

Does God Punish?

Mention of justice brings us back to the question we left aside
regarding the possible meaning of words like reward and punishment within these perspectives. The question, does God punish?
will bring us to the heart of the issue. It would seem obvious, from
numerous biblical references, that God does punish. Yet the perspectives we have been presenting lead us to a quite attentuated
understanding of the idea of God punishing.

Reflecting on the very idea of punishment, one former prison chap-
lain remarked that 'the act of punishing is a peculiarly human
phenomenon' without any divine precedent or any counterpart in
the animal kingdom, and that it is 'separated perhaps only by a
hair's breadth from the instinctive spirit of revenge'.[3] There is much
material for reflection in this, but what interests us here is the statement that punishment has no divine precedent. It suggests strongly
that punishing is something which humans do and then attribute to
God also. It suggests that if we speak of God punishing, we are
making presumptions about God based on things we do. When we
consider how violent our own practice of punishment actually is,
attributing punishment to God becomes all the more suspect.

But if God does not punish, just what does God do? One answer
would be to say that God only loves, does nothing other than simply love, because 'God is love'. This, however, does not mean that
there is no such thing as punishment in the divine scheme of things.
This will be evident if we reflect back again on our fourth way of
seeing morality. When morality is seen as love, then the terms 'communion-isolation' take the place of the pair 'reward-punishment'.

The difference is essentially that between the intrinsic and the
extrinsic. While we can say that 'the punishment fits the crime', the
relationship is extrinsic. There is no necessary connection between,
say, stealing a valuable painting and three years in prison. But the
language of communion-isolation sees outcomes as intrinsic to
actions. If one person betrays another so that the relationship breaks
down, the breakdown is not one of a number of possible punishments. Rather it is a consequence that is built into the act of betrayal.

We could say, then, that in the language of law, punishment is
inflicted by another, such as the judge; but that in the language of

love, punishment is self-inflicted. The punishment is contained within the action so that in a very real sense the person condemns or judges himself or herself.

This is a theme of Dostoyevsky's novel *Crime and Punishment*. The young student Raskolnikov is imbued with the *Übermensch* philosophy, that there are two types of people, the ordinary and those who are not bound by the laws of mere mortals. His murdering of an old woman is his putting his theory to the test. Of the book's 550 pages, the first 100 lead into the crime and the final fifty are about his time in prison – the punishment, one would suppose.

But in fact the 450 pages in between are about the punishment. They describe how Raskolnikov falls into a fever and then into an intense sense of isolation:

> '… stopping in the middle of the street at the crossroads and looking around, as though expecting a definite answer from someone. But he got no answer from anywhere; the whole world was dead and indifferent, like the cobblestones on which he walked – dead to him and to him alone.' (part 2, chapter 6)

This is to say that the punishment is already in the offence. Not everybody who does wrong will have Raskolnikov's sense of isolation. They may not feel isolated, but they are isolated, because this is the intrinsic implication of what has been done. This is the moral structure of the world we live in.

This makes perfect sense if we simply think of ordinary human relationships. If two people are close to one another and one does something that is quite hurtful, there is no tribunal set up for the meting out of punishment. Rather we would speak of damage to the relationship and of the need for repair, reconciliation, repentance. If there were no repentance, we would tend to speak of the person shutting himself or herself out from the relationship.

This guides us in the way to think about our relationship with God when it comes to morality. God does not punish but only loves compassionately and offers future. Punishment is isolation; it is self-inflicted and is perpetuated in the one who will not repent. But, because isolation means destruction of our relationship, it is the last thing that God wants.

This may be the context in which to consider the existence of hell. In the light of what we have been saying, hell comes to appear as something of our own making. It is not something that God created, as a teacher might set aside a corner of the classroom for disobedient pupils. It is simply the radical isolation and lovelessness that result from the wilful destruction of love. In this vein, the *Catechism* describes hell as the 'state of definitive self-exclusion from communion with God' (paragraph 1033). Whether any human being could ever wreak such havoc is another question.

Yet there is a sense in which it still makes sense to speak of God punishing. That is, the statement that God punishes may be more a statement that there is a moral order or structure to the universe, than a statement about how that order works out. It may be to say that there is punishment, in the sense that morality is intrinsic to actions, that each action reaps its own consequences – and that this is the kind of world that God has created. If this were not so, there would be moral chaos. But if this is so, then it is not necessary that it be God who does the punishing, on the model of some human tribunal.

We can go further by saying that the language of God punishing is in fact the obverse of the language of God loving. A necessary part of God's benevolence and compassion is God's aversion to sin. God's passionate desire for our happiness has as its corollary an abhorrence of whatever obstructs this. It is in this sense that we speak of the anger or the wrath of God. It is not the anger and wrath of a cruel, disciplinarian father. It is the anger of love.

What we forget about the wrath of God is that the Bible tends to speak of it in the context of social injustice – whereas we reduce it to a matter of a fearful relationship between God and the individual. One thinks of Patrick Kavanagh's poem, *War and Peace*, where the child asks what was the whisper that followed the sigh from 'the house of injustice':

>   'That was God raging, child,
>   Something to fright
>   More than the shouting
>   Of a whole drunken night.'

God is not the legalist God who has no time for human failure. God is the God who rages against all the injustice in the world. There is anger in the heart of God only because there is such intense love.

The idea of God judging deserves mention here also. Again we tend to reduce it to a fearful confrontation between God and the individual. In doing so, we forget that a significant part of what God's judgment means is God's judging in favour of the righteous and the oppressed. In this sense, God's judgment is part of God's love.

The biblical presentation of this is well illustrated by Psalm 73. The author knows of God's goodness to the upright, but observes and even envies the prosperity of the wicked, and thus comes to say, 'my feet had almost stumbled'. Their prospering prompted the thought that perhaps there is no moral order, that it does not matter what a person does. But the writer realises that to go on thinking like this would be a betrayal of the beliefs of the people's tradition. And so, 'I went into the sanctuary of God; then I perceived their end.' Remembering God brings with it clear vision, and the realisation that the prosperity of the wicked is only seeming success. In reality it is nothing, and their ultimate destiny is that they are nothing.

The biblical language of reward and punishment, of weeping and gnashing of teeth, is really meant as hope for the poor. It belongs most appropriately to the fifth way of looking at morality, morality as social transformation. It is saying that in God's universe there is a moral order and that goodness is vindicated. Its vindication is part of the meaning of the resurrection from the dead of God's humble servant. In this sense we can take the stern God seriously, in that anger is the obverse of God's infinite love.

Thus, different approaches to God converge in their imagery concerning God – the God of final judgment and the God of social justice, the God of wrath and the God of compassion. No one approach is sufficient for appreciating God, and all together reveal more fully the God of our morality.

CHAPTER 4

The Sense of Sin

In this chapter we will draw on the five approaches to morality to look at the theme of sin. We shall suggest that the variety of approaches makes for comprehensive thinking and avoids the distortion that comes from a preoccupation with one particular emphasis.

Sin Yesterday and Today

Many would say that the theme of sin has been far too dominant in our moral consciousness. While we can smile at light-hearted comments, such as that Catholics can easily be identified because of their feelings of guilt, we can also recognise the great harm that has been done to many a conscience, in terms of scrupulosity and an unreal sense of guilt, by an excessive focus on sin.

As against this, many have noted a trend in the opposite direction today. They speak of the loss of the sense of sin in our society, and see the evidence for this in a disregard for moral principles and a prevailing sense that 'anything goes'. They might sum it up by saying that the reign of the scrupulous conscience has ceded to the reign of the lax conscience.

It is reasonable, one might suggest, to see good and bad on both sides here. We can hope for a renewed sense of moral principle while at the same time not wanting a return to the sin- and guilt-ridden conscience of the past. And we can welcome the more positive moral outlook of today's world, while at the same time expressing concern over the laxity in moral standards. This is where the five approaches to morality may be of help. Because the five approaches bring together a diversity of emphases, they may help us towards a balanced and comprehensive perspective on the topic of sin.

From what has gone before, it is easy to predict in broad terms what the five approaches would say about sin. Seeing morality as law would lead to speaking of sin as breaking the commandments.

Seeing morality as inner conviction would translate into seeing sin as a matter of going against one's conscience. Seeing morality as personal growth would provide a basis for understanding sin as the expression of vicious attitudes and tendencies. Seeing morality as love would lead to seeing sin as doing harm in and to relationship. Seeing morality as social transformation would make for a definition of sin as injustice.

Even to say this much is to suggest that the contrasts between yesterday and today may not be as stark as they seem. These contrasts may be better accounted for by changing perspectives in our thinking than by assertions that we are either coming out of, or entering into, the dark ages. As we apply the five approaches to the topic of sin, we will find that they help make sense of what has been happening to the idea of sin in recent times. This in turn will provide a basis for thinking about sin today, one that integrates what is valid both in past and in present thought, and corrects what might be unsatisfactory in either.

Grave Matter

It will be useful to begin with the traditional definition of mortal sin. According to this definition, a sin is mortal if the act constitutes grave matter and is carried out with full knowledge and full consent. But if any of these elements is lacking, the sin might not be mortal; that is, if the matter of the act is light or if the person acts without full knowledge or freedom. It is a definition that stands the test of time because it makes good sense. It is about a person willingly doing something which he or she clearly knows to be seriously wrong.

If we ask what makes something 'grave matter', we come to another traditional way of speaking about mortal sin which hinges on the word 'mortal'. What makes a sin 'mortal' is that it is against charity and destroys the life of charity in the soul. The word 'charity' refers particularly to God, in the sense that being in relationship to God is the principle of life in the soul. The mortality of sin is the destruction it causes to this relationship. In the words of the *Catechism*, mortal sin 'results in the loss of charity' and if it persists it 'causes exclusion from Christ's kingdom and the eternal death of hell' (paragraph 1861).

Now, when we put these two definitions of mortal sin together, the issues begin to emerge. In our tradition we have grown up with the impression that there is quite a number of mortal sins and that mortal sin is something that happens quite frequently. But this is hard to reconcile with the definitions. To speak of the loss of the life of charity in the soul is to speak of the collapse of our relationship with God. If mortal sin is something that can happen frequently, we are then talking about a repeated collapsing of that relationship. This does not square with our experience of relationship. Likewise, it is hard to reconcile the idea of frequency with the first definition, in other words with the idea that people repeatedly and willingly do things which they understand to be seriously wrong.

If anything, Christianity would suggest the opposite picture. It is well established in our tradition that it is venial rather than mortal sin that is hard to avoid, so much so that venial sin is almost part of life. But for people in the state of grace, mortal sin is an unlikely event, because their whole disposition is opposed to it. So, how has this impression been formed, that people who are basically good are regularly engaged in mortal sin?

The problem, as with so much of what we are talking about, has to do with a neglect of certain aspects of the issue. In this case, one aspect of the idea of sin, that of grave matter, has become the focus to such an extent as to block out of the picture the more subjective dimensions of knowledge and consent. If mortal sin is identified with grave matter in people's minds, then we can readily understand how such sin could be seen as a frequent occurrence. Many things are done which are seriously wrong; but only a percentage of these can be said to have been done with full knowledge and full consent.

The problem is that, by being identified with grave matter, sin is being objectified. It comes to be seen as a matter of the action and nothing more. Take, for instance, somebody saying that it is a mortal sin to miss Mass on Sunday. Strictly speaking, this statement makes no sense. Missing Mass is an action (or rather, an omission). But a mortal sin is a seriously wrong action done with full knowledge and consent. To say that somebody missed Mass tells us nothing about these dimensions of knowing and willing. It does not even tell us whether the person was well enough to leave the house!

And that is the problem; because knowledge and consent are taken for granted we can slip easily into this objectified way of thinking. Strictly speaking, it does not make sense; but in a looser, more popular sense, it means simply that missing Mass is grave matter, a serious issue for a Catholic.

Again, a person might do something that ends up causing harm, yet do it with the best of intentions. Or a person might do something, thinking it to be right or at most only lightly wrong, though others think it to be grave matter. But if sin is understood in too objective a way, these considerations do not enter the picture. The action, what is out there, is all that counts.

It is this confusion that makes talk of sin from within the approach to morality as law seem so unacceptable. Within this approach one would speak of sin as breaking the commandments and this is quite legitimate, as long as it is not objectified in the foregoing manner. In chapter two we outlined the significance and value of the commandments, and the stories of David and of Ahab showed the sinfulness of breaking the commandments as graphically as could be wished. But just as the commandments become legalism when considered in isolation from the other approaches to morality, so it is with sin if it is seen only in terms of actions and their conformity to norms.

A further distortion of our understanding of sin is to found in the language that speaks of the Church forbidding something 'under pain of mortal sin'. This language gives the impression that the Church can decide what is right and wrong. This makes morality very arbitrary indeed, and further separates sin from anything that might be going on in the person doing the act. The truth, rather, is that the Church does not legislate over what is morally right or wrong; still less does it legislate over when and where the life of charity is lost in the soul. What the Church can do is to help its members identify what is right and wrong, what is grave matter, what is likely to endanger the person's relationship to God and threaten the life of charity in the soul.

It may be helpful here to distinguish between morality and Church discipline. For instance, stealing is against the moral law, whereas omitting to fast on an appointed day is against what happens to be the discipline of the Church. The Church could change the latter (and has done so), but it is not within the Church's power to change a person's obligations regarding the property of others. Therefore there is an important difference between going against what the Church says about stealing and going against what it says about fasting. One is an offence against the discipline of the community, the other an offence against the moral law. Which might be worse in a given case depends, of course, on the particular circumstances.

Action and Person

We are saying that the full definition of sin embraces both objective and subjective aspects. Sin is about both the action and the person. To say that something is a sin is to make a statement about both the act and the person, not about the act alone. If anything, it is to say more about the person than the act or, more accurately, about the person in the light of having carried out the act. For instance, the statement that lying is wrong makes no reference to any particular person or situation; it is a general moral evaluation of the telling of lies. But to say that lying is a sin brings the person into the picture by including the dimensions of knowing and willing. It is to say something about the state of the person who has knowingly and freely done this wrong.

This use of language will sound somewhat forced because we are so used to loosely saying that certain actions are sins, so some further illustration will help. Thomas Aquinas, in his *De Malo*, discusses in detail what we know as the seven deadly sins. As he goes through these sins, he asks about each whether it is a mortal sin. Let us compare what he says about envy and gluttony. About envy, he says that it is a mortal sin of its nature (*ex genere suo*), whereas he says that gluttony is not. This is because envy, which is defined as sadness over the happiness of another, is inherently contrary to charity, whereas gluttony is not necessarily a mortal sin because desire for food is not inherently contrary to charity.

Thus far it appears that Aquinas' language is at odds with ours, for he seems to be saying that certain actions are mortal sins. But he goes on to qualify. Even though envy is a mortal sin inherently, he says that it may not be mortal in a given case because of what he calls 'an imperfection in the act'. By this he means, either that the act does not proceed from deliberative reason, or that the matter of the act is not serious. These are the two aspects of our definition of mortal sin.

On the other hand, he says that gluttony could in a given case amount to mortal sin if what the person were doing amounted to putting something else in the place of God. What Aquinas is saying, therefore, is that if an action is contrary to charity, and if the matter is known to be grave, and if the person is acting with full awareness and deliberation, then we are talking about mortal sin.

We could make the same point in a less technical way by saying that it is only in the form of confession that sin becomes fully conscious of itself. To confess is to accept that this is not simply behaviour objectively contrary to the norm, but behaviour for which I accept responsibility and which, in the presence of God, I recognise to be an offence.

Consistent Sensitivity

With these clarifications in mind, we will proceed to elaborate on how all five approaches to morality can contribute to our understanding of sin. Within the objective focus of the approach to morality as law, we would talk simply about actions that are wrong. Indeed sin is also traditionally defined as a 'bad human act'. Here we bracket questions of intentions and responsibility so as to focus on the relative wrongness of different actions. The language of grave matter and light matter invites us to attend to the wrongness that resides in certain ways of acting and to discriminate between what is more and what is less seriously wrong.

An image that comes to mind here is that of a mountain range. The contents of our mind can be like a mountain range, and sometimes one peak can dominate so much that no other peak can be seen. This can be an image for our sensitivity to sin. For instance, there are people who are one-issue crusaders. They are so taken up with the perceived wrongness of, say, abortion or cruelty to animals or nuclear power that they cannot see anything else. Or again, there are people who are pathologically scrupulous about certain kinds of wrongdoing and quite unaware that other things they are doing might be much more wrong. Again there is our inherited tendency to equate the word 'immorality' with sex, a tendency that numbs our sensitivity to other kinds of immorality.

A correction to these tendencies is to be found in what Cardinal Bernardin of Chicago has described as a 'consistent ethic of life'.[1] He was thinking specifically of various ways in which human life and dignity are threatened, and in this context what he called for was a consistent sensitivity across the whole range of issues involved. Thus, for instance, it would be an inconsistent sensitivity to be opposed to abortion while not also concerned for the protection of all who are powerless or defenceless in society. Likewise, it could be argued that opposing abortion while advocating capital punishment, or *vice versa*, is inconsistent.

Looking at sin through the lens of the first approach to morality invites us to develop such consistency, to bring down to size the 'mountains' in our moral sensitivity so that our awareness of wrongness may be as comprehensive as possible. For some people it might mean seeing that immorality is as much, if not more, to do with issues of justice and truth as with issues of sexuality. For others it might mean that there are many more issues of wrongdoing in the world than the ones they happen to be obsessed with. For others again it might suggest the need for a more creative way of examining their consciences. Perhaps the ways in which they have learned to categorise wrong are those of a child, leaving them unable to access many areas that should be of concern to an adult.

Full Knowledge and Consent

If we move on to the second approach to morality, morality as inner conviction, we would now highlight, rather than bracket, questions of responsibility. Whereas morality as law would have us think of sin in terms of actions, this approach would shift our attention from 'grave matter' to 'full knowledge and consent'.

The first point is that the very idea of 'full' knowledge and consent requires some consideration. One can imagine all our actions to lie across a spectrum, ranging from those which are completely involuntary (such as a tummy rumble) to those that are done with complete awareness and willingness. The tendency often is to presume that most of our actions lie towards the latter end of the spectrum, to presume that people generally act knowingly and freely. But within the second approach to morality that is not taken for granted; if anything the opposite might be presumed. In fact, when we attend to the subjective aspect of action we begin to wonder just how much real freedom and responsibility there is.

When people confess their sins they are, of course, accepting responsibility, admitting that they could have done differently. But how many of our deeds can be confessed in this way? How often, rather, do we find ourselves saying, 'if only I had known…' or 'I was under so much pressure…'? Very often it is the case that people have so very little freedom, as when dominated by some habit or compulsion, that effectively it would have been next to impossible for them to have acted differently.

Think for instance of a habit of masturbation that has persisted over decades. Its roots stretch way down into the psyche. There are such cases where, despite the person's desire to confess, the act is not accurately described as deliberate. There are many comparable experiences where people are not so much in control of their own actions as in the control of their own past.

There are a number of factors that can prevent us from acting freely, with full knowledge and consent. There is ignorance of the situation; there is the inability to appreciate some aspect of what is involved; there is the presence of external force or threat; there is the internal pressure of fear or anxiety; there are unconscious motivations. Sometimes, of course, we can do something about these. Sometimes the pressure can be resisted; sometimes the ignorance is our own fault. But other times this is not the case, and when that is so, then we are not acting with full knowledge and consent. To that extent we are not 'sinning'.

In this area, psychology has much to contribute to our understanding of morality. We might compare the way a psychologist and a moral theologian would deal with lying or stealing. Moral theologians tend to speak in general terms about the rightness or wrongness of these actions, whereas psychologists are primarily interested in this particular kleptomaniac or compulsive liar and in what it is that explains the behaviour. This is something of a caricature but it makes a point nonetheless. To speak in general terms is valuable, but on its own it tends to disregard the subjective factors that inform action. But attention to the why and wherefore of a particular person's behaviour is likely to yield a lively awareness of just how unfree we can be at times.

In the light of these considerations, we can move from defining sin as a bad human act to defining it as going against one's conscience. Attending to the presence or absence of full knowledge and consent leads us to stress people's degree and quality of 'involvement' in what they are doing. It is only when awareness and willingness are present to such a degree as to make for responsibility that we can speak of sin.

Of course the approach to morality as inner conviction would also want to encourage people to grow in awareness and willingness, to inform themselves better as to the rights and wrongs of behaviours and to grow in their capacity to resist pressure and act freely. When people grow in knowledge and freedom, they actually become more aware of sin. The more conscientious we become, the more we are able to see the sin in ourselves.

This brings us to the question of guilt. Here again we might suggest a spectrum, this time ranging from an unreal sense of guilt, through a realistic sense of guilt, to an unreal lack of guilt. Guilt is itself a difficult word to pin down, but it is helpful to distinguish between *feeling* guilty and *being* guilty. It does happen that people feel guilty even though they did nothing wrong. It also happens that people do wrong and feel no guilt at all.

The thing to reach for is a convergence between our feelings and our actual guilt, in other words, a realistic sense of guilt. This is where we can weigh up both the gravity of the matter of this act and our own level of freedom and responsibility, so as to see what guilt applies to us. This is no easy task. It involves being able to make distinctions, such as that this action was very serious but that I am not to be held responsible, or that it was something insignificant in itself but that I was terribly to blame in doing it. This too is part of what is involved in learning to examine one's conscience well.

Act and State

The third way of looking at morality, morality as personal growth, expands this focus on the person acting. Here we go beyond, for instance, whether lying is right or wrong; we go beyond the awareness and willingness involved in telling this lie; and we ask the question, what is happening the person as a result of this deed?

Now we can see most clearly that sin is more a matter of what happens to a person than something that inheres in an action.

More accurately, sin refers to a state people are in as a result of the actions they do. Thus it is more precise to speak of a person being in a state of sin than to speak of a person committing a sin. The real tragedy is not just that a person does something wrong, but that the person thereby become a bad person or a worse person. By deceiving we become dishonest; through unkindnesses we become cruel; by doing wrong we become sinners.

This is especially important with regard to mortal sin. If sin is primarily about the state a person is in, the term 'mortal sin' describes a state of the soul where charity has died. Such a radical state is more than likely the result of a whole series and pattern of actions rather than the outcome of one momentous act. While the latter is possible, the more common human experience by far is of a gradual decline, of patterns building up until a critical point is reached. And, as the saying goes, it may be but a straw that breaks the camel's back in the end. In this perspective it is hard to speak of any particular act being a mortal sin; rather, we would be inclined to think of a whole pattern of more or less serious actions coming to constitute a state of mortal sin.

It is helpful in this context to think of sin in the singular – as 'sinfulness' – rather than just of 'sins' in the plural. This in fact is the thinking behind the seven capital or deadly sins. They are called 'capital' because they are root sins out of which all kinds of other sins grow. And they are cast in terms of things happening the person; becoming envious or lustful or greedy is going to set off a trail of other wrongdoings. What is important, then, is to get at the root, to get to what is happening in the person, the roots of sinfulness or sinful attitudes that are causing all these sins.

Such are the perspectives on sin opened up by the view of morality as personal growth. But there is one further point, which regards the very complex relationship between the person and the action. It is one thing to speak in general of moving from sin as act to sin as the state of the person, but it is quite another to do this in any specific instance. It is sometimes said that acts are symbolic of the person, that what we do symbolises or represents what we are. We talk of a good tree bearing good fruit. But we also say things like 'she wasn't herself' or 'I don't know what got into him'. We know too that, in the words of Shakespeare, 'one can smile, and smile, and be a villain' and that there are those who 'look like the innocent flower, But be the serpent under 't''.

When we think of sin in terms of what is happening the person, we learn not to presume a simple relationship between action and person, as if one could simply read off from the action the disposition of the person. Some examples will illustrate the complexity of this.

Thomas Kenneally's now famous documentary novel, *Schindler's Ark*, presents us with a most complex character. Living in Poland during the Second World War, Schindler was a businessman who was also in cahoots with the local Nazi officers. He engaged in black-marketeering, he was a very heavy drinker, he was grossly unfaithful to his wife (he was even unfaithful to his mistress). You might say that he was committing all the great mortal sins, and at quite a rate. At the same time, the book reveals, he was using his good relations with the Nazi officers to arrange that some of the Jewish prisoners could work within the better conditions of his factory. This eventually led to his saving something over one thousand of these people from death in the camps.

What, then, do we make of Schindler? Was he a good or a bad person? One thinks again of Shakespeare, 'The web of our life is of a mingled yarn, good and ill together.' But in this case, who is to say which is the dominant thread or what is the overall pattern? Things may not be what they appear. The complexity of this comes across forcibly in the words ascribed to Simon Peter, in Fabbri's play *Proces à Jesus*, as he reflects on his having betrayed the Lord:

> 'Despise me if you will! But what you cannot understand, what I shall never make you understand perhaps, is that a man can at one and the same time believe and betray, love and deny. Yes, I tell you, that is possible. And even as I stood in Annas' courtyard saying; 'I do not know him! I have never seen him!' at that very moment I loved him.'[2]

Even the act of betraying Jesus might not be mortal sin! For, when we think in terms of what is happening the person, we are not considering only discrete acts, we are also considering those acts in the context of the person's larger character and history. We are asking, where does this act fit into the picture? How does it affect the over-all picture? It is not enough to go by the act alone when talking about sin.

The words of Jesus himself on this are perhaps the most striking. Confronting the Pharisees with their unbelief he says: 'Truly I tell you, the tax collectors and the prostitutes are going into the king-dom of God ahead of you' (Matthew 21:31). The good deeds of the Pharisees conceal a self-righteous disposition, while the wrong-doings of the tax collectors and sinners have to be seen in the light of their repentance.

The complexity of these matters is actually reflected in the language we use about sin. Besides mortal and venial sin, in more recent times the term 'serious sin' has come into use. This makes for some confusion, but what is being expressed is the need for an intermedi-ate term between mortal sin and venial sin. Venial sin tends to mean something slight, while mortal sin refers to a radical loss of love. There is felt the need for a term that speaks about something which is seriously sinful but without destroying the person's rela-tionship to God. This is described as 'serious sin' and one can see the value of the term when one reflects on the examples of Schindler and of Peter and of the tax collectors and prostitutes.[3]

Sin and God

The language of love – the fourth way of looking at morality – opens up a further dimension of the meaning of sin. We have already used this language when we spoke of mortal sin as destroy-ing the life of charity in the soul. What this language highlights is that, at the heart of sin, is the breaking of relationship. If we take again the example of deceitfulness, the tragedy is not simply that people become dishonest (the language of the third way of looking at morality) but that relationships are becoming false, becoming a lie.

It is not that rare for somebody to come to confession after perhaps six months or a year and to say something along the lines of: 'I've nothing really to confess… I haven't broken any of the command-ments.' Such people's thinking about sin is confined to what is explicitly prohibited by the ten commandments. But if sin were

understood in terms of what damages relationship, their appreciation of the ten commandments would be deepened and their sensitivity to the presence of sin in their lives extended considerably.
Where previously, for instance, they understood that adultery was
sinful, they might now see that hurting one's wife or husband is
also forbidden by the sixth commandment!

We might go along with this to a point and then wonder: surely not
all sin involves the rupture of relationship? Is not some sin quite
private, in that it does not impinge on anybody else? At first sight
this would seem to be so. We would all be able to detect sinfulness
in ourselves of which nobody else is at all aware and from which
nobody else has suffered.

And yet, are we not all social beings? If we are essentially beings-in-
relationship, then the failure that we call sin must in some sense be a
letting down of others as well as of oneself, no matter how private or
secret the failure may be. This in fact is a fundamental, but little
understood, aspect of going to confession. Part of the meaning of
going to a priest lies in the priest's role as representative of the
Christian community, so that in confessing to the priest we are also
confessing that we have failed the community. Thus the examination
of conscience is always implicitly an examination of relationships.

But the relationship that primarily concerns us here is the relationship with God. It is this more than anything else which gives sin its
meaning – so much so that we could even say that only those who
believe in God can sin. This is not to say that non-believers can do
no wrong, but that the word 'sin' is essentially referred to God, as in
the definition of sin as the loss of the life of charity. If this is not part
of our thinking there will be something essential missing from the
definition of sin as grave matter, full knowledge and full consent.
To speak of sin is to speak of 'before God'. To confess sin is to
acknowledge a connection between our guilt and our faith. It is this
connection that the prophet Nathan pointed out to King David in
saying to him that by doing wrong he had despised the Lord.

It could be asked whether there is a link between the oft-remarked
loss of a sense of sin and the loss of a sense of God. Of course, what
is meant by a loss of a sense of sin may be simply the loss of a sense
of right and wrong. But if sin, properly speaking, is about our rela-

tionship to God, then the loss of a sense of God must entail a loss of a sense of sin. Then we no longer relate wrongdoing to a God before whom we stand. We could go on to ask whether this will also diminish our sense of right and wrong and whether, in the extreme, it will lead to the outlook Dostoyevsky prophesied, that if God does not exist then everything is permitted.

At any rate, there is a twofold sense in which sin is to be understood as damaging our relationship with God. There are, firstly, the cases of specific neglect of God. One thinks of the first three commandments, of the sinfulness of putting something in the place of God, or of not spending time attending to God in prayer, or of a neglect of or disrespect for the sacred dimension of experience, or of the sin of apostasy. The latter brings to mind the words of the second Vatican Council about those 'who wilfully try to drive God from their heart and to avoid all questions about religion, not following the biddings of their conscience' (*The Church in the Modern World*, paragraph 19).

Secondly there is the sense in which any instance of doing what we know to be wrong is indirectly a failure to love God. This is what we saw to be meant by the relationship between the first three and the remainder of the commandments. Or one might think of the words of Jesus: 'Just as you did it to one of the least of these who are members of my family, you did it to me' (Matthew 25:40). In this sense, when we say that sin means failure in relationship, we are referring to relationship with God and relationship with others at one and the same time.

Sin in the World

If sin is about relationship, then what makes something sinful is in large part the harm or suffering that it causes to others. This allows us to see further meaning in the term 'grave matter'. Talk of full knowledge and consent interests itself in the responsibility and culpability of the person doing the deed. But talk of grave matter attends to the action itself, not simply as a transgression of the law, but as something which causes suffering.

Thus sin is about suffering. It is about making people suffer or allowing them to suffer or ignoring their suffering. When our actions or omissions cause others to suffer or perpetuate their suffering, then God is offended, God is hurt. The seriousness or gravity of the sin is then to be measured by the pain and suffering it causes.

If we think of sin in this way, we can go on to speak of sin as being in the world and not just in the heart of the sinner. Sin is all too visible in its effects in society. This introduces into our discussion of sin the fifth way of looking at morality, morality as social transformation. Sin is now being seen as something that is felt in society and which is blocking the transformation of society.

Contemporary theology speaks of this as 'social sin' or 'structural sin'.[4] In one sense, the word 'sin' is being used analogously in such terms, for it is only individual persons who can sin. But what such terms seek to convey is that the results of the sinful actions of individuals and groups of individuals can become embedded in the world and remain long after the perpetrators themselves have gone.

A useful comparison is provided by what we call 'passive smoking'. If one individual smokes, the effects literally stay in the air to affect others. Likewise our sins linger after us and the lingering has two consequences. On the one hand, there is the suffering that is caused either immediately or subsequently. On the other hand, when the effects become embedded in society, it means that others will be contaminated in a way that inclines them to sin as well.

Thus, for example, if a society becomes violent or if it becomes aggressively competitive, people are going to suffer. But also, those born into the society are going to be brutalised. The effects of the sins of others will seep into their attitudes and behaviour, just as the smoke of others gets into our lungs. The idea of sinful social structures means that the ways in which people relate in society have become contaminated by the sin of some, such as to both cause suffering and engender further sin.

So sin is not just something we do; it is also something of which we are victims. It is a power from which we suffer. It can be understood as a power working within the person (as in Paul's well known account in Romans chapter seven), or as a power present in the world and in the structure of society. In the latter sense, contemporary theologians speak of 'the sin of the world'. The idea here is that, just as sin leaves behind its effects, so those effects accumulate or snowball through history. One glimpses something of this in the words of Gerard Manley Hopkin's *God's Grandeur*:

'Why do men then now not reck his rod?
Generations have trod, have trod, have trod;
And all is seared with trade; bleared, smeared with toil;
And wears man's smudge and shares man's smell: the soil
Is bare now, nor can foot feel, being shod.'

Something like this lies behind the story of Adam and Eve also. The writers of this story are not like journalists at the scene, giving a blow-by-blow account of what happens. Rather, they belong to a much later time and are seeking to give an explanation of what they see around them. One thinks of the words of Jeremiah (5:1); 'Run to and fro through the streets of Jerusalem... Search its squares and see if you can find one person who acts justly and seeks truth...' This sense that sin was pervasive led the biblical writers to the insight that it had always been thus, its origins to be located as far back as could be imagined.

Subsequent Christian theology would coin the phrase 'original sin'. Cardinal Newman once remarked that he found the doctrine of original sin the easiest to believe, almost as certain as that the world exists. He came to this, not by reading about Adam and Eve, but by reflecting on the world about him and seeing how out of joint it was with the purpose of its Creator. In the same way, our awareness of the suffering caused by sin can help us understand sin as 'original', that is, as universal and as embedded in our origins.

Our concern is not to attempt a full discussion of original sin; that would deserve a study in its own right. It is the more modest one of suggesting the usefulness of thinking in terms of a history of sin in the world, where each generation is born into a sin-determined situation and soon feels the effects of this inheritance. As traditional Catholic doctrine would have it, knowledge is dimmed, the will is weakened and we ourselves are inclined to sin.

But it is thinking in terms of the view of morality as social transformation that opens up for us this dimension of the meaning of sin. In doing so it also performs the valuable function of reminding us that sin is not simply a private affair between the sinner and God, but also something very public, embedded in society as much as it is embedded in the heart.

In this perspective, the examining of conscience shades into what is known today as 'social analysis' Besides the examination of our own deeds, attitudes, motivations, there is required a sensitivity to the suffering that sin is causing in the world and to the causes of that suffering. A story is told of a village in the mountains where one morning the body of a baby came floating down the stream. Villagers retrieved the body and tried to save it; but the next day more babies came floating by and the next day more again. Finally one of the villagers left and started heading up the mountain. They asked him where he was going. He said he wanted to find out where all the babies were coming from. In examining our conscience, we too start to ask 'why?'

The Sense of Sin

Some of our language about sin has been so oppressive that not alone do we see ourselves as sinners, but also we think that this is how God sees us too. But we can seriously doubt if this is what God sees. It is more likely that what God sees is God's children. It is more likely that God sees suffering and rages at the sin that causes suffering. If this is so, then it has implications for how we should think about sin.

We should first of all think about love, that we are the focus of attention of the infinite and infinitely faithful One who *is* love. We might then think about sin as all that is wrong in God's creation, and then seek to attain a sharper consciousness of how sin causes suffering. We could go on to reflect on how we ourselves are affected by the power of sin, how sometimes we accede, how sometimes we are too weak. But we might remember too that we are more than our actions, and that, while our sinfulness makes us sinners, God's grace makes us new.

CHAPTER 5

Jesus' Liberating View of Morality

Up to this point we have been considering five ways of looking at morality and exploring their application to a number of themes. In this chapter we wish to add to this some ideas about how Jesus saw morality, and then to relate Jesus' view to the five ways. We shall also see how looking into Jesus' understanding of morality brings us further into the heart of what Christian morality is all about.

Redeeming the Word

There is much more to New Testament morality than what will be considered in this chapter. There is, for instance, the teaching of Jesus on marriage and divorce, or on sin and forgiveness. Again, there are the different perspectives on Christian moral living presented by the different New Testament authors, such as Paul, John, Peter and James. Our concern is simply what we can glean from the gospel presentation of his words and deeds as to what Jesus thought about morality itself.

The starting point for our investigation is the Sermon on the Mount (Matthew 5-7), which has traditionally been taken as containing the nucleus of Jesus' moral teaching. It is notable, though, that in the parallel section of Luke's gospel (Luke 6) the sermon takes place on a plain. So where did it take place? In a sense it does not matter, because what we are being given is theological, not geographical, information. The mount in Matthew's gospel is intended to correspond to Mount Sinai in the Old Testament. As Moses was given the ten commandments on Mount Sinai, so now Jesus is presented as the new Moses and his teaching is the new law. What Jesus says is to occupy the central place in our understanding of the moral life.

It is not surprising, then, that much of the sermon in Matthew's gospel should hinge on Jesus' attitude to the Jewish law. Although the Jewish people never forgot the covenant, but continued to see morality as a response to God's revelation, nevertheless at the time of Jesus there had emerged a tendency to see morality in a legalistic way. Legalism began to set in as laws were multiplied in an attempt to define every detail and cover every eventuality of living. In the process, morality was coming to be understood as dependent above all else on the observance of the law. As we read the gospels we tend to identify this legalism with the Pharisees.[1]

But this does not mean that the law is to be set aside. Jesus introduces his teaching by saying: 'Do not think that I have come to abolish the law or the prophets; I have come not to abolish but to fulfil' (Matthew 5:17). His attitude is that the moral law needs to be 'redeemed', needs to be restored to its proper context. From our own experience of how the word 'morality' can be impoverished both by moral legalism and by moral relativism, we can readily appreciate such an effort to redeem the word.

Jesus' stance is not that the law should be relaxed in any way; he goes on to say this quite clearly in the passage just quoted from. His desire is not the relaxation but the perfection of the law. What he attacks is not the law and the commandments, but the legalistic way in which they were being observed. So he says to his disciples; 'unless your righteousness exceeds that of the scribes and Pharisees, you will never enter the kingdom of heaven' (Matthew 5:20). His concern is for the radicalisation of law and morality; he wants to work back to the roots of what morality is all about.

We will present an account of how he does this under six headings. We will suggest that Jesus sees morality in terms of the maximum rather than the minimum, of the internal as well as the external, of putting people before principles, of the spirit rather than the letter of the law, of humility as opposed to self-righteousness, of the detachment that opposes possessiveness. The reader may well wish to add to these categories or to state them in other ways; but they do appear to capture much of what is at the heart of Jesus' own sense of what the word 'morality' means.[2]

The Minimum and the More

Matthew 5:21-48 divides into six units and all have the same structure. Each begins, 'You have heard that it was said…' and continues, 'But I say to you…'. The first part of each unit presents something of how the requirements of the law had come to be interpreted, and the second presents Jesus' radical re-interpretation. The six might be summarised as follows:

You have heard that you shall not murder; but I say that you shall not even be angry with another. You have heard that you shall not commit adultery; but I say that you shall not even lust in your heart. You have heard that you should give a divorced wife a certificate of divorce; but I say that you should not divorce. You have heard that you should not swear falsely; but I say that you should not swear at all. You have heard 'an eye for an eye'; but I say not to resist an evil-doer. You have heard that you should love your neighbour and hate your enemy; but I say that you should love your enemy.

All this has been described as a morality of 'the more', a morality of going beyond the strict demands of the law, asking us to think instead in terms of the maximum that is possible. This is particularly striking in the last two units, in their exhortation to the serious practice of non-violence and enemy love, even at the cost of personal suffering and humiliation. In the final unit, the word 'more' actually occurs:

'For if you love those who love you, what reward do you have? Do not even the tax collectors do the same? And if you greet only your brothers and sisters, what more are you doing than others. Do not even the Gentiles do the same?' (Matthew 5:46-47)

When morality is seen as a matter of laws laid down, life is often lived on the thin line between what is prohibited and what is per-mitted. 'How far can you go?' is the classic phrase that sums up this approach. It thinks in terms of the minimum that we are obliged to do and the maximum we can get away with.

The alternative is to think in terms of what is possible, the maxi-mum, the ideal – what I *might* do rather than what I *must* do. It is illustrated by the conversation between Jesus and Peter in Matthew 18:

'Then Peter came and said to him, "Lord, if another member of the church sins against me, how often should I forgive? As many as seven times?" Jesus said to him, "Not seven times, but, I tell you, seventy-seven times".' (Matthew 18:21-22)

In effect, what Jesus is saying is that there never comes a stage when any of us can say, 'Now I have done all that the law requires; now I have done enough.' That attitude might possibly be sufficient in relation to the law of the land, but in morality we must think without limits. We call this 'idealism', and indeed there is very high idealism in the words of Jesus in the Sermon on the Mount. But in this context 'ideal' is not the same as 'impracticable'. Jesus means what he says to be practised seriously.

To understand this idealism, it may be helpful to distinguish between two different kinds of moral demand. Some moral demands are to be observed perfectly right away, for instance, that we should not injure another or steal from another. But in the case of the other kind of demand, we will spend a lifetime responding ever more perfectly, for instance the demands of integrity or of enemy love. The idealism of Jesus refers to the latter. But his emphasis is not so much on the gradualness of the achievement as on treating the ideal as serious and urgent.

Another way of putting this would be to say that what is demanded in morality is not that I do this or that; what is demanded is myself. And self-giving has no limits, for if limits are put on it, then it ceases to be a giving of self. This perhaps was what made the rich young man sad. He was observing the commandments but something more was required and he was not ready for the self-giving involved (Matthew 19:16-22). We might think too of the story of the widow's mite (Luke 21:1-4). Others gave out of their abundance but she gave all that she had; meaning that they gave of what they had and that she gave of herself.

The final words of Matthew 5 are: 'Be perfect, therefore, as your heavenly Father is perfect'. Seeking to do 'the more' is in fact seeking to be like God, in the sense of imitating God's way with people; 'for he makes his sun rise on the evil and on the good' (Matthew 5:45). We already spoke of the spirit of the ten commandments as treating others the way God would treat them. Here we find Jesus advocating that same spirit, the spirit of imitating God in a way that is unending.

The External and the Internal
Jesus' view is that morality is a deep-seated inner affair, and not just about externals. As we shall see, this is far from meaning that the

external action does not matter. What it means is that externalism in morals forgets the great significance of what goes on within.

In the very next section of the Sermon on the Mount, we begin to understand Jesus' thinking on this. In Matthew 6:1-18, he is talking about the three pillars of Jewish morality, namely, giving alms, praying and fasting. He says that these things should be done 'in secret', in other words, not so that they may be seen and praised by others, as is the case with the hypocrites. If we do them in secret, the Father will see, and that is what matters.

There is a tendency within the legalist mentality to misplace the emphasis by putting it on external performance, on what can be visibly observed. Morality becomes a matter, not just of doing what is required, but of being seen to do it. It becomes something to take pride in. Jesus criticises the Pharisees for this:

> 'They do all their deeds to be seen by others; for they make their phylacteries broad and their fringes long. They love to have the place of honour at banquets and the best seats in the synagogues, and to be greeted with respect in the marketplaces, and to have people call them rabbi.' (Matthew 23:5-7)

Now, we all value recognition and affirmation and it is good that we experience these from others. If they were completely lacking we could well be discouraged from persevering. But the problem is when they become the objective of our striving. When Jesus says to practise morality in secret, he means to focus on the true objective, which is to develop the right interior dispositions, particularly the disposition of doing the right thing because it is the right thing. As Gandhi observed about his own practice of non-violence, the person acts thus not because it works but because it is right. This is morality from a pure heart.

'Heart' is in fact the biblical word for this. In the Bible, the heart is suggestive of far more than affectivity. It means the inside of a person in the deepest sense. It is the centre of the person's being whence actions flow. It is the source of consciousness and of freedom, where we enter into dialogue with ourselves and where we open or close ourselves to God. Jesus spoke thus of the heart when responding to the hypocrisy of the Pharisees:

'But what comes out of the mouth proceeds from the heart, and
this is what defiles. For out of the heart come evil intentions,
murder, adultery, fornication, theft, false witness, slander. These
are what defile a person...' (Matthew 15:18-20)

And it is the heart that God sees. As the Lord said to Samuel when
calling the unlikely David: 'for the Lord does not see as mortals see;
they look on the outward appearance, but the Lord looks on the
heart' (1 Samuel 16:7). When God sees the heart, God sees the disposition from which the action came. In a very real way it is the disposition that forms the action, and so it is only when we see the
heart that we truly understand the action.

Thus, what is objectively a misguided gesture assumes a different
significance when one appreciates that it was done with a loving
heart. On the other hand, there is what T.S. Eliot speaks of in *Murder
in the Cathedral*: 'The last temptation is the greatest treason: to do the
right deed for the wrong reason.' In either case, the external deed
provides insufficient data for understanding.

No wonder then that the Sermon enjoins us not to judge (Matthew
7:1-5). We have enough trouble understanding the roots of our own
behaviour without presuming to grasp the hidden motives of
another. Our concern should shift from being judgmental, towards
being open and sympathetic to what may be within a person, holding out for what is best within that person. And it should move into
an effort to discern where our own hearts lie. 'For where your treasure is, there your heart will be also' (Matthew 6:21).

There is, then, a deep appreciation in Jesus for the inner aspect of
morality. But this is not to say that externals do not matter.
Notwithstanding the importance that is attached to being sincere in
whatever we do, sincerity is not enough. As we saw in the last chapter, sin is about more than intentions, it is about that which causes
suffering. The matter of the action is not to be neglected. When we
read the gospels we find that Jesus is very sensitive to the rights and
wrongs of what people actually do and he is especially sensitive to
the suffering that is caused.

So we are not suggesting that Jesus stands for the internal over and
against the external. He stands for both and what he stands against
is legalism and the hypocrisy it produces. Because legalism sees lit-

tle beyond the visible action Jesus points to the heart. If the heart is rightly attuned to God and rightly attuned to good, the actions will take care of themselves.

Principles and People

A third aspect of Jesus' way of seeing morality comes across from a number of passages in the gospels, most notably from those that describe him healing people on the sabbath and thereby coming into conflict with the religious authorities. What comes across in these passages is the way in which he puts people before principles, not in the sense of detracting from moral principles, but in the sense of correcting the aberration that results from a legalistic clinging to principle.

The gospels include quite a number of stories of healings on the sabbath. There is a story about a man with a withered hand (Luke 6:6-11), another about a man who suffered from dropsy (Luke 14:1-6). There is the account of the healing of a woman who had been bent over, crippled for eighteen years (Luke 13:10-17), and that of the healing of a man who had lain ill and helpless for thirty-eight years (John 5:1-18). As we listen closely to these stories, we sense years and years of pain and quiet suffering. The mention of long numbers of years is further suggestive of the hopelessness of these cases.

However, the question arises: if these people had been ill for so long, what difference would another day make? Why heal on the sabbath? Why not wait till the next day? We begin to suspect that there is a point being made above and beyond the healing itself. It is as if Jesus is deliberately acting provocatively, so as to bring some issue to a head. And that issue is in part the issue of principles *versus* persons.

Indeed he is told that there are six days in the week for working. His response is: would not any of you go to the help of an animal that was in difficulties on the sabbath, yet for some reason it is actually unlawful to do good and save life when it comes to people! He sees the hypocrisy that over-strict, legalistic interpretation of the commandments has led to; that it has actually become wrong to do good. He is challenging the place law had assumed, where external conformity had led to people being forgotten. He is pointing out that the concern for principle can miss out on what really matters, that morality is in the end quite simply about the person standing next to me.

The story of the Good Samaritan (Luke 10:25-37) portrays the same truth. The priest and the Levite pass on by for reasons of ritual purity and the fear of becoming defiled. In other words, they are obeying the law, doing what they think is right. But the Samaritan is 'moved with pity'; and so he sees and responds to human need. It is the non-Jew, not encumbered with the law, who alone can see. This is quite a critique of the religious morality, to think that religion could actually have become an obstacle to seeing what morality is all about.

Mark's gospel has Jesus conclude: 'The sabbath was made for humankind, and not humankind for the sabbath' (Mark 2:27). It is a very radical saying, subordinating the observance of the sabbath to the needs of people. People do not exist in order to obey commandments. Rather, the moral law exists in order to promote the well-being of people. It is a guideline as to the directions in which growth is possible. This is akin to what we saw earlier, when considering the ten commandments as ultimately a gift, setting forth the path to life. So what comes first is people and what people are for. If the moral law is not serving people, making for their entry into life, what then is its purpose? Has it come merely to serve itself?

Such absolutising of the law is another of the dangers of legalism. When we think only in terms that 'this is always and everywhere to be obeyed no matter what', the danger is that people are forgotten. A preoccupation with observance can make for an insensitivity to suffering. This is not to impute malice, simply to point to the paradox that a certain kind of devotion to the law can blind us to the very purpose of the moral law.

Another thread of all this has to do with freedom. The first of the sabbath confrontations pictures Jesus and his disciples on the sabbath making their way through the grainfields and plucking and eating some of the grain. The confrontation with the Pharisees ends with Jesus saying, 'The Son of Man is lord of the sabbath' (Luke 6:1-6). There is a sense of Jesus being a free spirit, free from legalistic entanglements, free to enjoy God's creation and to respond to God's creatures. The obverse is that those who confront Jesus are in fact enslaved by the law and blind to what really matters.

But it should be clear that Jesus is not here saying that people can just do what they want. He is not rejecting the law but putting it in its place. It is noteworthy that sometimes, as in healing on the sabbath, he relaxes the law, but that on other occasions, such as the six 'But I say to you...' teachings, he tightens the law to the point of being called idealistic and unreal. But he is being consistent. Both the relaxing and the tightening are for the same reason, namely, whatever is for the well-being and flourishing and more-being of people. It is not a matter of whether Jesus is for or against the law; it is that he is on the side of people.

The Letter and the Spirit

The contrast between people and principles leads easily into a closely related contrast between attention to the letter and attention to the spirit of the law. If the ten commandments constitute the summary statement of the morality of the Old Testament, then Jesus' twofold command to love God and love one another is the corresponding summary in the New Testament. But in presenting this formulation, Jesus is also recovering and revealing again the very spirit of morality.

This is particularly evident in the manner in which he presents the commandment of love in Matthew's gospel (22:34-40). Stating the love of God and the love of neighbour as the greatest commandments, he concludes: 'On these two commandments hang all the law and the prophets.' The two tablets of the law are reduced to their essence, the love of God (the first three commandments) and the love of neighbour (the remaining seven). The implication is that if these loves are not present, the commandments are not being practised.

Paul says the same in the famous passage on love in 1 Corinthians 13. No matter what heroic heights I achieve, if I have not love I am nothing. And again in Romans: 'Owe no one anything, except to love one another; for the one who loves another has fulfilled the law' (Romans 13:8). It is not that the commandments are annulled, but that the commandments are specifications of what love is.

Therefore, if we truly love we will be obeying the commandments; but if we seek to observe the law and are without love, then we have missed the point. It is in this sense that we are to understand also the famous saying of St Augustine: 'Love, and do what you will'.

Here again we find a paradox, that if the effort to be moral becomes too intense it can destroy itself. Excessive concentration on detail and on detailed conformity, on getting it right and even being in the right, ends up as a project of self-perfection that loses sight of what morality is all about. It is the letter without the spirit. In its essence morality has become something other than love. In fact it has died in the process, as Paul hints when he speaks of 'a new covenant, not of letter but of spirit; for the letter kills, but the Spirit gives life' (2 Corinthians 3:6).

The image of missing the wood for the trees comes to mind. If we look in detail at every single tree and branch and twig and leaf, and document everything, we will end up with nothing more than masses of detail. We need to look around, to get the feel of the forest. We need to stand back and look from a distance to see how it enhances the landscape. Likewise we will not understand morality by entering immediately into the minutiae and applications of every norm and precept. We will need to look around and stand back if the whole picture is to present itself. And it is only when we see the overall picture or pattern of love that we really begin to appreciate the details, as well as the range and limits of their application.

Self-Righteousness and Humility

In the end, Jesus' view of morality comes down to two contrasting attitudes. We shall call the first of these the stance of self-righteousness and self-sufficiency, and the other the stance of humility and openness to God. Perhaps the place where Jesus presents these most clearly and vividly is the story of the Pharisee and the publican (Luke 18:9-14).

As so often in Luke, the meaning is given in the introduction. 'He also told this parable to some who trusted in themselves that they were righteous and regarded others with contempt.' The contrast between the Pharisee thanking God that he was not like others, and the publican refusing to even look up, but beating his breast and imploring God's mercy, is the contrast between self-righteousness and humility. And the introduction suggests that this opposition has not a little to do with the divisions that exist between people.

Self-righteousness is about morality being seen as entirely our own achievement. When morality is seen only in terms of the observance of law it easily becomes self-sufficient, because all the emphasis is on what we ourselves are doing. Because of this, any reward or just-ification is something that we ourselves bring about also. There are good grounds for saying that Jesus regarded this as the fundamen-tal sin, underlying all sins. Indeed it is the very antithesis of coven-ant morality. That morality is a morality of invitation and response; anything we do is entirely dependent on the invitation that makes response possible.

This is what humility or openness to God sees. And so, when Jesus says that it was the publican and not the Pharisee who went home justified, it makes perfect sense. Justification is something that God achieves in God's covenant invitation, and it is ours if we allow it into our lives. This makes for something of a paradox. We can be failures, morally speaking, and yet be able to see our need. On the other hand, we can be morally quite upstanding and see this simply as a credit to ourselves. Thus Jesus could say to the Pharisees that tax collectors and prostitutes were making their way into the king-dom of God before them (Matthew 21:31). The statement is shock-ing and can only be understood when we appreciate that all hinges on openness, on the sense of needing God.

Not only does self-righteousness or pride not need God, but it is also the source of individualism and divisiveness. We refer here to the poison of comparison in morals. It is as if, in order to appear in the right, we must be able to point to others who are in the wrong. This is the significance of the Pharisees' despising the prostitutes and publicans. Humility can see that the line between good and evil runs through each heart. But self-righteousness draws the line between people, building a wall between so-called good people and evil people, loading all the wrong onto 'them'.

Gandhi once asked the question: how can they who think they pos-sess absolute truth possibly be fraternal? He saw that, if some peo-

ple think that they possess the truth, this inevitably leads into per-
secuting others who are regarded as outside the truth. But humility
recognises that, if anything, the truth possesses us, that we all participate in truth, each of us just as needy as the next. Openness to
God and openness to others go hand in hand.

Attachment and Detachment

With this final pair of terms we are entering more into the specifics
of morality, but this is warranted by the attention given by the
gospels, particularly by Luke, to this theme. Jesus comes across as
seeing morality as having to do with getting our attachments and
detachments right and very often he thinks of this with specific reference to wealth and possessions.

This theme presents morality as a matter of single-mindedness. 'No
one can serve two masters', Jesus says, and 'no city or house divided
against itself will stand' (Matthew 6:24; 12:25). Again, 'No one who
puts a hand to the plough and looks back is fit for the kingdom of
God' (Luke 9:62). At the very heart of the moral journey, then, is the
question of our commitments and attachments.

Jesus would seem to see the basic choice as being between the
things of God and the things of the world. God and wealth are seen
as the two masters in the passage quoted above. Depending on
where our hearts lie, we will store up treasure on earth or in heaven.
This leads us into the teachings on wealth and poverty in Luke's
gospel. For instance, there is the story of the rich man building bigger barns for his goods, and the chilling words of Jesus:

> 'But God said to him, "You fool! This very night your life is
> being demanded of you. And the things you have prepared,
> whose will they be?" So it is with those who store up treasures
> for themselves but are not rich towards God.' (Luke 12:20-21)

The folly of storing up treasure is again evident in the story of the
rich man and Lazarus (Luke 16:19-31). In the later chapters of Luke
we see the contrast boil down to a fundamental choice. When Jesus
invites the rich man to sell what he has, the man goes away sad
(Luke 18:18-25), but a few paragraphs later we see Zacchaeus gladly
take up the challenge with remarkable generosity of spirit (Luke
19:1-10). After the rich man walked away, Jesus remarked what an

obstacle riches can be, but the story of Zacchaeus encourages us to think that the obstacle is not insurmountable.

So we have the sense that for Jesus morality is about a basic decision as to where our hearts will lie, in devotion to God or in devotion to the things of this world. But it is not just that people whose hearts are in God are not attached to possessions. Rather, they experience a more general detachment. Trusting in God, they are not anxious – about what to eat or drink, about what to wear, about how long they will live. Preoccupation with these things can mean that God is forgotten and that life becomes dominated by anxiety. But preoccupation with God frees our spirit from enslavement to the material and thereby frees our generosity, as it did for Zacchaeus.

Morality as Liberating

Under six headings we have outlined something of the picture of morality that can be built up from the teachings and interactions of Jesus. If we go on now to compare this picture with the five ways of looking at morality which we have already outlined and illustrated, we will find some striking points of convergence.

Firstly, the shift from thinking of the minimum to thinking of the more deepens our appreciation of morality as law. It tells us that the moral law is not a minimum set of requirements but the call for a response that knows no limits. It is ultimately the very law of our being and becoming. Secondly, Jesus' emphasis on the heart corresponds to the view of morality as inner conviction, telling us that morality is a matter, not of external conformity, but of interior commitment to the truth about living. Thirdly, his putting people before principles calls to mind the understanding of morality as personal growth, where morality is primarily about what is happening persons.

The fourth way of looking at morality was in terms of love and it is this perspective that highlights the significance of invitation-response as the structure of Christian morality. This relates obviously to what Jesus says about the letter and the spirit of the law. But also, when Jesus speaks of the opposition between self-righteousness and openness before God, we can see that he is talking about love, about a sense of the priority of God's loving initiative and of a grateful response to it, in contrast to the individualism of

the self-righteous. Finally, Jesus' further contrast between possessiveness and the detachment that trusts in God can be linked to the
view of morality as social transformation, given that what he says is
so focused on the dangers of possessions.

There is, then, great convergence. But we would suggest that Jesus'
teaching goes further, in that it is indicative of an integrated way of
holding together all these different aspects and emphases. We
might put this in terms of a composite profile of the moral person
that emerges from the words and deeds of Jesus.

Perhaps the place to begin that profile is with the word *freedom*. It
comes across, from much of what we have said, that morality can be
a very confining and constricting experience. But the teaching and
practice of Jesus offer something much more positive. In what he
says and does, there is a great sense of freedom from the slavish,
minimalistic and scrupulous observance of the externals of morality
that also puts principles before people and appearances before the
reality.

Further theological reflection on this is to be found in Paul's letter to
the Galatians, where the law is presented as enslaving. The contrast
is developed between being enslaved to the law and being liberated
by the promise of Christ. 'For freedom Christ has set us free. Stand
firm, therefore, and do not submit again to a yoke of slavery'
(Galatians 5:1).

Thus, freedom comes with transcending that in which freedom had
been thought to reside, namely, the self-reliance and self-justification of the law. In humble openness we place our trust in God. We
learn that true morality is within, so we learn purity of heart and we
learn to live from the heart. We come to appreciate the centrality of
love, so that we become responsive to the needs of people in an ever
more generous giving of self that contrasts with the small-minded
minimalism that has lost sight of what people are for. All this is
God's free spirit working in us, liberating us into our own true
being.

Discipleship

The pivotal point in the gospels is when the concentration shifts
from what Jesus says and does to who Jesus is. We notice it, for

instance, in the reaction to his calming of the storm: 'Who then is this, that even the wind and the sea obey him?' (Mark 4:41). This observation brings us to the heart of the moral vision of the gospels.

One way in which the concentration shifts is that people appreciate that the picture of morality presented by Jesus is an articulation of what he himself lives by. People see that his heart is open to God (they will go on to call him the 'Son of God') and that he transcends legalism in his unstinting response to the needs of people and his compassionate love for them. But the real shift comes when people experience themselves as the recipients of this grace.

The pivotal point is when, to quote a famous phrase, 'the proclaimer becomes the proclaimed'. People experience for themselves the liberating effect of Jesus. Paul says that for freedom Christ has set us free. John's gospel has Jesus himself saying: 'if the Son makes you free, you will be free indeed' (John 8:36). The sinner woman of whom Jesus said, 'her sins, which were many, have been forgiven: hence she has shown great love' (Luke 7:47), knew the meaning of this release.

But the raising of Lazarus is perhaps the great symbol. Lazarus has been bound in the tomb for four days. Jesus shouts to him, 'Lazarus come out!' and to those around, 'Unbind him, and let him go' (John 11:40-42). The drama of the story has great symbolic meaning. It is not only about raising from the dead; it stands for the whole of the liberating effect that Jesus has on people's lives, bringing them up out of their tombs.

As people experience this liberation, Jesus becomes more than an enlightened moral teacher. This is the significance of the language of 'discipleship' in the gospels. When Jesus 'calls' somebody to 'follow' him, the word 'disciple' assumes new meaning. In Judaism at that time, it would have referred to following the teaching of a Rabbi, joining his school of thought and studying his teaching. But in the case of Jesus, what was involved was not so much subscribing to a teaching, as attachment to a person. People might well move on to a different Rabbi, but here fidelity and commitment were key. Again, the pupil of a Rabbi might guard or pass on his master's insights; but a disciple witnesses to Jesus himself.

The difference is grasped by noting that we do not speak of 'following' Francis of Assisi or Vincent de Paul or Mahatma Gandhi or Mother Teresa. What all have in common is that we would want to internalise the vision and values these people lived by, so that the vision and values would become the internal source of our own acting. At this level, there might not in fact be a great deal of difference between, say, Jesus and Francis. But it is only Jesus that we speak of 'following', as his disciples.

Thus, in the end, the Christian moral life is more than respect for principles, more even than being driven by a vision. It is attachment to Jesus, thinking of 'we' rather than of 'I' and living out of that relationship. Of course, discipleship still refers to the internalisation of Jesus' values so as to imitate him from within – what the last paragraph spoke of. But discipleship means more; it refers to a sharing of being and particularly a sharing in the being of Jesus as the Son of God. Thus discipleship is understood as a becoming one with him in the life of the Trinity. This is what St Paul understood when speaking of our 'adoption':

> 'And because you are children, God has sent the Spirit of his Son into our hearts, crying, "Abba! Father!" So you are no longer a slave but a child, and if a child then also an heir, through God.' (Galatians 4:6-7)

One implication of this for catechesis concerns the inadequacy of presenting Jesus as an enlightened moral teacher or as the model profile of the moral person, revealing and enacting the best of humanity. If this is all that Jesus is, then Paul's words resound: 'If Christ has not been raised... If for this life only we have hoped in Christ, we are of all people most to be pitied' (1 Corinthians 15:17-18). Rather, Jesus' enlightening vision and practice of morality should lead us to the question he put to the disciples, 'But who do you say that I am?' (Matthew 16:15) – and to their answer.

CHAPTER 6

Is there a Natural Law?

Our reflections on the approach to morality as law have shown that this is an essential perspective on morality. In this chapter we seek to deepen our appreciation of this perspective by reflecting on the theme of the natural law. This is the theme that reveals what it means most fundamentally to see morality as law.

Natural Law Today

A brief note about terminology may be helpful, as the term 'natural law' is itself confusing. At first sight the term might suggest the laws of nature such as are formulated in the natural sciences. It is, for instance, a law of nature that mass can be converted into energy, or that moths are attracted to light, or that daffodils bloom in the springtime. These are laws about what is the case in nature. They define inevitabilities or probabilities that are built into how things are.

In morality, natural law refers to human beings specifically; it is more accurately spoken of as natural moral law. Here 'law' is not a description of what is, but a formulation of what should be. It is a normative rather than a descriptive term. To speak of the natural moral law is to say that the basis for moral law, for what people should do and what they should avoid, is to be found in our nature as human beings. This means that what we are, our nature, contains indications as to how we should live. There is no such 'should' at any other level of created being.

Frequently when the idea of law is used in moral discourse, it is understood as something that somebody decides, rather like the way legislators might determine laws on divorce or drink-driving or the prevention of terrorism. Such laws might be otherwise, and are indeed different in other countries, but they are what they are because this is what has been decided. But the natural moral law is not the outcome of human determination. It is a law in the sense of something inbuilt and prior to our decisions, something we discover rather than something we determine.

For all its prominence within the Catholic moral tradition, there are a number of difficulties with the natural law theory. Firstly, there exist different versions of what natural law means, and we shall refer to a couple of these below. Obviously, it makes critical discussion of the idea of natural law very frustrating if it is not clear what people are actually talking about or if they are talking about different ideas.

Secondly, in an age when change is so much our experience of history, the idea of a natural law can sound quite frozen. We have almost got used to rapid and accelerating change as part of human life. This change brings with it previously unimaginable ethical dilemmas, but it also throws up new perceptions on the meaning and possibilities of human existence. For many, this conflicts with the idea of a natural law formulated for once and for all, reflecting a permanent and unchanging human reality.

Thirdly, it can be hard to reconcile the idea of a natural law with the fact of cultural variation. The diversity across different cultures concerning the moral rights and wrongs of issues, ranging from polygamy to cannibalism, renders it difficult to argue that all humanity shares a common morality. One is tempted to conclude that morality is culturally determined rather than universally prescribed and that there is in fact no such thing as a universal moral truth. This would reduce what is moral to what is conventional.

This relates to a scepticism today about the very possibility of moral truth. To say, for instance, that contraception frustrates the proper functioning and true purpose of human sexuality, or that the needs of the poor are prior to the right to private property, can seem to be no more than one group's version of what the moral truth is. It might well be that others agree broadly on what it is to be a human being, and yet are puzzled or unconvinced by, or vehemently disagree with, such conclusions. They do not see why what we are necessarily implies that this is how we are to behave. They suggest that directives for living cannot be read off so simply.

As against such difficulties, there remains the suspicion that without some kind of natural law there may be no morality at all. It is hard to imagine, for instance, how we can come to terms with the ecological crisis or with the challenge to international peace without some universal ethic and universally applicable values. If, with the transformation of communications, we live in a 'global village' then we would expect that there would be some global ethic to guide our life together. Despite all the pluralism that exists in morals, the way the world is going seems to demand some basic morality in common for all humanity.

But even apart from that, it makes sense to think that if there is a common human nature then there would also be some common human morality, however general or specific it might be. And if there is no universal basis for moral discourse, it does not seem to make sense to speak of a human nature that is shared by all of humanity, and whereby we are all moral beings.

A Way of Thinking

There are two ways of approaching the idea of natural law. It can be seen as a theory which tells us what is right and wrong, or it can be seen as a theory which tells us how to go about finding out what is right and wrong. It is probably more helpful to start with the latter, as it is the more fundamental.

Natural law is basically a way of going about the business of ascertaining right and wrong. It says that we come to moral truth by using our reason to reflect upon our human nature. Natural law is this method, of reason reflecting on nature, through which we discover moral truth. Here the word 'reason' is not meant to sound excessively rationalistic. In moral reflection it is good to think in terms of 'the reasoning heart', that is, of a form of reflection that integrates thought and affectivity. Again, the word 'nature' is not meant to thingify personhood. Reason reflecting on nature means people reflecting on their own human being and their own experience of being human. It means reflecting on what it is to be a human person.

This method stands out more sharply if we contrast it with other ways of finding out what is right and wrong. There are two in particular which are prominent in contemporary moral consciousness. One is sometimes called subjectivism or emotivism. It sees moral statements (statements that such-and-such an action is right or wrong) to be no more than statements of subjective preference. Here, deciding what to do depends on consulting our feelings and convictions. If two people then disagree, for instance, about the morality of euthanasia, it is essentially no different from their disagreeing about the merits of Indian food. There is no accounting for taste, and there is no accounting for moral viewpoints. In other words, there is no further court of appeal.

Where this method sees moral truth as no more than the truth of what one feels, another method for determining right and wrong finds moral truth by weighing up the consequences of different courses of action. It is sometimes called consequentialism or utilitarianism. The action that offers the best outcomes for all concerned is the one with the greatest utility value, and is therefore judged to be right. The outcomes in question are sometimes defined by the phrase, 'the greatest happiness of the greatest number'.

Now it is eminently sensible, when deciding what to do, both to consult our feelings and to consider the consequences of possible courses of action. So we do not wish to suggest that a choice has to be made for one of these methods and against the other. Indeed, the ideal might well an integration of the different methods. That is to say, when deciding what to do in a given situation, we would have regard both for our own feelings and convictions, and for the likely consequences of the various choices available, as well for the significance of the choices in relation to the meaning of human existence.

But the natural law method would see the last of these as more fundamental. That does not mean that every decision has to be preceded by an explicit and prolonged reflection on what it is to be a human being; that would be paralysing. More often than not, all that we are doing in the concrete is consulting feelings and weighing up consequences. But there is an underlying stream in our thinking, less often explicit but none the less real, that has to do with how we understand the meaning of being a human person in the world. Though it may be more implicit than explicit, it is the most decisive ingredient in our moral decisions.

Thus, when people disagree about right and wrong, it may be a conflict of feelings or convictions that leads to their difference. Or

their disagreement may represent different estimations of the consequences of the various options. But it may also be due to a difference in perceptions of what being a human person is all about. For
instance, if people disagree about the rights and wrongs of sex outside marriage, they will argue in vain about what harm sex outside
marriage might or might not do, if their real difference is about the
significance of sexuality within personal and interpersonal existence.

When we reflect on what it is to be a human person, we may in fact
conclude that certain of our feelings or convictions were misguided, or that certain consequences we thought desirable are out-
weighed by other considerations. For instance, we might feel very
strongly like executing the perpetrator of a brutal killing, or we
might be very tempted by the potential outcome of torturing a terrorist in order to elicit where the bomb has been planted. Natural
law would simply advocate that we reflect on what the nature and
purpose of human existence might have to say about such courses
of action. Otherwise we may find that we have done something that
we find in retrospect to have contradicted what we are. We may torture the terrorist only to find ourselves asking ourselves: what does
it mean for us as a society, now that we have introduced torture?

To tease this out further, let us take the issue of terminating the life
of somebody who is terminally ill. Some family members may want
to end the agony of their loved one, while others may regard it as
wrong to take life. Feelings and convictions are divided, and no
doubt each point of view would argue that its line of action would
produce the most desirable outcomes. There is a need to look at
underlying and perhaps quite unreflected views about the meaning
of life and death. Is life to be preserved at any price? Is death a good
or an evil? Is there anything after death? Does suffering have any
meaning or value?

It is quite possible that all those concerned could discuss all these
questions and end up agreeing about the broad meaning of life,
death and suffering, yet continue to disagree about what to do in
the situation. This tells us that general reflections on the meaning of
the human reality do not translate simply into deductions about
what to do. But the reflection is vital for a different reason. Without
it, how are we to know what is a good consequence as opposed to a

bad one? Without it, how are we to know what to feel strongly about? Without it, the convictions we feel and the consequences we seek lack a rational basis.

In other words, there is a basis for moral thinking to be found in reflection on what it means to be a human person. This reflection may not tell us concretely what to do, but it provides directions for thinking. It orients our feelings and forms our convictions in certain directions. It leads us to seek and to value certain kinds of consequences over others. It means that we will tend to feel strongly about what is conducive to human self-realisation. It means that we will look for options for action that have the consequence of achieving the purposes of our existence.

Room for Creativity

Often there is a suspicion about natural law, that if we base our ethical reflections on the nature of the human person we will end up with a very rigid kind of moral thinking. For this reason it is important to note the balance contained in the definition of natural law as reason reflecting on nature. If we neglect to consider our 'nature', then we will be reasoning without any reference frame or foundation, and our conclusions may be quite arbitrary. But if the element of 'reason' is neglected, the natural law can appear not to require any reflection at all, but only the application to particular situations of directives that have already been worked out elsewhere and which are quite fixed and unyielding.

That this latter has often been the case is the reason for much dissatisfaction with natural law theory. Take for instance the issue of lying. According to a version of natural law which fails to appreciate the role of reason, the purpose of the faculty of speech is clearly that of communicating to others the contents of our mind. While there will be occasions when this would not be appropriate, so that we might withhold the truth, to communicate something contrary to what we know in our minds to be the case would be a misuse and abuse of this faculty and therefore morally wrong.

The reason why this version leaves so little room for human reasoning is that human nature is understood in this case as no more than a physical functioning of the faculty of speech. If, instead of this, we were to think of the natural moral law for humans as a matter of

communicating in ways that are faithful to the demands of relationship and the building of communion, we would have a very different picture. The values of fidelity and communion would give us a
far stronger and deeper motivation for being truthful. But we could
also imagine situations where saying what is not true might actually
be the most faithful and truthful thing to do. In discerning when
and how that might be so, there would be great demands made on
the creativity and imagination of the reasoning heart.

Thus, to say that natural law begins with reason reflecting on
nature does not mean that everything is already written into our
human nature, simply to be read off. That would correspond to the
first version above and it would reduce human nature to something
like a computer programme, where all the instructions are written
in beforehand. In such a case there would be no room for creativity,
but only for applying formulae or deducing from what is already
fixed.

The complexity of human nature and of the human reality is of a
different order. It is not the complexity of a computer's extraordi-
narily intricate, but nevertheless pre-written, set of instuctions. It is,
rather, the complexity of a being which finds itself in this world as a
certain kind of being, and yet has to find out what kind of being it
should be.

The complexity might be expressed by saying that, as reason
reflects on the human reality, it discovers that the human being is
both pre-determined and undetermined. This introduces the theme
of freedom, and touches on the debate between those who say that
human beings are radically free and those who argue that we are
fundamentally determined, whether by our environment or by our
genes or by our unconscious. Without entering into that debate, we
wish to suggest that human reality is a combination of both the
determined and the undetermined.[1]

A comparison with the animal world clarifies this. Animals are pre-
programmed to a great extent, with ranges of agilities and reactions
that unfold relatively automatically. Animals blindly follow the
instincts and tendencies of their nature. But people are different.
Whatever other troubles they might have, dogs do not have to
agonise over the meaning of their dogginess. But the experiences

that people have in life confront them with questions as to who they are and what it all means. They have to think about what they could be and what they should do. Unlike animals, people will not realise themselves by blindly following their instincts, but only by reflecting on their experience and discovering the imperatives of their nature.

As we reflect, we will discover that in some senses our human nature is something pre-given. In particular, we will discover that there are certain fundamental possibilities that define human existence. These possibilities might be expressed, for example, in the language of virtue. We might speak of virtues such as integrity, love and justice as representing what is both highest and most distinctive about human nature. This much is given, pre-determined; at this level we do not decide about ourselves but rather discover what we are.

But as we reflect, we will also discover that what is given is primarily a task, the task of becoming such a person. It will not happen automatically. Rather, we are free in a very deep sense. We may assent to or reject what we discover to be the deepest possibilities of our nature. As well as that, the times we live in may modify our understanding and appreciation of what it is to be a human being. And then, having gained some insight into what we are to become, there is the task of figuring out what ways of living and relating and behaving will best promote this becoming.

Thus, at the human level creation, is not governed by necessity; there is room for manoeuvre. We find out for ourselves that we have to decide for ourselves what to make of ourselves. We each have to carve out our own personhood from what we are given. We might think of the analogy of a sculptor working on a block of stone, needing both to respect the raw material and to imagine creatively what it might become. We too must shape what we are given; so much so that it can be frightening at times and we would sometimes prefer to have it as easy as the animals.

The Law of our Being

The fact remains that, even if we base our morality in reflecting on the nature of human reality, people still differ about what it is to be a human person. One school of thought will say that, when we reflect on what we are, what we find is simply the inclination to seek pleasure and avoid pain. In contrast to this, traditional natural law theory speaks of the inclinations to preserve life, to procreate and educate offspring, to seek the truth and to cooperate in society. Another philosophy will hold that we find nothing pre-given, but that our human nature is nothing more than what we create through the exercise of our freedom.

But is there anything more fundamental that underlies such various interpretations? One promising approach would be to say that common to all such interpretations is the human spirit in search of moral truth. Natural law is about reflecing on human nature; but if reflection and deliberation are what is distinctively human, then natural law means most fundamentally our reflecting on our own reflecting. Whether our conclusions converge or diverge, we all seek and question according to the same pattern. If so, this pattern is itself the most basic natural moral law. Let us elaborate on this.[2]

At the heart of our moral consciousness there is questioning. First of all, our human experience of good and bad, right and wrong, raises questions for our understanding. As we seek to understand our experience, we come up with different ideas and insights, so that there arise questions for our judgment, which search to see if our understanding is true. This in turn raises questions for deliberation. These questions bring us beyond knowing and feeling to the moment of decision and commitment.

This is the pattern of how we operate as morally conscious subjects, a pattern of experiencing, then understanding, then judging, then deciding. We can say that the pattern is invariant in that, if another were to disagree with the outcomes of our reflections and delibera-tions, that person would do so by coming to different understand-ings, judgments, decisions, commitments. Whatever the outcome, the pattern would be the same. Thus we can say that it is our natural orientation to inquire into our experience, to seek insight, to strive to arrive at what is true and what is good, and to commit ourselves to the good that we find.

One can readily see the 'law' that is contained in this pattern and how the pattern can be experienced as a source of obligation. It is the law of being open and attentive to our experience, of being intelligent and insighful in our inquiries, of being reasonable and comprehensive in our judgments, of being detached and responsible in our deliberations, of being committed to the good that we discover. If we observe these 'precepts' well, we will arrive at the true and the good. And this is what the natural law fundamentally is.

In the formulation of Thomas Aquinas seven centuries ago, the basic precept of the natural law is that we should do good and avoid evil. It may sound obvious, but what he was stating is that we are moral beings, that we are by nature oriented or inclined towards the good. The above formulation simply develops this, by elaborating on the pattern of our moral consciousness. It is this pattern of consciousness that differentiates us from the animals. They do not have to decide about themselves and about what is good. But we do, and this is how we go about it. For this reason, the human person might be described as 'the moral animal'.

From this we can say that the first thing that reason learns from reflecting on human nature concerns the 'how' rather than the 'what' of morality. Our basic learning concerns how to go about being moral beings, namely, by being attentive to our experience, insightful in our thinking, reasonable in our judgments, responsible in our deliberations, committed in our living. This is our nature, our natural inclination as moral beings. What this will tell us about right and wrong is a further question, but this is the path whereby we activate our nature as moral animals.

This much does, however, offer an explanation for at least some of the disagreement that exists about human nature and moral principles. That is to say, people attend, think, reflect, deliberate differently. People attend to different data; they understand differently and come to different conclusions. Some of this is due simply to the enriching fact of diversity. And some of it is the result of ignorance, inadvertence, oversight, blindspots, bias.

Some of the latter in turn has to do with the context, for it does happen that the blindspot or bias may affect a whole community or culture. It may be simply that the individual person has a distorted understanding of, say, property or of sexuality; or it may be that the person is a victim of the distorted understanding of the times he or she lives in. We do not reflect in a vacuum, apart from the culture we live in; on the contrary, that culture significantly modifies our moral sensibility.

This formulation also allows us to affirm a natural law while at the same time taking account of the centrality of change. The world we are in is constantly changing and so too, our perception of ourselves is on the move. But there is a bedrock, namely, our nature as experiencing, inquiring, understanding, knowing, deliberating, loving human beings. This bedrock makes for continuity amidst all the changes in our situation, in our perception of ourselves and in our moral awareness.

A Future Achievement

The focus of our reflections has been on process rather than on content. We have been exploring the fruitfulness of thinking of natural law as the law of how we think about morality rather than as the results of that thinking. An advantage of this approach is that it avoids the impression of natural law as an immovable set of moral directives and emphasises instead the central role of the reasoning heart in the discovery of moral truth.

However, this approach is bound to feel frustrating to those who simply want a statement of what is right and wrong. The basic answer to that sense of frustration is that there is no way of setting forth what is right and wrong that bypasses human minds and hearts. There is no 'objective' formulation of the natural moral law, set in stone for all times and places and requiring nothing more than simple acquiescence on our part.

This is because of the nature of objectivity. In any area of inquiry there is no objectivity without subjectivity. We do not reach the objective truth without successfully negotiating the subjective processes of inquiry, understanding, judgment, decision. But in morality these processes are further complicated by the fact that what we are investigating is ourselves. Some of the phenomena that scientists seek to understand are outside the scientists themselves. But in moral reflection, we ourselves are the phenomenon that we are trying to understand.

There is no formulation of right and wrong that can be advanced so as to end all debate. Reflection on and debate about human experi-

ence is the only solution. If we start with people reflecting on what
it is to be people; if we enter into conversation about our various
viewpoints; if in a spirit of dialogue we grow to appreciate what has
been called 'the light of disagreement', then we will be progressing
towards truth.

For this reason the natural law, in the sense of the outcomes of our
reflecting and conversing, could be said to lie ahead of us. It is
something we strive towards rather than something we possess. In
a sense it does not yet exist, because humanity has not yet attained a
converging viewpoint as a result of its experiences, insights, judgments and decisions. Put more positively, the natural law exists
insofar as people have come to a common perception of and commitment to the truth about themselves. The natural law is future
because we as a race are still in the process of discovering who we
are and learning to agree on what it means to be a human being.

One modest illustration of this comes from a gathering of people
from the variety of world religions in 1993. The gathering styled
itself the 'Parliament of the World's Religions' (though those present were not necessarily officially representing their religions),
and it produced a declaration on what it called a 'global ethic'. The
ethic consists of a 'fundamental demand' and four 'irrevocable
directives'. The fundamental demand is that every human being
must be treated humanely. The four directives are: commitment to
a culture of non-violence and respect for life; commitment to a culture of solidarity and a just economic order; commitment to a culture of tolerance and a life of truthfulness; commitment to a culture
of equal rights and partnership between men and women.[3]

To the enlightened this will seem unremarkable, yet something
new is happening. People from vastly different cultures are beginning to come together and to agree on fundamental moral values.
The values they articulate are very much what the natural law is
about, or will be about in the future. These values are what emerge
when people join together to attend and inquire, to reason and
deliberate, in loving commitment. The results are not so much
human constructions as what people discover when they activate
their moral consciousness.

One thinks also of the United Nations Human Rights Declaration as a similar process in a secular context. But what it all amounts to is convergence. In one sense the natural law is there already, in the way we are and what we are for. But in another way it lies ahead of us, its unveiling hastened by the convergence of minds and hearts coming together from very varied backgrounds.

This is something that has never happened before in the history of the world. Whenever the natural law was formulated or articulated before, it was from within a single culture, that of Europe. Perhaps that is why the phenomenon of conflicting practices in far-off cultures was so hard to embrace. But now the world is becoming a single unit, a global community. The focus is on dialogue between different perceptions of the moral truth, on different accounts of our moral being coming into conversation. Here, truth is born from the enrichment of diversity.

The outcome of this emerging dialogue is not the kind of standardisation that capitalism is imposing on the world community, nor the kind of moral uniformity that might have characterised single cultures in the past. Rather, the possibility presents itself of diversity being recognised and cherished within a common perception of what it is to be human.

Nevertheless, to think of natural law in this way as a future achievement attendant upon the unity of humankind is far from implying that such an achievement is in any way imminent. Even though there is now a global context for ethical debate, it remains that some of the most intractable difficulties in moral discourse today stem from humanity's inability to agree on fundamental aspects of what it is to be a human being. It is one thing to speak as we have of natural law as being in the future; how short-term or long-term a future is another matter.

All of this echoes points that have always been acknowledged in the Catholic tradition about natural law. That tradition has acknowledged that we do not come to a knowledge of the natural law without difficulty, and that we should not expect that most people would agree on how to understand the natural law. The prospect of hordes of people easily recognising the rights and wrongs of whole ranges of issues, or even agreeing on the underlying principles, is not what natural law means. Confusion and disagreement are much more what is envisaged. The idea of natural law is that there is a moral truth to be found and that we will find it by activating our moral consciousness in communion with one another.

If this is the case, then the clear need is that 'reason' be given the same attention at least as 'nature'. The idea of natural law holds that there is a law of our being that we are called to discover and to cherish. But it does not envisage an easy discovery. The key, then, is that we learn how to reason well with our reasoning hearts, and how to reason well together in a world that, for all its pluralism, is converging into a single community.

The Autonomy of Morality

To speak of natural law is to speak of morality as coming out of who we are. It is to say that we are moral animals and that the kind of being we are is a source of revelation as to how we should live. The question we would now raise is: how does God fit into this way of thinking about morality?

The question is important because we can easily misconceive God's relation to natural law, thereby both discrediting the idea of natural law and distorting our picture of God. In particular, the language of God 'giving' the natural law can be misleading, however valid the intention behind the language. Such language can have the effect that those who do not believe in God are alienated from the idea of a natural moral law.

Much of the misconception comes from the way religion and morality can be bound up together within a given culture. It often happens that people leave the Church because of disagreement over what they obviously regard as significant moral issues. Usually these people still believe in God and are still hungry for spiritual nourishment, and yet departing from the morality and departing from the religion have become almost the same thing. The Christian religion has become identified with its moral teachings, with the resulting tendency in people not to see themselves as part of the religion if they are in disagreement on certain moral issues.

Meanwhile, and the more so the more pluralist society has become, we are confronted with the phenomenon of high morality manifested in people of no religious affiliation or no religious belief. This has led theologians to speak of the 'autonomy' of morality. The fact of morality present in people of no religious conviction suggests that morality can and does exist independently of religion. Just because people give up their religion is no reason for them to give up their morals. Being moral is part of being human, whether a person is religious or not. Some would go so far as to argue that morality is even more fundamentally part of us than is religion.

The alternative to the autonomy of morality is some kind of morality of authority. Rather than morality being part of being human, it is located in an authority figure who 'gives' it to humankind. This could be the crude understanding of what God was doing in giving Moses the ten commandments. Or it could be the crude understanding of God 'giving' us the natural law.

In a morality of authority, the rightness or wrongness of a course of action tends to be seen to reside in the will of the authority figure rather than in the nature of things. Why is it wrong to steal? Because it is against the commandments. Why is killing wrong? Because God has told us. Why is abortion wrong? Because the Pope says so. Sometimes this is as far as it goes. But the real questions are only beginning. Why is it against the commandments? Why does God tell us so? Why does the Pope say so? One could even ask flippantly: what if God had a change of mind tomorrow? Would that make something right when today it is wrong? Or are rightness and wrongness inherent in the nature of things (as God has created them)?

The problem with a morality of authority is that it threatens the idea of any universally common morality. If morality is to be found in the will of God, or in the Bible, or in the teachings of the Pope, then what is the situation of one who has not read the Bible, or does not subscribe to the Pope, or does not believe in God? It would seem that such a person has no access to moral truth. For the believer this would mean that God goes on creating millions of human beings who have no way of knowing what God wants from them.

A much more satisfactory view of the matter is to be found in a text we have already quoted from Paul's letter to the Romans. Some very immoral practices were going on in that community, yet, being

Gentiles, they did not have the law of Moses. But for Paul there is no excuse. When Gentiles do what the law requires. they show that 'what the law requires is written on their hearts' (Romans 2:16).

On this basis, morality is not a set of obligations whose only sense lies in the will of the authority figure, and which is not accessible to those beyond the range of that authority. It is, rather, accessible to all because it is part of what we are as moral beings. That does not mean that its demands are easily known, but it does mean that they can be known by all and that they can be justified on their own grounds, without reference to God or religion.

Natural Law and God

Where, then, does God come into the picture? One way of answering this is to speak, not of God, but of the question of God that arises from within our moral experience. The idea of natural law is the idea that reflection can find an order and a direction within human reality. The drives and orientations it finds in the human person suggest there is a purpose to things. The experience of value, and the drive to realise moral values, prompts us to think that the world is not indifferent to the moral struggle. It has been said that moral commitment is 'the womb of hope'. The experience of morality generates the hope that the order one senses is not a delusion. And this, the question of an ultimate meaningfulness and worthwhileness, is the question of God.

But the sense of a moral order that reason finds in reflecting on nature seems to be contradicted by the further experience of moral negativity. There is the evil in the world and there is the evil in ourselves. There is the persistence of injustice and the repetition through generations of the same cry, why do the wicked prosper and the just suffer? From this the question of God arises in another form, as the question of salvation and justification. Is there mercy for those who sin? Is there justice for those who are dispossessed of their future?

This question of God also makes it clear what we should and should not expect from a religious morality. If all that religion can provide is its own version of the moral law that is already written on all hearts, or further refinements of or additions to the same, then the big questions remain unanswered. However, the morality of the Bible operates at another level, where it offers a response to the question about God, to the question of whether the universe is on our side, to the question of ultimate justice.

In this way we might suggest that it is not so much that God reveals the natural law as that the natural law reveals God. Our reflection on what it is to be a moral being throws up questions that demand God as their answer. A helpful way of looking at the 'moral teaching' of the Bible might be to see it as meeting this demand.

Christian morality can go on from this to speak of God as the foundation of the natural moral law. The traditional way of putting this was to say that the natural law is our participation in the eternal law of God. In other words, when we reflect on our human reality and discover its moral structure, what we are discovering is no less than the plan or design of God. The hope it engenders in us is not in vain.

To say that God is the foundation of the natural law does not mean that God has written into our nature a set of instructions on how to live, but simply that God has created us the way we are. It is also to say that God, in creating us the way we are, created freedom. God does not so much tell us what to do, as call us to accept our freedom by discovering what we are, by appreciating what it is to be a human being, and by discerning in concrete situations how to be faithful to and how to realise what we have come to appreciate about ourselves.

The moral laws we then formulate are nothing other than formulations of what freedom has come up with in the process of self-discovery. Thus, to say that God gives us the natural law is to say that God gives us our freedom, as a task and an opportunity.

The Five Approaches

Some concluding comments will relate this discussion of natural law to the four other approaches to morality presented above. For, even though we have been presenting natural law as an elaboration of the first way of looking at morality, it has clear links to the other approaches also.

The definition of natural law in terms of reason reflecting on nature makes a clear reference to the understanding of morality as inner conviction. This approach stresses the role of conscience in the personal discovery of and commitment to the moral truth. Not losing sight of this approach will mean that the word 'reason' in the definition is not under-appreciated as it was in the past when the approach to morality as law was seen in isolation.

The approach to morality as personal growth is also intimately connected to the idea of natural law. For the natural law is about our reflections revealing to us the law of our own being – 'law' in the sense of the inner dynamic structure and orientation of the human spirit. What the natural law says in the light of this discovery is: become yourself!

Further elaboration of what the law of our being is will bring us to the fourth and fifth approaches to morality. For that law is most deeply a law of love, whereby we discover or realise ourselves in the gift of ourselves. This logic of love, when transposed to a social context, leads into the language of solidarity and social transformation, where the natural law appears more clearly as the law of our common being, the law of humanity in which we participate.

So, the five approaches continue to interpenetrate. But there is more to it. If each of the five approaches can be seen as contributing to an account of natural law, then each of them can help fill out what has been only hinted at in this chapter. Most of our attention here has focused on natural law as an approach to morality, rather than on what that approach discovers. The chapters that follow can be seen, not only as elaboration of the other ways of looking at morality, but also implicitly as elaborating on what is the natural law of our existence, on what it is to be a human being.

CHAPTER 7

The Small Print in Moral Theology

In the last chapter we elaborated on the fundamental meaning of seeing morality in terms of law and obligation. In this chapter we go on to show how this approach to morality can take account of the complex situations in which people find themselves having to make moral decisions. While the tradition's emphasis on morality as law often appears quite unbending, in fact it is much more nuanced than is often realised.

Black and White, and Grey

Catholic morality can be very imposing. It can be imposing in the way it confronts and challenges us with the high ideals of the gospel. But in a more negative way, it can be imposing because it can appear so unbending. 'Objective' morality can mean a morality that is worked out already, worked out in some abstract manner, long before we arrive on the scene and independently of our circumstances. The moral law can appear invulnerable, as if nothing concrete can affect it in any way. The language used often supports this impression – terms such as 'intrinsic moral evil' and 'grave moral disorder' and 'absolute norms' come to mind.

For all that, there is much nuance in moral theology and in the Catholic tradition of moral teaching, though it is largely unknown (that is why we are calling it 'the small print'). Here we are leaving aside for the moment the other four approaches and simply taking morality as law. We are saying that within this moral understanding there is a great deal of appreciation for the complexity of real life and concrete decision-making. Why this is not better known is itself an interesting question, particularly since most of the nuances and qualifications we are about to present have been part of the moral tradition for centuries.

In presenting his *Ethics*, Aristotle said that the 'discussion will be adequate if it has as much clarity as the subject-matter admits of, for precision is not to be sought for alike in all discussions' (book one, chapter three). This is a point that discussions of ethics need to attend to. The kind of exactitude that we can expect is far from that of mathematics or the natural sciences. Morality is not black-and-white: much of it is about the grey areas in life. This is why the answer, the only answer, to so many questions about right and wrong is simply 'it depends...'. The small print in moral theology is where this appears most clearly.

The term 'casuistry' (meaning case-study) is worth mentioning here. Frequently the word is used to denote a legalistic, scrupulous, nit-picking kind of moral theology. But, while casuistry can be of that kind, it has a more positive meaning also. It is a recognition that generalities and absolutes are not enough when it comes to moral issues, because situations and circumstances are so complex in their variety. Thus casuistry recognises the need to look into the grey areas of particular cases in order to understand properly.

Nine instances of what we are calling the small print will be presented. However, we can expect some overlap, perhaps even repetition in this presentation. Sometimes it will be debatable which of the nine is most suitable in discussing a given issue; it could be that a number of them might be equally suitable. Perhaps this very abundance of resources may be taken as an indication of how significant a part of the moral tradition these nuances and qualifications have been.

Absolutes and Exceptions

The first point concerns the natural law, and it says that the more we get down to details the more likely it is that there will be exceptions. A moral principle that is stated very generally may be indisputable or of universal validity. But when we enter into discussion of concrete cases, things become more complex. It is in this sense that we are talking here about the idea of exceptions being a valid part of our moral thinking.

This idea is to be found in the *Summa Theologiae* of Thomas Aquinas. In his discussion of the natural law, he argues that the general principles of the natural law are the same for all, but that 'the more we descend to matters of detail, the more frequently we encounter defects'. He gives as an example the general principle that goods should be restored to their owners, and then considers the case of somebody claiming back what is his own in order to use it to fight against his country. Aquinas concludes that the principle is true 'for the majority of cases', but that in this case it is not to be applied because it would be 'injurious, and therefore unreasonable'. He adds that the more detail we descend into, the more the principle will fail (*Summa Theologiae* I-II, 94, 4).

By way of illustration, we might advert to the acceptance from very early on in our moral tradition that one person might legitimately kill another in self-defence. We would be hard pressed to find a general principle as sacred as that of respecting life and not killing any other. And yet this applies only in the majority of cases. In other words, while at a general level killing is always to be avoided, the picture changes when we begin to consider concrete cases. If this is the case with killing, then presumably exceptions to most moral principles would be conceivable.

We can say this and, at the same time, say that killing is always 'wrong'. What we are saying is not meant in any way to discredit moral principles. They lose none of their sanctity by our recognising that, in the complexity of concrete situations, they may not always apply in the same way. Neither is this to say that exceptions are common. It is to say that our thinking has become too rigid if the possibility of exceptions has been eliminated from our considerations.

This is not to say that exceptionless norms cannot be formulated. But the way they are formulated is by making the definition less general and more specific. For instance, the norm 'do not kill' admits exceptions. But if the norm were to read 'do not deliberately take innocent human life', we would be approaching something exceptionless. This is because we are building the detailed into the general, thereby excluding certain sets of situations.

In the same passage, Aquinas says that principles can also fail because they are not known to all. This leads us to reflect on just how difficult moral knowledge is, even as regards fundamental principles. Think of how, for so many centuries, huge segments of humanity, such as women and slaves, were regarded as inferior.

Think of how much disagreement there is in our own society about the moral meaning of property or of sexuality. Think of how people across the board, even though they agree that life should be cherished, disagree vehemently on the rights and wrongs of euthanasia, both those for and those against claiming that they are cherishing life as best they can.

We recall again the words of Aristotle: expect only that precision of which the subject matter admits. We may expect that, at a general level, moral principles will apply universally, although even here we will not be surprised at the lack of knowledge there can be. And as we descend to concrete cases, we will positively expect both cases where a particular principle does not apply and cases where there is intractable disagreement about how it should apply.

Equity

The idea of equity goes back to Aristotle's concept of *epieikeia* (of which the English word is a translation). It is usually used in the context of positive law and concerns situations that were not sufficiently taken into consideration, or even envisaged, when the law in question was being formulated. In such cases this principle (Aquinas called it a virtue) would interpret the law according to its spirit rather than go by the letter of the law.

The presence of this idea in our moral tradition is a recognition that law is too universal to be able to cover everything, that it can only attend to what commonly happens, and that we would be unrealistic if we expected it to do more. So something is needed to supplement the law and ensure that it does not end up in some cases defeating its own purpose. In such cases, according to Aquinas, 'it is good to set aside the letter of the law … To follow the letter of the law when it ought not to be followed is sinful' (*Summa Theologiae* II-II, 120, 1).

We need more clarity, though, on what the word 'law' refers to here. Obviously it refers to laws made by the state. It can also refer to laws made by the Church, where a person concludes that a certain obligation of Church discipline does not encompass his or her particular situation. But it could also apply, beyond the area of Church discipline, to matters of the moral law. This refers, not so much to the natural law itself, as to our formulations of the natural law. It is to say that our formulations of the demands of the natural law cannot envisage everything in the way that God does, so that *epieikeia* becomes a possibility.

One reason for this is that times change. For instance, when Ambrose and Augustine formulated their versions of the theory of the just war some sixteen hundred years ago, they could not have envisaged the prospect of nuclear war. Many today would say that the availability of nuclear weapons renders the concept of a just war obsolete. Again, when Aquinas argued the rationale for capital punishment seven hundred years ago, he could hardly have envisaged the level and sophistication of prison security widespread today, whose presence makes execution simply unnecessary.

Common sense would concur with this view of the moral law. Thus today, when the demands of the natural law are formulated or interpreted in a particular way, we can legitimately ask: is it conceivable that these formulations or interpretations may not be able to embrace every possible eventuality?

It should be noted that *epieikeia* is not equivalent to a relaxation of the moral law. While in some cases it may excuse a person from the requirements of some law or discipline, it other cases it makes more stringent moral demands, as in the examples of war and capital punishment. It is not that *epieikeia* weakens the law, but that it improves the law. It is not that *epieikeia* is a weakness; it is the law itself which is imperfect, in its incapacity to cover every eventuality.

A useful image is that of a ruler. The law without *epieikeia* is like a wooden ruler, only able to measure even surfaces. But the law with *epieikeia* is like a tape measure, which can follow both straight and undulating surfaces without strain. It is the difference between adapting the real to the rule and adapting the rule to the real. The ideal, then, is a moral law that can be conceived flexibly – not in the sense of being easily manipulated, but in the sense of being capable of reflecting the real. The principle of *epieikeia* gives this capability.

It might be suspected that, because it will usually be up to individual conscience to apply this principle, the principle would be vulnerable to abuse. This of course is true, though, no doubt, a wise conscience would consult others where this was possible. However, the reason this is part of the small print in moral theology is that there has been a preoccupation with law and conformity to the law, to the neglect of the role of reason. For this reason, to reassert *epieikeia* is also to reassert the role of the reasoning heart in moral decision-making.

Objective and Subjective

One of the more familiar parts of the small print concerns the distinction between the objective and the subjective in morals. This says that when something wrong is done, it is of the utmost importance to make a distinction between the action and the person. It has long been part of the moral tradition to see a significant difference between saying that a given action is wrong and saying that the person who did it is to blame.

This distinction is already present in what we have said above about sin. We spoke of sin as a combination of relatively grave or light matter and of knowledge and consent on the part of the agent. We emphasised that grave matter alone does not constitute a sin, for sin resides more in the person than in the action. Without knowledge and consent, that is, without freedom and responsibility, a person cannot sin – even though what that person does is wrong.

The distinction is also present in the ordinary language we use. We talk of mitigating circumstances, of extenuating circumstances, of exonerating circumstances. 'Mitigating' means making something milder, 'extenuating' means making something thinner; in this context the 'something' is the responsibility and culpability of the person. 'Exonerating' means lifting a burden and here refers to situations where culpability is not simply reduced but actually eliminated.

Let us take an example. Abortion would commonly be regarded as grave matter, a serious wrong. But according to this distinction, it is possible that in a given case we could say both that abortion is terribly wrong and that this woman is entirely without guilt – not that she will not feel guilty, but that there is no blame to be attached to her. This might be because she received no support or understanding, or because her partner deserted her, or because her family condemned her, or perhaps all of these. It might be that what was done was done as the only remaining option, carried out under intense threat and pressure and anguish. If there is sin in anybody in this case, it is probably in those whose lack of compassion left her in this anguish.

Even though the Church would be more noted for its condemnation of the evils of abortion, the 1995 encyclical of John Paul II, *Evangelium Vitae*, also acknowledges the aspect we are presenting. The encyclical speaks of those cases where the abortion is not carried out for selfish reasons, 'but out of a desire to protect certain important values', though it is not being suggested that these sometimes 'serious and tragic' reasons actually justify abortion. The Pope then goes on to say that 'there are often other people too who decide upon the death of the child in the womb':

> 'In the first place, the father of the child may be to blame, not only when he directly pressures the woman to have an abortion, but also when he indirectly encourages such a decision on her part by leaving here alone to face the problems of pregnancy... Nor can one overlook the pressures which sometimes come from the wider family circle and from friends. Sometimes the woman is subjected to such strong pressure that she feels psychologically forced to have an abortion: certainly in this case moral responsibility lies particularly with those who have directly or indirectly obliged her to have an abortion.'[1]

The passage goes on to mention the responsibility of all in society who encourage abortion and also the attitudes of sexual permissiveness that make it such a problem. In this way, it says, the responsibility for abortion goes beyond individuals and 'takes on a distinctly social dimension'.

We have dwelt on this particular illustration but we would also, in order to be consistent, have to apply the principle to every other human action, though we might prefer not to. We would have to say that some of those who perpetrate the horrific abomination of sexually abusing a child could be lacking in culpability because of not being completely responsible for their actions. We would have to say that the one who pushes drugs on young people might not be acting completely free from pressure. We would have to say that the young paramilitary recruit might not have made his or her decision with full knowledge and consent.

The distinction in each case is between gravity and culpability. When we are horrified by the gravity of a wrongdoing, it is hard to see the wrongdoer as other than culpable. In many cases the wrongdoer is in fact culpable, but in some cases he or she is not. In some cases people are in the power of others, or under unimaginable emotional strain, or quite ignorant in their moral judgment. If we impute culpability in such cases, our justified moral outrage has exceeded its bounds.

This is what is implied by Jesus' saying that we should not judge. All we see in most cases is the external visible action. We do not see the heart and therefore we do not know whence the action springs. The knowledge and consent present in what we might think a light matter could render it seriously sinful, just as the lack of knowledge and consent in what we would think grave matter might mean it is only lightly sinful or no sin at all. All we are saying here is that these things are possible. Condemning the deed and pronouncing on the moral state of the agent are two different things.

It can be hard to get the balance right. When a very objectivist, legalist morality holds sway, the subjective can become totally lost. One thinks of older people coming to confession to say that they had missed Mass (in other words confessing that they had sinned) even though they were sick in bed at the time. On the other hand, when the moral fibre of society is weakened, conscience can become very lax. With goods from the workplace under his or her coat, the worker mutters that 'it'll make no difference, they've so much of the stuff anyway' or 'everybody's doing it'. We need to be able to tell the difference between right and wrong, but we must make sure not to confuse this with the difference between guilty and inculpable.

The Moral Meaning of an Action

The fourth distinction goes even further. To distinguish between objective and subjective is to say that something may be objectively wrong but that subjectively the person is not to blame. Now we would add that in some situations, not alone is the person not culpable but he or she could actually be right to do what would in normal circumstances be wrong. This might sound like saying that it can be right to do wrong, but that is not what it means. It means that circumstances alter cases, and that in certain circumstances the very moral meaning of an act can change.

A classic example would be that of a starving person stealing. It is not simply that the circumstances relieve the person of all guilt for doing something wrong. That is not an adequate description. It is that, because of the circumstances, it could be right to steal. But even that is not enough. It is that, in the circumstances, 'stealing' is no longer an accurate description of what is happening. The action is far more accurately described by some such phrase as 'preserving human life'.

Traditionally it would have been said that in such a situation of emergency 'all things are common property', that a value higher than that of private property is at stake so that in effect property is for the moment no longer private (*Summa Theologiae* II-II, 66, 7; cf *The Church in the Modern World*, paragraph 69). What is happening is not stealing in the moral meaning of that term.

In a passage where he is speaking about the ten commandments as being unchangeable, Aquinas continues: 'but as to any determination by application to particular actions – for instance, that this or that be murder, theft, or adultery, or not – in this point they admit of change' (*Summa Theologiae* I-II, 100, 8). What this means is that it is one thing to say that stealing is wrong, but quite another to say that what happens in a particular instance satisfies the definition of stealing.

Likewise we could say that killing in self-defence is a different kind of act than killing in order to steal or killing in order to exact revenge. Indeed we reserve the term 'murder' for the latter kind of cases. But 'murder' does not capture the moral essence of what is happening in the case of self-defence. Again, telling a lie in order to save somebody from grievous harm when no other option is available, is radically different from what we usually understand by lying. Materially it is a deception, as all lies are, but the circumstances render 'lying' an unsatisfactory description of the act. Words like love and justice would have to be part of an adequate description.

This is far from implying that *any* circumstance changes the moral meaning of an action. Some circumstances are completely accidental and of no moral significance, for instance, the time of day at which the lies were told. But other circumstances, such as the imminent danger of death, are far from incidental and enter into the moral fabric of the action. Aquinas put it technically by saying that a circumstance 'so long as it is but a circumstance, does not specify an action, since thus it is a mere accident: but when it becomes a principal condition of the object, then it does specify the action' (*Summa Theologiae* I-II, 18, 10).

Some aspects of the discussion of contraception could benefit from this perspective. What are we to call the using of a condom when a person's partner has AIDS? Perhaps the most obvious thing to call it is risky, but it is not accurate to call it contraception. The moral essence of contraception has to do with frustrating the potential for conception, but that is incidental in this case. Because of the presence of a deadly disease, the condom has assumed a different purpose, that of preventing AIDS. That does not decide what should be done, but at least it clarifies what we are talking about.

Again, there is the dilemma of the woman who must decide whether to use contraceptives when her drunken husband is regularly forcing himself upon her. Would this be better described as contraception, or as an effort to lessen the damage being done by such an invasion of her body? In this context there comes to mind Pope John Paul's saying some years ago that there is such a thing as rape within marriage.

We might recall also the statement of the Irish bishops following the Health (Family Planning) Act of 1979, which noted that 'As a moral act – and this presupposes freely chosen sexual intercourse – contraception is wrong' (paragraph 11). The qualifying clause is there for a reason. There would seem to be an implication that if intercourse is not freely chosen, the moral scenario is decisively changed.

This question of circumstances is a complex one in the Catholic moral tradition. In the 1993 encyclical, *Veritatis Splendor*, it is stated that circumstances cannot change the 'moral species' (what we have been calling the moral meaning) of an action. However, the context shows that it is *consequences* specifically that are meant, and not all circumstances. The concern is lest the consequences come to be seen as potentially justifying any means.[2] This, of course, is a valid concern.

What we are talking about, however, is not *consequences* making a bad action good but *circumstances* making an action morally different. We are saying that actions do not exist in isolation but are always embedded in a context of circumstances, and that those circumstances can be either incidental or can enter into the very meaning of the action. Of course, this can also happen in a way that makes a bad action worse. Stealing when starving takes the action out of the realm of stealing properly speaking; but stealing from a holy place turns it into sacrilege.

Grave and Light Matter

The distinction between grave and light matter is an old one but unfortunately is very seldom heard of today. It is a distinction to do with the action rather than the person, and what it says is that not all wrong actions are equally wrong. There is a hierarchy among wrong acts, from the more to the less serious. To put it another way, we can say that something is 'wrong', but we can also ask, how big is the 'w'? Something may be wrong with a capital 'W', while something else may be wrong with a very small 'w' indeed.

Of course the circumstances will enter into such judgments concretely, but we can still speak in a general way about actions. We can say, for instance, that taking somebody's character is in itself a far more serious thing than taking their property. We can say that abortion is much more serious than contraception. Thus, speaking in a very general way, some actions come to be classified as grave matter and some others as light matter.

There has been a tradition within Catholic morality that any offences against the sixth commandment – that is, to do with sex – are always grave matter and that there could be no light matter when it came to sex. Offences in the area of sex, it has been argued, are always serious business. Today this view is discredited. Sexual sin is same as any other sin in this regard; there are both grave and light matter when it comes to sex, just as there are when it comes to justice or honesty or whatever. As Bishop Murphy O'Connor of Arundel and Brighton put it once when speaking about contraception:

> 'Married people who practise artificial birth control for good motives are judged by the ordinary norms of Catholic pastoral theology. Sometimes the practice may be lightly sinful, sometimes no sin at all; rarely, if ever, should it be an obstacle to the reception of holy communion.'[3]

The phrase, the 'ordinary norms of Catholic pastoral theology', is a reference to the small print that we are setting out here. However, the discrediting of the tradition that sexual wrongs are always grave matter has not been widely communicated. Why would so many people have given up the practice of their religion, deprived themselves of holy communion, were it not that they thought their use of contraceptives to be grave matter? Even though this tradition has been discredited, somehow it continues to come across in the moral teaching, with this lamentable consequence.

So there is great need to recover the distinction between grave and light matter. While this applies particularly to the area of sex, its recovery would be of more general benefit. For it would provide a tool that would help us ask ourselves; what really are the bad actions in the world today? Are they to do with sexuality? Or are these just some of them? Might there others of equal or far more serious concern?

Conflict and Compromise

There are situations where you are 'damned if you do and damned if you don't'. A married couple with an elderly and infirm parent living in the house, trying to decide whether it is best that this parent go to a nursing home or stay in the house, will feel that any decision will be unsatisfactory. There is a conflict of values and no decision will realise all the values involved.

The point is that this is a situation not of the couple's own doing. While the onus of deciding rests on them, it is with respect to a situation in which they find themselves, a situation not of their own making, yet one which they feel compromises them. In such a situation they will seek to choose the lesser evil. They will find themselves having to choose among values, having to sacrifice the realisation of a lesser value for the sake of what they judge to be a greater one. Whatever guilt they may feel does not mean that they are actually to blame in any way.

Moving on to a somewhat different situation, it may even be the sin of another or others that leaves us compromised in our moral decision-making. This is another way of looking at killing in self-defence, or at lying in order to protect another from harm, namely, that the evil actions or intentions of one person leave the situation compromised for another. One powerful example here is that of the German Lutheran minister, Dietrich Bonhoeffer, a committed pacifist, yet who became part of a plot to assassinate Hitler. We can see that the options left to him by the situation lay between this and looking on powerlessly as hundreds and thousands more went to their death.

Some theologians speak of 'a theory of compromise' in relation to such situations. Perhaps this is an unfortunate choice of term, as it can suggest some kind of acceptance or tolerance of the situation, or even a compromise of one's principles. Clearly we cannot condone the sin that has brought the situation about and we must show this by fighting against the situation. Nevertheless, as Bonhoeffer judged, we may also have to respond immediately, if intolerable harm is being threatened immediately.

Perhaps instead of *compromise*, we might speak in terms of trying to be realistic and yet faithful. The important point is that the situation we are left in may have compromised us, in the sense that it has become impossible to realise all values, but that this is not our own fault. The only fault would lie in not responding as best we can. Once we do respond as faithfully as possible, we should resist the feelings of guilt that the situation makes almost inevitable.

Indirect Intentions

Next, there is the distinction between direct and indirect intentions. This may be familiar because of certain issues that have been the matter of public debate. It is relevant when the same action has both good and bad results. The familiar issues have to do with pregnancy. When a pregnant woman has cancer of the womb, or when the foetus is lodged in the fallopian tube, it may be necessary to remove the womb or the tube in order to save the woman's life, even though that will entail the death of the foetus.

But these are not the only examples. Think, for instance, of a factory that decides on a programme of computerisation and automation in order to ensure survival in a competitive market, although this will mean redundancies. Here too we are talking about a course of action that seems necessary, but where unfortunate ramifications seem inseparable from what must be done. These latter may be in no way intended, nor are they a means to the end, but are better described as regrettable side-effects.

Or are they? Perhaps the redundancies are not that much regretted and could be avoided. Perhaps they are unavoidable but not a justifiable price to pay. Or if the situation were that the redundancies were announced as a way of improving competitiveness, then they would be a means to an end. All this will depend on the situation.

All these considerations are addressed in what moral theology knows as the theory of the double-effect.[4] What concerns us here is simply the point that sometimes doing what must be done carries with it undesired side-effects which cannot be avoided. Such side-effects are said to be 'indirectly intended', whereas they would be 'directly intended' if they were positively brought about as a means to some end. The theory of the double-effect elaborates guidelines for distinguishing between the two cases. The point is that when undesired side-effects cannot be avoided, we may feel intense regret or sorrow, but we should not feel guilt.

Gradualness

Earlier we quoted the phrase, 'the truth looks different from here'. We could add that sometimes it feels different too. The ideals and demands of morality feel different to different people. We do not come to the starting blocks equal. Aristotle even said that some people are maimed from the start in their capacity for virtue. The principle of gradualness recognises the need to differentiate between different people in different circumstances as to what the moral call expects of them.

The idea was used by John Paul II in his encyclical on marriage. He spoke of the moral progress of married couples seeking to realise the values of God's law in their marriage. While insisting that gradualness does not mean any dilution of the moral truth, such that there would be different truths for different people, he did recognise 'what is known as 'the law of gradualness' or step-by-step advance'.[5]

Take anger as an example. The demand not to be angry is different for one person who has had a splendid day and then flies off the handle at some trifling matter, than it is for another who has had a disastrous day and then arrives home to find that a burglar has ransacked the house. The moral demand to overcome anger is still the same demand, but one person may be in a better position to respond than another. Certainly we do not expect the same of everybody.

Somewhat like the idea of each marching to a different drummer, we might speak here of 'the practical ideal'. The ideal of overcoming anger is one thing; but the *practical* ideal is what can realistically be expected of the particular person in the particular situation. Sometimes a lot will be expected, sometimes very little. And, while God expects a moral response from all of us, God does not expect the impossible. The words of Gibran's *The Prophet* resonate here: 'You are good when you walk firmly to your goal, and with bold steps. Yet you are not evil when you go there limping; even those who limp are not going backwards.'

If morality is too objectively focused on the demands of the law, it can lose sight of what it is like for people striving to do the good. As Jesus said with reference to the Pharisees: 'do not do as they do, for they do not practise what they teach. They tie up heavy burdens, hard to bear, and lay them on the shoulders of others' (Matthew 23: 3-4). So the idea of gradualness in the moral tradition is to be welcomed for its recognition of what moral progress is really like and of the need for expectations to be realistic, lest people be discouraged or driven away or driven mad with guilt.

Following your Conscience

The view of morality as inner conviction would lead to the conclusion that the essential moral demand is simply to obey one's conscience. Indeed, sin could be defined as doing what is known to be wrong. Yet it can happen that, if the view of morality as law is so predominant that this other view is lost sight of, the significance of following one's conscience could be obscured.

The theme of conscience seems to be treated in different ways within the Catholic moral tradition. In issues of sexual morality it tends to be played down. The emphasis is on the moral law and on the need to be informed concerning it. But in social morality, conscience seems almost to have a different status. We recall what the documents of Vatican II had to say about people being free to follow their religion, or how, in the context of discussing peace and war, they expressed admiration for the conscientious objector.

But what the moral tradition ultimately says is that if my conscience obliges me in a way that I know would be wrong not to obey, then I must follow it. I may discover subsequently that I was mistaken. Everybody around me may be telling me I am wrong. But if all that I am able to see as wrong is not to follow this particular command of my conscience, then not to follow would be for me the sinful option. This applies equally whether we are talking about disobeying what is judged to be an unjust law of the state or if we judge ourselves obliged to act contrary to a formulation of the moral law.

Strangely, a place where one senses some recognition of this is in *Humanae Vitae*. Perhaps it is because Pope Paul VI felt himself obliged in conscience to go against a majority view of the Commission that had reported to him on the issue of the regulation of birth. At any rate we find the following in the encyclical:

> 'It is to be anticipated that not everyone perhaps will easily accept this particular teaching... And yet there is no doubt that to many it will appear not merely difficult but even impossible to observe... We have no wish at all to pass over in silence the difficulties, at times very great, which beset the lives of Christian married couples.'[6]

Throughout these passages, the Pope insists on the truth of the teaching he is proposing. For this reason, what he intends in what he says might be better considered under the theme of gradualness. And yet there is something about conscience here too. It is not just that the Pope appreciates that what he proposes may not be easily attained. There is also the awareness that some may find themselves unable to agree. This does not imply that 'anything goes'. We may regard another's view as quite wrong, but we cannot fail to acknowledge how people seek the moral truth with often painful commitment.

A Style of Thinking

We recall again what Aristotle said about the kind of precision or exactitude to be expected from the study of morality. Some presentations would give the impression that the study can be almost mathematical in its precision, but this is false. There are too many grey areas and any proper presentation must recognise this. What we have been presenting is the way in which the moral tradition, despite operating mostly in terms of morality as law, has been quite sensitive to the grey areas and quite replete with nuance and qualifications. Even if thinking in terms of law is not the only way or the best way, at least the thinking that has been done appreciates the complexity of life.

It adds up to a style of thinking about morality that lies between absolutism and relativism: between the rigidity and the black-and-white quality of everything being worked out abstractly, and the relativism of saying 'do as you sincerely feel is best'. This style is one that is able to speak in terms of 'right and wrong' and also in terms of 'it depends'. It has a high regard for moral principles and a firm conviction that the person must do no wrong. But this is combined with a real sensitivity to situations in which people find themselves having to decide and to act. It knows good and evil, not in some abstract or bookish way, but in what life is like for people as they struggle with the moral call.

Some of the small print we have discussed brings us beyond the objective style of morality. For instance, in speaking of objective-subjective, or of gradualness, or of conscience, we are already moving into the more subjective considerations of a person-centred approach to morality. We take this up in a more substantial way in the next three chapters. There we will consider some aspects of looking at morality from the point of view of the person, in contrast to what we have been doing, looking at morality from the point of view of the action. We would also note that, even as we discussed natural law, we were really talking about the law of our being as persons. Perhaps it is only the understanding of morality from a personal (and then also from a social) perspective that fills out what the moral law is.

CHAPTER 8

Freedom to Love

The last two chapters have been leading us to the conclusion that to talk about the moral law is to talk about the human person, for our understanding of moral obligation is based on our understanding of what it means to be a person. In the next three chapters we look more closely at the moral call from the point of view of the person, and we begin in this chapter by taking up the themes of freedom, love and virtue.

Thinking 'Subjectively'

Recent decades have seen a shift of attention in moral theology from the act to the person. Since before Vatican II, the benefits of scripture scholarship were being felt in a new appreciation of the person as called by Christ, called to conversion and a life of discipleship. This harmonised well with the contemporary style in philosophy which emphasised the theme of the meaning and authenticity of human existing.

Parallel to all this there has been a swing in popular moral consciousness from a morality of authority to a morality emanating from the subject. The beginnings of this go back a few centuries. The rise of the natural sciences begot a new faith in the powers of human reason, and dependence on religion diminished. Humanity began to sense itself as being in control of its own destiny. Part of all this was that freedom became and remained a central theme in philosophy and ethics.

Today we benefit from the fruits of these developments. After thinking for so long that morality was simply a matter of doing what we were told, we now have a new appreciation of our own freedom and responsibility and creativity in the moral sphere. We have a new confidence in ourselves as moral agents.

But we can also observe how naïvely this freedom is frequently understood. Sometimes it can seem as if freedom is an easily accessible and unproblematic power, involving little more than people consulting their feelings. It can seem that deciding what to do, and carrying out the decision, come readily to the individual. We get a glimpse of this mentality when people speak of wanting to be left alone by an authoritarian morality, as if such interference were the only obstacle in the way of their realising their moral selves.

All this feeds into the idea that morality is the individual's own private affair. Morality is seen to be about each person acting upon his or her own feelings and convictions. The value of tolerance is prized because it advocates leaving the individual free in this way. By way of reaction, many feel that such individualism is going too far. It is one thing to celebrate human freedom, but quite another to suggest that morality amounts to no more than each individual doing what he or she thinks best. Such a suggestion goes too close to equating being right with being sincere. It is too subjectivist.

One response to this trend is to reassert an objective moral order and a respect for the moral law. Undoubtedly this is the concern of those who ask: 'Where have the ten commandments gone?', or 'What has happened to the sense of sin?' However, this response often comes across as a retreat into the past, so that one is left with the feeling that it has not adequately come to grips with the spirit of the age.

But this is not the only response possible. It has been said that in such situations four options are available. We can *ignore* what is happening and pretend that nothing has changed. We can *deplore* all that is new and all that is changed. We can seek to *restore* things to the way they were. And if all these fail, we can begin to *explore* other possibilities.

In the spirit of exploration, we would seek to capitalise on the current interest in the subjective. We can accept that this is the spirit of the age and that we have to speak in the language of freedom and tolerance. But we can go on to transform this language from within.

To take this approach would be to say that the times we are in have both got it right and got it wrong. They have got it right in bringing freedom to centre stage, but what they have got wrong is their understanding of what freedom is all about. We can welcome the move to looking at morality from the point of view of the person and we can welcome the prioritisation of freedom. But we can question how adequate are the view of the person and the understanding of freedom being put forward or implied.

What we need, then, is a better account of the nature and scope of human freedom, one that does better justice to the nature of the human person. Just as others can describe, for example, the workings of the brain or the workings of the immune system, so we need an account of the workings of the person's internal 'moral system', an account of what is involved in our exercise of freedom and responsibility. For surely there is much more involved than just 'doing what you feel is best'.

We might see this as the search for a better way of talking about subjectivity in morals. Subjectivity often seems to be no more than subjectivism, no more than an assertion that the person's own feelings and convictions are the only arbiters of moral truth. Such subjectivism is a reaction to its own opposite, the objectivism that thinks of morality as 'out there', already formulated by somebody else, with little or no place for the person's subjectivity, little or no place for thoughts or feelings or convictions.

But we can also think of subjectivity and objectivity in another way. We can think of what is objective as being 'in here' rather than 'out there'. We can think of objectivity as a quality of subjectivity, a quality of the person's deliberations and decisions. That is to say, when a person performs well the subjective operations of experiencing, understanding, judging, deliberating and deciding, objectivity is what results. Objectivity and subjectivity are not either-or; they are both-and. Objectivity is the fruit of authentic subjectivity, of the proper functioning of our internal moral system.

Thus the focus of the person-centred approach to morality is on the dynamics of our deliberating and deciding. One of the great strengths of this approach is that, in shifting attention away from the rights and wrongs of actions themselves, it allows us attend to what is going on in people, in between their actions. It allows us grow in sensitivity to what it is actually like for people to respond to the moral call.

Oddly, both subjectivism and objectivism are at one in missing this dimension. Subjectivism tends to presume too optimistically on the presence of freedom. Objectivism, because too focused on the requirements of the law, tends to take it for granted that there is nothing other than bad will in the way. In this manner, both lack appreciation for what is concretely involved in striving to be moral.

Are we Free?

Freedom is among the most cherished words in the moral vocabulary. We uphold the dignity of freedom, we cry out when it is denied or unduly restricted. But freedom is also a very vague word, as a few questions will illustrate. For instance we can ask: Is everybody free? Can a person be both free and committed? Is freedom easy or difficult? Is it something we have or something we acquire? To begin to tackle such questions would bring to light the great complexity of human freedom.

Consulting the dictionary, we find that the principal meaning of freedom has to do with being unrestricted, unfettered, not in bondage, in a released state. This can be meant in a very general way, or it can refer more specifically to our personal and social rights to freedom of conscience, freedom of expression, freedom of movement. We are aware of how these rights are restricted or denied under oppressive civil and religious regimes.

The danger with this ordinary usage of the word is that it can leave us with a picture of freedom as no more than being able to do what we want, without being confined. We might imagine a bird in a cage that is then released to soar freely. We might imagine two weeks on the sunny Mediterranean, totally free to do as we please. It is a picture of what might be called *outer freedom*. The factors that might limit or expand freedom are all outside the person.

Another image might be that of a supermarket, where the range of commodities available makes the shoppers more free than others who shop in the local grocery store. This is the idea behind some advertising also: the same manufacturers offer a second line in chocolate bars or washing powder and tell us that now we are free to choose. One advertising jingle some years ago went: 'Knowing my options, life's mine to live'. Again, freedom is outer, a function of outward circumstances. It expands with an increase in the options available.

As a picture of freedom this is true up to a point. There is a dimension of freedom that is external, where the extent of freedom depends on the situation. Thus, for example, the limitations of space and time are an external limitation on freedom. We say that we cannot be everywhere at once, or that there are only twenty-four hours in the day – meaning that we simply cannot do a lot of what we want to do. Other outward constraints are the weather, the law of the land, the cash in hand. Here there are things that we are able to do, but cannot because of the situation. Then there are the constraints others put on us, including physical force and emotional pressure.

But if this is all that freedom is thought to involve, it is quite an unreal picture. It is true to a point, but not as an account of the whole, or even the greater part, of human freedom. For, of the many significant ways in which freedom is limited, only some are outward. Besides these, there are limits imposed on freedom from within the person. Most obviously there are the limits of human nature itself. We cannot fly or live underwater. Again, the particular make-up of some people may mean that they will never grasp quantum physics or play the piano or win a medal for football.

More significant still are the limits imposed by the unconscious. There are factors influencing our exercise of freedom that we can hardly control, let alone understand. There are irrational fears and dislikes. There is the mixture of motives that feeds into our actions, some of which we are unable to access consciously. As well as this, there is the influence of our past, only some of which we are aware of, yet which can effectively decide how we will react in some situations. All this can mean that sometimes we do not know what we are doing, even though we seem to ourselves to be acting quite deliberately.

On reflection, these inner aspects add up to quite a delimitation of human freedom. Especially when we appreciate some of the unconscious influences, we might be forgiven for wondering to what extent we are free at all. In theory, we are free to do all kinds of things, such as giving up smoking or not flying off the handle or taking prayer more seriously. But in practice it is not so easy. There is more than good will or will-power involved. Within ourselves, there is difficult ground between the intention and the action, and much of it is uncharted.

Inner Freedom

Consideration of the ways in which freedom is limited might make for pessimism, but it is meant to yield a starting-point from which to understand freedom realistically. Freedom is not the capacity to do what we want. Ours is but a human freedom. Certain things are predetermined. The situation we find ourselves in includes much that cannot be otherwise, however much we might wish it could be. And we ourselves are predetermined to a significant extent. Much of what we are, cannot be changed. Much can be changed only very slowly and laboriously. Much of what we are, we do not even understand.

This suggests that freedom is firstly about recognition of the way things are. It is the capacity to respond from within what is given, about making what we can out of a set of circumstances that were not themselves chosen. But the capacity to respond is rooted in the capacity to see things as they are. The starting-point has to do with recognising the situation for what it is. Without that foundation, our efforts to act upon our situation will be founded on illusion and misapprehension.

All this is reflected in the popular prayer: 'Grant me courage to change what can be changed, serenity to accept what cannot, and wisdom to know the difference.' This prayer represents a realistic recognition of the situation of freedom. When this recognition is lacking, we speak of somebody living in a fool's paradise, or spending his or her waking life in a dream world. We speak of somebody forever wishing things were otherwise, or pretending something never happened. Such people cannot see, for instance, that their hopes are impossible or that their illness cannot be cured. They cannot see or accept what is there, and to that extent they are not free.

Freedom might be described as 'response-ability', where the ability to respond depends on recognising where we are starting from. Once we recognise and accept the situation for what it is, we can then begin to transform the situation. The transformation in question is not a changing of what cannot be changed, but it is real nonetheless. By proceeding in this way, freedom in fact declares its dignity and superiority over the situation.

This leads us to contrast inner and outer freedom. The contrast might be illustrated from Brian Keenan's account in *Evil Cradling* of his captivity in Beirut. The account brings home vividly the truth that a person can be in prison and yet free. What makes sense of such a paradox is the idea of inner freedom, of freedom as a capacity to recognise the situation for what it is, to respond creatively within the limits, and thereby to assert its own transcendence.

Obversely, it should then be the case that a person might not be in prison but not be free either. Indeed the book hints strongly that those guarding Keenan were the real captives. A person might be relatively free of outer constraints and yet unfree in a far deeper sense, because unable to recognise and respond to the situation for what it is. The example of Brian Keenan even suggests that it is often in the context of severe outward limitation that freedom attains its deepest dignity.

All this implies that freedom is more achieved than given, more a task than a possession, more a power than a choice. If freedom is about seeing and responding, then what we possess is no more than a capacity, a potential. Actually to be able to see things as they are and respond creatively is a challenging task and, to the extent that this capacity is realised, it is high achievement. It is a power the person now possesses. If freedom were simply outer, then it would expand with the range of choices available. But insofar as it is inner, an increase of freedom is a development in the person.

Freedom and Love

Most of what we have been saying concerns the negative side of freedom, about what we can seek to become free from. There is also the question of what we are free for. This will be described in terms of love.

Freedom is not simply about the capacity to see things as they are. It is ultimately the capacity to see things lovingly. In talking about freedom, we are talking about a moral kind of seeing. This kind of seeing comes about, not through just opening our eyes, but through self-transcendence. In order to see lovingly we need to be able to transcend ourselves, to get out of ourselves. We need to escape from the weight of our own egoism. For it is the short-sightedness and blinkered vision of our egoism that prevents us from seeing lovingly.

Egoism takes the narrow view. It asks, 'what's in it for me?' Because of its narrow focus it cannot appreciate the situation or relationship in its entirety, but only those aspects that pertain to its own interests. It is more or less blind, for instance, to the perspectives of other people in the situation. Or if it is not, it may well see its own interests and theirs as in competition.

Loving vision, in contrast, is alive to the fact and implications of interdependence. It understands the fact of our interdependence as what John Paul II called 'a moral fact', that is to say, a fact that carries with it moral obligations.[1] Interdependence could be seen to demand co-operation with others from a purely pragmatic motivation, out of enlightened self-interest. But as a moral fact, it is seen to reveal the moral truth about ourselves, that we exist for the sake of one another and that the purpose of our existence lies in unity and communion.

An illustration will serve to show how this is indicated by our experience of life. (We already referred to this in chapter one when introducing the idea of morality as love.) It is a common human experience that responding to the needs of others and realising the potential of our own humanity go hand in hand. This is because our relationships call forth our humanity and our gifts. If there were not relationship and interdependence, it is hard to envisage how this potential would ever be unlocked.

The calling forth happens in all kinds of ways. Somebody who approaches me to talk, when I am preoccupied with something else, calls forth my patience, my generosity, my sympathy. A friend who is afraid calls forth my courage and my powers of encouragement. A difficult relationship calls forth endurance and hope and perhaps the ability to love the unlovable. An invalid or disabled relative calls forth compassion. The cry of the poor calls forth my sense of justice. These qualities that are called forth are what is deepest in me; yet without the call of the other they would remain dormant, perhaps never to be adverted to even as possibilities. In this way, responding in relationship and self-realisation happen either together or not at all.

To see things from this perspective is to see lovingly and to see truthfully. With such vision we are impelled to commit ourselves to quality of relationship across the range of relationships that involve us. With loving vision we are inclined to see situations in terms of the well-being of all and not just of ourselves; though, of course, to think of the well-being of all includes thinking of our own well-being, but in a larger context. With loving vision we are committed to this view as being the truth about ourselves.

The paradox in all this is that freedom is measured, not by the extent of our independence, but by the quality of our commitment. We saw that freedom begins by appreciating the limits or unfreedom of its situation, and now it completes itself in the further unfreedom of commitment. As Paul images it in the letter to the Galatians, freedom finds itself by enslaving itself. He says that 'For freedom Christ has set us free', and then goes on to exhort us to become slaves of Christ. In like spirit are the words of *The Church in the Modern World*, that 'human persons discover their true selves only in a sincere giving of themselves' (paragraph 24).

Thus freedom cannot be imagined as a splendid isolation, or invulnerability, or self-sufficiency. For without others it is cut off from its own fulfilment. This is not to say that others are but a means towards our moral progress. That would reduce morality to an egoistic process of self-perfection. It might be nearer the mark to think of the other as our salvation, and to see that it is only in relation to others that we have access to the truth about ourselves.

At this stage we need to say something more about the kind of thing that love is. The basic point we wish to emphasise is that love is a different category of activity from any other. Some acts are kind, others hurtful or reconciling or violent or honest, and so on. But a loving action is not another in this series. It is of a different order.

This is reflected in the New Testament, in what Paul says about love. When he says that 'the one who loves another has fulfilled the law' (Romans 13:8), he puts love into a different category from all the commandments. This is even clearer in the famous passage in the first letter to the Corinthians:

> 'If I speak in the tongues of mortals and of angels, but do not have love, I am a noisy gong or a clanging cymbal. And if I have prophetic powers, and understand all mysteries and all knowledge, and if I have all faith, so as to remove mountains, but do

not have love, I am nothing. If I give away all my possessions, and if I hand over my body, so that I may boast, but do not have love, I gain nothing.' (1 Corinthians 13:1-3)

One could paraphrase by saying that love is the essence of morality which must be present in every act. Hence it is not another kind of act, but a quality that is to characterise all human activity.

Another way of putting this would be to make a distinction between the *freedom to be* and the *freedom to do*. Generally we think in terms of the latter, for instance, of not being free to meet somebody or of not being free to overcome some compulsion. But underlying the freedom to do this or that is the freedom to become a certain kind of person in and through what we do. This is our freedom, not to choose this or that, but to choose ourselves, to say yes or no to the meaning and possibilities of our existence.

It is at this level that love belongs. Because love demands not only our actions but ourselves, the freedom to be is confronted with only the two alternatives of assent or refusal. In many of our concrete decisions and actions we are faced with a multiplicity of choices. There may be a dozen different things we could do on a given afternoon. There might even be a few different ways we could expend our energies for the coming year or for the rest of our lives. But the fundamental issue throughout is whether or not the choices we make add up to and represent a commitment to being and becoming love.

The preface for the marriage ceremony captures this when it says that love is our origin, love is our constant calling, and love is our fulfilment in heaven. Love concerns the freedom to be rather than the freedom to do. It is what freedom seeks to become, and what freedom does is done in order that it may become love. In this way the significance of love goes beyond the meaning of any specific action.

Feelings

This reflection on the themes of freedom and love is really an expression of the natural law, in terms of the dynamics of what is happening in the person. If morality is considered only in terms of actions and their rightness or wrongness, the person may be forgotten. Or rather, there may be an unconscious tendency to see the person almost as a moral computer that can respond immediately to any moral command. Response may be seen as a simple matter of the will, where the only obstacle to responding is bad will. The machine is presumed to be in perfect working order.

But if morality is seen from the point of view of the person, in terms of freedom and loving vision, things become far more complicated. There is much more involved in responding than good will and bad will. There is the complexity of our internal moral system, what one theologian called 'the tangled undergrowth of character', the 'fascinating country' of our interior life, 'the vast underground life of feelings and emotions'.[2] The image shifts from that of a machine to that of a jungle. Thinking moves away from a simple sequence of knowing leading to acting.

The Greek philosopher Socrates is reported to have thought that the person who knew what was good would simply act accordingly. But it all depends on how strong a sense is attached to 'knowing'. We have all had the experience of knowing what should be done and then doing something else. Clearly then, if knowing is only an intellectual apprehension of the good, it will not necessarily lead to our doing the good.

The idea of loving vision, however, suggests a knowing that is heartfelt, a motivated knowing. It suggests the conviction and commitment of the 'reasoning heart', which is both an intellectual apprehension of what is good and an affective apprehension whereby we are drawn and moved towards the good. To know in this sense means that our feelings also are oriented in the direction of what is good.

But such an orientation is far from automatic, not just because there might be bad will, but more often because of the complexities we have spoken of regarding the inner life. This shifts our attention from our actions to what is going on within us in between our actions. Iris Murdoch has said that we are like 'an obscure system of energy out of which choices and visible acts of will emerge at intervals in ways which are often unclear and often dependent on the condition of the system in between the moments of choice'.[3] This focuses our attention on how we come to see and feel as we do.

It is also a further corrective to the naïve view of freedom which thinks that morality is a matter of doing what we feel is right. For feelings are not that simple. Rather, morality is about coming to feel strongly about the right things and in the right way. It is more than spontaneous feelings. It is about the refinement and integration and reorientation of our feelings and instincts so that they truly serve the cause of love in our lives. If feelings are not refined in this way, then we will be prey to our emotions, and not free at all. We will be the victims of our own partial vision and misapprehensions and prejudices and fears. We will confuse strength of feeling with truth.

But the refinement of feeling does not come easily and sometimes it may not come at all. Take, for instance, the sermon which presents the gospel ideal that we are to love one another. It sounds friendly and encouraging. In some hearts it may meet with bad will, with an 'I won't'. But more hearts than we might imagine will whisper, 'I can't'. 'Things have been too hard, life has been too cruel.' 'I have known only unkindness.' 'I have been wounded, morally disabled.' 'I want deeply to love, but cannot.' To a greater or lesser extent in each case, life has left many of us unable to love.

Once on radio, a woman in her twenties, who had been sexually abused as a child, was asked what damage it had done to her. She said that she was 'incapable of compassion'. These are chilling words that should teach us not to underestimate the difficulty there may be in responding to the moral call. Many times there is no lack of good will. It is simply that people are often not able, incapable, inadequate, needy.

If freedom is to realise itself in loving vision it must attend to and not bypass feelings. Perhaps two conclusions can be drawn as to how feelings might be reoriented. Firstly, self-knowledge will be central. Loving vision will not come simply out of knowing the good. It also depends crucially on our knowing ourselves, the 'tangled undergrowth', the 'obscure system of energy' that is our inner life. Such self-knowledge can be the beginning of something new; just as we said earlier that freedom begins in the recognition of the situation for what it is.

Secondly, an attention to healing as well as preaching is indicated. It is not enough for preachers, teachers and leaders to point out what is right, as if that was all that was required for people to respond. If the problem is about people not being able, and not just about people not wanting, to respond to the moral call, then what is called for is enabling and healing, as well as an appreciation for the courageous way in which people struggle on while carrying such deep wounds.

Virtue

Freedom is a lifelong task of becoming love. If love is such an over-arching category, standing for the whole of the moral call, it would make it more manageable if we could break it down into its components. And indeed, while love in itself is a simple reality, that of the giving of ourselves, its richness of meaning makes it a multifaceted reality also. It is this multifaceted nature of love that the idea of virtue refers to.

The word 'virtue', however, has been impoverished in our understanding. We have only to think of the images suggested by virtues such as prudence, temperance, chastity, charity, humility. In the popular mind these words can convey a picture of piety, caution, self-depreciation, even repression. But the idea of virtue, which has been central to our moral tradition as far back as the Greeks, is much richer than this.

In the becoming of love, different elements of the picture emerge on the way. These different elements are the virtues. They are partial aspects of the person's self-realisation as love. Love is the self-realisation itself; individual virtues are the constituent parts, the different faces of love. Each virtue realises loving vision with respect to a particular area or dimension of human experience. For instance, truthfulness is the face of love with respect to communication, patience and courage are its face with respect to adversity, chastity (if that is still the best word) with respect to sexuality, honesty with respect to transactions, integrity with respect to our decision-making.

We can see this as a two-way movement between love and different virtues. On the one hand, it is in and through the growth in a particular virtue that you or I become more fully a loving person. On the other, in order for virtue to be truly virtuous, it must already be an expression of love. It would seem that virtue is both the by-product of love and its midwife.

But love is the key. The formulation of Aquinas was to say that 'love is the form of the virtues'. It is what gives them their intelligibility, what makes them virtuous. Without love, what seems to be virtue may in fact be vice. This is the case when, for instance, a thief shows great courage or patience in the pursuit of evil ends, or when a rich relative is showered with compassion in the hope that the will might be modified.

Another way of putting this would be to say that virtue is evoked or elicited by love. What matters is that we respond to love's demands. If that is happening, virtue will be formed. The danger would be to focus our attention on acquiring virtues in a process of self-perfection – as if the world were a kind of moral gymnasium where each of us worked on strengthening our own character. The focus of morality is not such self-perfection; such a focus is in fact self-defeating. The focus, rather, is on responding to the demands of love – then virtue takes care of itself.

With this overall picture in mind, we can think of specific virtues such as courage or integrity as moral habits. They are habitual patterns of feeling and acting at the moral level, which do not come easily but have to be acquired through practice, repetition and correction. But when they are acquired they then come easily. They become what we call 'second nature'. It is quite easy now to be patient in adversity, or not to retaliate, or to give generously. Such virtue greatly expands our moral freedom. We can each of us more easily be more of a human person.

What counts as Virtue today?

In answering this question we will start from the concrete by thinking of virtue simply as what a particular community or society or culture regards as 'success', as a perfection of freedom, as what being a person is all about. Obviously this means thinking critically. A particular society might get things wrong and be quite misguided in its understanding of some aspect of being human.

For example, we might compare what Aristotle says about the virtues with what the New Testament has to say. We will find in the New Testament a special regard for the virtue of humility, based on the self-emptying of Christ in his incarnation and crucifixion. But Aristotle sees humility as a distortion of virtue, an undesirable self-depreciation. Clearly the cultural context in each case is influencing what is understood to constitute virtue.

This invites us to look critically at our own culture. It may not use the word virtue, but it is nonetheless holding out to us a picture of what counts as success and failure, of what it is to be a successful human being, of the qualities and characteristics that are to be sought after. Such critical reflection is again an exercise in expanding our freedom, as we seek to recognise the situation for what it is and to appreciate the ways in which it is influencing our own grasp of what it is to be a human being.

Presumably the reflection would yield both positive and negative valuations. We might, for instance, welcome the manner in which the virtue of justice has come to the fore in moral consciousness, as new generations grow more concerned about the inequalities and suffering in the world. On the other hand, we might worry about a lack of justice at an interpersonal level, as evidenced in the lack of respect there is for the property of others, or for honesty in dealings. Again, we might welcome the flourishing of the virtue of compassion where previously society could be much more judgmental. Or on the negative side, we might deplore the encouragement of greed and the aggressive individualism of our consumerist culture.

These are only indications of the potential of the theme of virtue as a tool for the moral analysis of society's appreciation of what it is to be a human person. Another part of the exercise might be the setting of our own culture's account of virtue and vice in dialogue with other accounts to be found in the moral tradition.

For example, there is a classic account of the virtues that stretches from the philosophers of ancient Greece right down through the Christian tradition. We know this account as the 'cardinal virtues'. As one finds it in Aquinas, it sees the person as a multi-level being. The highest levels are those of intellect and will, beneath which are the emotions and appetites. Moral virtues have to do with the will, and with the manner in which the emotions and appetites are integrated by this higher power. This will resonate with some of what we have been saying above.

The key virtue of the will, of the deciding person, is called prudence, but the word does not have our connotations of cautiousness. It is the disposition that makes for good decision-making. This would include open-mindedness, a contemplative attitude, a resolute commitment to serve the good rather than the self. It is about being able to distinguish between what promotes and what hinders growth. It is about making the connections between moral values and overall goals on the one hand, and this particular situation on the other.

The cardinal virtue of the person acting is called justice. It is defined as the constant determination to give others their due. Thus it is the virtue of other-centredness and solidarity. It suggests that the other is to be the rule of our actions, that what we do is to be well 'adjusted' to others, so as to ensure right relationships. Thus it is the virtue that transcends self-interest.

Courage is the cardinal virtue that pertains to the emotional part of the person and thus has to do with mastery at the level of feelings. It is about not being controlled by feelings and, more specifically, about not being pinned down by fear. Courage is not fearlessness, but rather the affirmation of our essential nature in situations of fear. The real fear of the courageous person is the fear of betraying love.

The fourth cardinal virtue, temperance, concerns appetites and instincts. With this virtue, there is an inner order whereby we act according to what is highest in us, our desires subject to a higher control. Temperance is more than no drink or no sex. It is about integration, the integration into our love of our assertiveness, our anger, our sexual desire, our hunger and thirst, so that appetites and urges are not leading a life of their own to the detriment of our love.

We can see the value of thinking in terms of these virtues. They portray a person who is integrated as regards desires and instincts, who is able to deliberate well, who is focused on the other and able to act accordingly. This temperance, prudence, justice and courage greatly expand the person's freedom and self-mastery.

Another approach would be to ask what counts in the New Testament as virtue. We are used to thinking of faith, hope and charity as the Christian (or 'theological') virtues, but it is worth looking again to see what else the New Testament says. One schema is that offered by Bernard Häring, and it is structured according to virtues that refer to the past, to the future and to the present.[4]

In relation to the past, he identifies the virtues of gratitude and humility. Both of these share a sense of dependence on the grace of God and of living life as a grateful response to God's graciousness. In a context where the focus is on what God does as primary, rather than on human achievement, humility and gratitude are valued highly.

In relation to the future, Häring speaks of the virtue of hope. Christians look to the kingdom of God as the future of humanity, a future already initiated in the death and resurrection of Jesus. This yields a disposition of confidence that history has a direction, and of rejoicing in the ways in which God's future is becoming a reality. This is not to gloss over the pain of history, since it is a hope emanating from the cross of Jesus. Rather, it experiences all adversity, evil and suffering in the power of his cross.

In relation to the present, Häring speaks of the virtues of vigilance, serenity and joy. Vigilance means listening in hope to the world around, being alive to what is going on, and seeking to interpret what we find in the light of the gospel. It is a way of being in the world, of carrying our gratitude and hope into the present. Serenity and joy refer to the way in which this gratitude and hope free us from worry and anguish and fear, so that we are free to live to the full in God's redeemed world.

Again these are only indications, and there is far more to virtue than what these two accounts offer. There is, for instance, the virtue of integrity. There are the gospel virtues of non-violence and forgiveness. But what we have said may be sufficient to demonstrate the potential of the theme of virtue for opening up new perspectives on how our freedom might be expanded and how love might be manifested and realised in our lives.

CHAPTER 9

The Grace of Conversion

In this chapter we continue to reflect on morality from the point of view of the person, but this time in the context of the person's relationship with God. This leads us to focus our attention on the themes of conversion and grace.

The Idea of Conversion

The word 'conversion' will have different connotations for different people. For some it will evoke the conversions from Anglicanism to Catholicism of such figures as John Henry Newman, G. K. Chesterton and Ronald Knox. Others might be reminded of William James' classic study, *The Varieties of Religious Experience* (1902), which presents all kinds of cases of the psychological phenomenon, an equivalent to which today would be the phenomenon of conversions to religious sects, with people torn from their families and changed dramatically. Others again will think of the conversion of St Paul or the conversion of St Augustine.

What we are talking about is different from all these. We are talking about a conversion that usually happens without any change of religious denomination. It is not rare and out of the ordinary, but it can and does happen to anybody. It is not normally dramatic or spectacular, although it is always highly significant in the life of the person concerned. It is not usually sudden but rather ongoing, continuing in fact through a lifetime – as John Paul II has remarked, what is needed is 'a continuous, permanent conversion'.[1] In other words, conversion is about everybody and it is meant to be an experience, an issue and an opportunity that persists through life.

The theme of conversion is at the heart of the gospels. The very first words of Jesus proclaim that the kingdom of God has come near and that our response should be to repent, to be converted (Mark 1: 15: 'repentance' and 'conversion' can be used interchangeably). The word used here *(metanoia)* means a change of heart or a change of mindset. The other word used in the New Testament *(epistrophé)* pictures conversion as a turning round. It focuses on the exterior aspect of conversion, on the change in conduct that accompanies a change of heart (e.g. Acts 3:19; 9:35). It also has the suggestion of homecoming. One thinks of the story of the prodigal son as the story of a change of heart that unfolded as a coming home.

The conversion envisaged is both religious and moral, but is fundamentally a religious reality. It concerns the stance that a person adopts towards the gospel of Christ, but the acceptance of the good news of God's grace must also express itself in moral performance. This contrasts with the confessional conversion of such figures as Newman and Chesterton, where the change of religious allegiance need have no great implications for moral behaviour. What the New Testament is talking about is a basic spiritual experience that is the core of a new way of living.

Because conversion is fundamentally a spiritual or religious event, it includes the dimension of grace. Indeed, grace is the heart of conversion. Within Christianity, the moral life is envisaged as a co-operation of the person with the grace of God, and the term conversion refers both to our co-operation and to the grace that makes it possible. We could say that conversion is the grace of God; we could speak of the grace of conversion.

The word conversion might also be contrasted with the word 'development'. Much contemporary discussion of moral change is in terms of development. This is inspired by Lawrence Kohlberg's already mentioned work on identifying stages in the development of moral judgment from childhood to adulthood. That work suggests that we progress morally according to a linear pattern. The prominence of the image of development is also inspired less consciously by the emphasis on never-ending growth and development that is central to capitalism.

Conversion is a somewhat different image. Whereas development suggests a continuous unfolding, conversion suggests a change of direction, discontinuity, tension, decision. The images of turning and of homecoming also lead us to think of conversion more as a centring than as a thrust forward. When the prodigal son physically sets off for his father's house, what is happening spiritually is that he is 'homing in' on himself, returning to himself and to what he most deeply is.

But we do not have to choose between development and conversion. One might think of conversion as a breakthrough within a process of development. All the time there are going on the ordinary processes of operating and relating, by which we are being affected and being formed. Now and then things culminate or come to a head. There is a breakthrough or conversion whereby we enter more deeply into the mystery of existence. Often this happens at moments of weakness, such as sin or pain. But the actual moment is embedded in a before and after.[2]

This is very similar to the way in which we described the opposite of conversion, mortal sin, as the culmination of a process rather than one isolated and spectacular event. And just as conversion might be seen as a circling in on the core of what we are, so the 'aversion' that is mortal sin can be seen as a form of losing ourselves or losing touch with ourselves. One thinks of Jesus' words about losing our life and finding our life.

Self-Righteousness

If conversion is a turning, then it is a turning from something. That something Christianity calls sin. What is meant, though, is not so much sins in the plural, the various wrongs we might be guilty of in life. Rather, what is meant is sin in the singular, the root of sinfulness in the human heart, from which wrongdoings arise.

It would seem from the gospels that Jesus understood this fundamental sin or sinfulness to be the sin of self-righteousness. (We have already seen something of this in the chapter about how Jesus saw morality.) We might look on it in the following way. In the gospels, conversion happened to people in whose hearts the words of Jesus found an echo. There was a resonance with their own felt need. To those who felt burdened by sin or imprisoned in guilt, the call to conversion was real. They knew the inadequacy of their situation and the inadequacy in themselves, and could therefore appreciate what Jesus was holding out to them. They were the ones who had 'ears to hear'.

The way Jesus put it, on an occasion when he was eating with tax collectors and sinners and thereby scandalising the Pharisees, was: 'Those who are well have no need of a physician, but those who are sick; I have come to call not the righteous but sinners' (Mark 2:17). By this he did not mean that he accepts the sinner and not the upright; that would be a perverted sense of justice. It is more like what we mean when we say that sinners are closest to God – not because they are sinners, but because they know they are sinners and bitterly regret it. They are open to something new, open to God. They are ready for conversion.

Being self-righteous means exactly the opposite. It means no openness, no sense of needing God. Though the self-righteous of the gospels were the ones who were considered morally upright, their exterior uprightness betrayed a deeper malaise. G. K. Chesterton, in his *Heretics*, remarked that the most damnable pride is the pride of somebody who has something to be proud of. Being proud of your ancestors, he continued, which reflects no credit on you, does little harm. Being proud of the money you have made is a little more serious, and more serious still is intellectual pride. But most pernicious of all is taking pride in your goodness.

This suggests that the hardest people to convert may well be the good people, because they do not see that there is an issue. It is not their goodness that is the problem. It is the sense that can go with it of being self-made and therefore self-sufficient. The only role left for God is to admire their achievement! When Jesus says that everything will be forgiven except 'blasphemy against the Spirit' (Matthew 12:31-32), this is at least part of what he had in mind. To deny the action of the Spirit is to close oneself off. There can be no forgiveness, not because forgiveness has been refused, but because the need for it has been denied.

Earlier we noted how self-righteousness makes for prejudice, for despising others and for division. The way *The Church in the Modern World* put it was to say that 'once God is forgotten, the creature is lost sight of as well' (paragraph 36). Once there is self-righteousness there is no need of God; and once there is no need of God, there is no sense that we all stand before God as similarly needy people. Instead of all existing under the Truth, some feel they possess the truth over and against others.

In the Christian tradition, the more common word for self-right-eousness is pride. It is often mistakenly thought that this is one of the seven capital sins, but in fact two things are being confused. The capital sin in question is the sin of vainglory, which concerns an inordinate desire for one's own prominence. But pride is more basic. It is the root which, with desire, is common to all seven capital sins. Here, pride means a turning away from God and desire means a turning towards some other attachment in place of God.

In the Latin of Aquinas, turning away from God is *aversio* and turning towards something else is *conversio*. In other words pride means that conversion and aversion are reversed. Pride or self-righteousness means that a person is converted to the very contrary of what he or she should be converted to. For this reason it is the fundamental sin.

Self-Negation

However, there is a sense in which self-righteousness is only half the picture. The language of pride, with its implications of arrogance, self-sufficiency, self-assertiveness, will to power, is about placing too much trust in ourselves. But there is also the self-depreciation that does not trust enough in itself. Besides those who exalt themselves, there are others who belittle themselves and surrender their own concerns too willingly.

It is sometimes said that men can identify more easily with the language of pride than women can, at least traditionally. In the past, with women not having had to take much responsibility outside the home, pride and arrogance were hardly likely to have been the specifically feminine forms of sin. Much more likely was the self-depreciation which, according to Valerie Saiving, would have been reflected in:

> 'triviality, distractibility and diffuseness; lack of an organising centre or focus; dependence on others for one's own self-definition; tolerance at the expense of standards of excellence; inability to respect the boundaries of privacy; sentimentality, gossipy sociability, and mistrust of reason – in short, underdevelopment or negation of the self.'[3]

However, for our purposes, we need not see this only in a masculine-feminine context. Instead, we can see both self-righteousness and self-negation as human problems, each as problematic as the other, each an obstacle to conversion for both men and women. Besides those who trust too much in themselves and see no need of conversion, there are those who cannot believe either in themselves or in the possibility of conversion, so that this then becomes a self-fulfilling prophecy.

We tend to neglect this side of conversion. With all the emphasis on sin and conversion, we can forget that for many people the problem is less that they have sinned than that they cannot believe themselves forgiven. They cannot believe that a new beginning is possible. Conversion or repentance is the most revolutionary force in the world because, while we cannot change what has happened in the past, we can change the meaning of the past. Conversion adds another chapter to the story of our life; the plot shifts and previous happenings assume a new context and a new meaning. Self-negation cuts itself off from this possibility, or at least cannot believe that this is possible.

It is hard to know whether or not this self-negation should be called sin. Compared to self-righteousness, sin seems too strong a word here. Self-negation suggests helplessness rather than arrogance. And yet it is also a 'blasphemy against the Spirit', because it too denies that the action of the Spirit is possible and that to God all things are possible. Aquinas says that to think that a given sin cannot be forgiven is an offence against the infinite mercy of God (*Summa Theologiae*, III, 86, 1). In that sense, self-negation could perhaps be considered to be another face of pride.

We might reflect also on the original words of Jesus: 'The time is fulfilled and the kingdom of God is come near; repent, and believe in the good news' (Mark 1:15). To believe in the good news means transcending our narrow vision of ourselves as sinners. It means learning, as did the prodigal son, to drop the 'I am sinner' and listen to the 'You are son/daughter'. As one prayer puts it: 'O Lord, help me to believe the truth about myself, no matter how beautiful it is!'

Origen, a theologian in the early centuries of Christianity, said: 'I beseech you therefore, be transformed. Resolve to know that in you there is a capacity to be transformed.' In some cases the transforma-

tion will be from self-righteousness, in other cases from self-negation, and it is a moot point which is the harder change to negotiate.
In many cases the latter is the harder kind of conversion – simply to
believe that I am loved, to allow myself to be forgiven, without having to prove anything or to be anything. But both are encountered
by Jesus in the gospels. He came up against self-righteousness in his
dealings with the Pharisees, and he encountered self-negation in
the tax-collectors and sinners he associated with.

Common to both self-righteousness and self-negation is what
Eamonn Bredin speaks of as the temptation of familiarity. We tend,
he says, to domesticate Christ. Instead of moving out into his
world, we settle him down in our own, making him into our image
of what we would be comfortable with, so that we will not be disturbed. This is self-righteousness and self-negation in the form of
complacency. When we are self-righteous we are satisfied with ourselves as we are and we seek to justify this. Equally, when we do
not believe in ourselves we resign ourselves to what we are and
argue that any change is futile. Either way, the gap between what
we are and what we might be is collapsed. The source of challenge
is dried up; there is no longer any point seen in conversion.[4]

A Question of Openness

The *Catechism* (paragraph 2091) speaks of the sins against hope as
presumption and despair. This relates very well to what we have
been calling self-righteousness and self-negation. Self-righteousness presumes too quickly and easily in its own salvation. Self-
negation despairs of ever being saved. This tells us that there is
something common to both, namely, the sin against hope. Both
refuse to let God be God. Both refuse to let God be our future, the
God of our future, the God of hope.

This means in turn that the essence of conversion has something to
do with openness and willingness. Because closure is at the heart of
both self-righteousness and self-negation, the way forward lies in
the opening up of a new horizon. Conversion is made possible by
an openness to the possibility that we may have got things wrong,
that there may be a further perspective which we do not possess,
that we may have to change. Such openness makes for a willingness
to be persuaded and to see anew.

There is a vivid sense of such openness and willingness in the words of Augustine describing his own conversion in his *Confessions* (book seven): 'When first I knew you, you lifted me up, so that I might see that there was something to be seen, but that I was not yet the man to see it.' This is not yet conversion but it is the beginning of the process. It is conversion in embryo because it affirms that something more is needed, while acknowledging that this something more is not yet possessed. It sees that there is an issue.

Common to self-righteousness and self-negation, in their lack of hope, is the absence of such openness. They do not want to see further, they are not willing to be persuaded, but prefer to rest as they are. Even though it may be painful in some cases, particularly in cases of self-negation, each is actually comfortable in its familiar world and would be insecure at any prospect of change.

Because of this, conversion is often an experience of dread and resistance. It evokes dread because we are being asked to see ourselves in a new and different way. When we reflect on how difficult it can be to change a routine or a habit, and how threatening a feeling it may be, we can appreciate how much more difficult it will be to envisage our very selves differently, whether it is to see ourselves as in need of God where previously we did not, or to see that we have a future where previously we did not.

Perhaps this is part of the logic of Jesus in saying: 'For those who want to save their life will lose it, and those who lose their life for my sake will find it' (Matthew 16:25). Could this mean letting go of myself as I am for the sake of what I may be? Is it a matter of letting go of what I *think* I am, in order to discover what I *truly* am? It would seem that conversion is no less than a process of myself dying and rising.

The image of seeing has been recurring in the above discussion. In the last chapter we saw that freedom begins in seeing things as they are and that freedom expands with the expansion of loving vision. In this chapter we have been implying that the expansion of freedom is a matter of conversion and that conversion is a change in how we see. Both those who are self-righteous and those who negate themselves are called to see themselves differently. Their present vision is enslaving and without hope; it brings them death. They do not desire to see truthfully. In contrast, the experience of

Augustine indicated a shaft of light coming through, the beginning of new vision.

Seeing also occurs in the gospels as an image for conversion. Mark 8:22-26 tells the story of the gradual healing of a blind man (the only one of such gospel stories where the healing takes place gradually). Jesus puts saliva on his eyes and lays his hands on him. The man can now see, but only in a blurred way – 'I can see people, but they look like trees, walking.' When Jesus put his hands on him again, 'he looked intently and his sight was restored, and he saw everything clearly.' The story is a symbol for the enlightenment that comes with recognising who Jesus is. This is what both the self-sufficient and the self-belittling need to see, for neither can recognise Jesus' power as Saviour.

The fact that the healing is gradual is also further indication that the conversion we are talking about is more often an ongoing process of enlightenment than a sudden spectacular event. In this regard, mention might be made of the detail in the story of Paul's conversion that 'though his eyes were open he could see nothing' and that for 'three days he was without sight' (Acts 9:8-9). Conversion is a disorientation, in that we lose our familiar way of seeing things and have to learn to see as if for the first time.

Grace

Openness to new possibilities is not all that openness involves. Ultimately the openness that is the core of conversion is openness to another. It is openness to the perspectives that another brings to our situation and a willingness to be guided by these perspectives. It is openness to how God sees us and to God's action in our lives.

The great danger in thinking about conversion is that we will be tempted to think of it as something we do ourselves. After all, even when we think along the lines of invitation-response, we still tend to regard the response as all our own. In one sense this is true: if the response were not our own then it would hardly count as a free and responsible, hence a moral, act. The danger, though, is in losing sight of the fact that the response is only possible by virtue of the invitation. How else would it be a response? If this is forgotten, then thinking about the conversion as our own doing can slip imperceptibly into a mindset of self-righteousness and self-sufficiency.

Thus we would speak of conversion as the experience of grace, or of the grace of conversion. Conversion is a process of submitting to grace. Just as opening the door allows in a light infinitely brighter than the flickering light we can manufacture for ourselves, so conversion is the end of self-reliance. Or rather, it is the end of the illusion of self-reliance, the illusion that the only power is the power whereby we have made ourselves the self-righteous or self-negating creatures that we are. It is this opening of the door to grace that we see in the words of Augustine and in the dawning recognition in the blind man's eyes.

Conversion is a co-operation with the grace of God. It is a co-working with the One of whom Paul said: 'We are what he has made us, created in Christ Jesus' (Ephesians 2:10). When we speak of grace we are talking about the love of God for us. By this we mean God's participation in our lives, God's affirmation of the value of each one of us, be this value actual or potential, and God's commitment to the realisation of the good and the value of our lives, even where there is presently visible little other than sin or failure. Such is God's love for us in Christ, affirming us, forgiving us, revealing to us our innermost selves, calling forth what is deepest in us.

If God's grace is this loving liberation of us into our own true selves – so that, in the words of Irenaeus, the person, the living person, is God's glory – then conversion is our learning to see ourselves as God sees us, learning this loving vision of ourselves as love, so that we may then become love. In this way, conversion is a co-operation with the grace of God.

But there is a further power affecting our conversion besides the power of grace, and that is the power of sin. Paul knew this when he spoke of not understanding his own actions and not being in control of what he did. 'Now, if I do what I do not want, it is no longer I that do it, but sin that dwells within me'. He goes on to contrast this 'law' with the 'law of God in my inmost self' in which he delights. He thus experiences a struggle between two powers within him. The law, which was good and spiritual, was ineffective against the power of sin which Paul felt within himself. In conclusion he exclaims: 'Wretched man that I am! Who will rescue me from this body of death? Thanks be to God through Jesus Christ our Lord!' (Romans 7:14-25).

From a theological perspective, our exercise of freedom is defined by the two powers, of grace and of sin. These two powers constitute the situation freedom finds itself in, the situation it must recognise if it is to realise itself. Conversion, then, is nothing other than freedom's recognition of both the need of grace and its availability. On the other hand, it is the power of sin that underlies our self-righteousness and our self-negation. And just as grace is more than our self-justification, so sin is more than our self-destruction. It is also a power to which we are subject.

Contemporary theology would say that the power of sin is outside as well as inside, embedded in the world in which we live as well as embedded in our hearts. Just as smoke lingers in the air we breathe and enters our lungs, so there is a power of sin in the world which enters into us to corrupt us, drag us down and bring out the worst in us. It is this power, both within and without, that is experienced by both the self-righteous and the self-negating person. Both are victims of sin, though they experience it very differently. The one finds in the power of sin the possibility for self-assertion, the other reacts to the experience of sin with self-depreciation.

In the New Testament, Paul understands the structure of our personal existence as defined by these two poles of grace and sin, and he symbolises this in a rich variety of ways. We live, he says, between darkness and light: 'children of light and children of the day; we are not of the night or of darkness' (1 Thessalonians 5:5; cf. Colossians 1:13). We live between estrangement and reconciliation: 'he is our peace... [he] has broken down the dividing wall' (Ephesians 2:14).

We live between death and life: 'you also must consider yourselves dead to sin and alive to God in Christ Jesus' (Romans 6:11; cf. Colossians 2:12-13). We live between the old self and the new self: 'You have stripped off the old self... and clothed yourselves with the new self' (Colossians 3:10; cf. Ephesians 4:22-24). We live between flesh and spirit: 'you are not in the flesh; you are in the Spirit' (Romans 8:9; cf. Galatians 5:16-25). We live between slavery and freedom: 'You are no longer a slave but a child... children, not of the slave, but of the free woman' (Galatians 4:7, 31; cf. Romans 8:2).

Arching over all these is the contrast Paul draws between being in Adam and being in Christ. He contrasts Adam, through whom sin

came into the world, with Christ, who is the source of the free gift of
grace (Romans 5:12-21; cf. 1 Corinthians 15:21). Adam symbolises
the power of sin whereas Christ is the power of grace. Together
they represent the two possibilities of existence. To speak of being
in Adam and being in Christ as the fundamental possibilities of our
existence is the theological equivalent to what the previous chapter
spoke of as saying yes or no to our existence, deciding for or against
ourselves.

But the two powers are not equal. The contemporary idea of 'original blessing' is a statement of the victory of the power of grace over
the power of sin. It means that, while ours is a wounded humanity
because of the power of sin, the world we are born into is saved and
we are born blessed by God. As Augustine said: 'Because you love
us, you have made us lovable'. Perhaps there is a link between this
idea of original blessing and the doctrine of the Immaculate
Conception. The doctrine says that Mary, the first person to know
the grace of Christ, existed in that grace from the first moment of
her existence. The link might be the principle that anything we say
about Mary we also say in some way about every human being.

But if our existence is founded in grace, it is only in the unfolding of
our lives that the victory of grace over sin will become ours, as we
determine to live up to the dignity which our baptism proclaims.
And thus the journey of our lives is a journey of continuing conversion, because so much of it will be a moving back and forth between
these two possibilities of sin and grace. To refer again to the contrast between conversion and development, the pattern of our lives
is less likely to be one of straightforward, linear progression and
more likely to be along the lines of 'three steps forward, two steps
back' – the pattern of permanent striving, recurrent failure and
gradual attainment.

Our Feel for Ourselves

We have been identifying three elements in Christian moral existence, namely our own human being, the grace of God in Christ, and
the power of sin. Because of this complexity there is a question of
balance involved. Already we have seen examples of imbalance.
Self-negation may be understood as an over-emphasis on the
power of sin, while self-righteousness can be seen as over-emphas-

ising our own human power. The balance that is desirable might be described in terms of having the right feel for ourselves as Christian moral subjects.

The history of the Christian tradition indicates that the balance is not easily attained or retained. For, arguably the greatest and most prevalent theological controversy through the whole Christian tradition is that concerning the relationship between nature and grace. We can see in the history of that debate the repeated misunderstanding of the relationship and an unending struggle to get the balance right.

Going right back to Paul's correspondence with the Romans and the Galatians, we find there the controversy between law and grace. Paul asks the Galatians (3:2): 'Did you receive the Spirit by doing the works of the law or by believing what you heard?' It is not observance of the law that saves, but grace. We do not make ourselves righteous, but we co-operate with God's activity of justification.

Four hundred years later saw the controversy between Augustine and Pelagius. Pelagius' argument was that we are able to do good of our own power, and that Christ was no more than a good example. The debate ended when Augustine asked, why then are we baptised? For baptism is the sacrament of God's justifying grace redeeming us from the power of sin. As such it testifies to our need of grace.

However, there was another strain in Augustine. It is notable that both Augustine and Paul experienced a quite dramatic form of conversion and it is often the case with such experience that it leads to a considerable emphasis on the grace of God, even to the point of downplaying human nature. There would seem to be something of this in Augustine. His awareness of the need for God's grace was such as to leave him with a rather negative view of human nature apart from grace.

If there was a thread of this in Augustine, it was far more explicit one thousand years later in the theology of Martin Luther. Again the background was an intense spiritual experience of conversion. But this time the outcome was a theology that saw human nature as so corrupt and under the power of sin that even God's grace did not change it. Justification is 'imputed' to us. We are not really changed; it is just that God does not count our sinfulness against us. Thus, in Luther's eyes, we are both justified and sinners at the same time.

In the following centuries there were further controversies over the balance between human nature and God's grace. And again the pendulum swung between those who displayed too glib a confidence in the powers of human nature with too little appreciation of the power of sin, and those whose sense of the need for grace was such as to belittle their estimation of the goodness of human nature.

In particular, there was the Jansenism of seventeenth century France. This school of thought put no trust at all in human nature: apart from grace we can only sin. Its view of things made for a rigorist, scrupulous morality, as well as for a very severe spirituality of abnegation and flight from the world. While the movement was partly a reaction to too lax an approach to morality and an overly optimistic view of human nature, it is obvious how such thinking tilts the balance far too much in the other direction.

While the theology of Aquinas, and the Council of Trent's response to Luther, might be seen as examples of a more balanced position, it is probably fair to say that the overall tendency of the tradition has been more in the direction of downplaying rather than exalting human nature (even though such downplaying is usually seen as a fault of Protestantism). We might wonder if this accounts for even a little of the reliance on authority in our moral tradition. In other words, it would hardly be surprising if a lack of trust in human nature and freedom went hand in hand with a corresponding emphasis on conformity to a teaching authority in matters of morals.

The question, in other words, is: to what extent can we trust ourselves or to what extent must we be suspicious of ourselves? Are we basically good or basically sinful? Can we rely on ourselves or must we depend upon another? What is our feel for ourselves as moral agents? To which end of the spectrum does our feel for ourselves tend – towards glorifying ourselves or towards condemning ourselves?

An adequate balance is one that can hold things in tension. It is one that can speak of both grace and sin. Here, conversion is about knowing both that we are loved in the depth of our being and that there is also a dark side. Our deepest self is a place inhabited by God's love, so that at our core we are good, healed, at one with God. But the power of sin has weakened and wounded us, so that we must struggle. We have grounds for confidence, but if we forget about sin, confidence turns into presumption. We have grounds for being humble, but if we forget how much we are loved, humility slips into self-negation. Shakespeare captured something of this balance in *All's Well that Ends Well:*

> 'The web of our life is of a mingled yarn,
> good and ill together:
> our virtues would be proud if our faults whipped them not;
> and our crimes would despair
> if they were not cherished by our virtues.' (IV, 3, 83)

Idealism and Gradualism

Another way of posing the question would be to ask: when it comes to moral conversion, are we too hard on ourselves or too easy? Given the overall tendency in our tradition to emphasise our sinfulness over our goodness, to be suspicious rather than trustful, the chances are that being too hard on ourselves may be a greater problem than being too easy.

Of course both are there in us, and that is why we would see the conversion as a matter of both idealism and gradualism. Idealism is required because the gospel presents an ideal that is very high indeed. Jesus' proposal of enemy love ends with the words: 'Be perfect, therefore, as your heavenly Father is perfect' (Matthew 5:48). When we spoke above of Jesus proposing the maximum rather than the minimum, we saw that he had in mind a response that is unending.

Perhaps it is even the case that there is not enough of the ideal being preached. If the view of morality as law prevails then, notwithstanding the value of that perspective, morality will almost inevitably be seen as something to be observed rather than something to be sought after. Obeying will replace striving, satisfying the requirements will replace seeking the goal. Perhaps we need to hear more about the challenge of discipleship and less about the requirements of conformity.

At the same time, because the ideal is something that is being constantly sought after, never fully attained, its pursuit is the source of an ever-present dissatisfaction. So the dissatisfaction must be tempered with an appreciation that progress is gradual and according to present capacity. The ideal is what beckons; but what is demanded is no more (and no less) than what is possible today – what we earlier called the practical ideal. Gradualism takes people where they are at. This is what an objective morality is ever in danger of forgetting.

Given the need for both idealism and gradualism, the call to conversion should be experienced as both challenging and comforting. It needs to be challenging because we often need to be disturbed out of our complacency and confronted with the gap between the actual and the ideal. But other times the call to conversion needs to be comforting because sometimes we can do no more than limp along. Sometimes people are tired or broken, unable for anything more than the weakest response. They need to know that the response is none the less real for that.

Oddly, it can be we who are unrealistically demanding of ourselves, and not some moral authority. Often the conflict is in our own hearts. We can find it hard to accept our own inadequacy or failure. Perhaps we even refuse to tolerate ourselves as we are, thus bringing much discouragement upon ourselves. This refusal is itself a subtle form of self-righteousness.

While we come down hard on ourselves, it is God who treats us humanely. While the gospel does call us to be perfect, God does not expect the achievement to be overnight. God knows that conversion is gradual and that what matters is that we are turned in the right direction (what conversion literally means), that our hearts are in the right place, and that we are responding according to present capacity.

There was a film entitled *On Golden Pond,* which described the 'conversion' of an elderly man who had always been very hard on his own daughter. As the daughter lamented to her mother about the pain it had caused her, the mother said that sometimes you have got to look at a person and realise he is doing the best that he can. Something like that is what God can see in us, often in our worst moments. God can see and appreciate our heart better than we can ourselves.

Cardinal Newman once said that to live is to change and to be perfect is to change often. The gospel call to perfection is not about arriving at the end-point or destination. It is about a quality of the journey, the quality of being open to change and grace and transformation. There are often times when being open is all that is asked – and when that is everything.

Sacrament of Conversion

Only two of the seven sacraments accompany us through life. They are eucharist and reconciliation, and one of these, the sacrament of reconciliation, is being experienced by less and less people. Yet one of the central aspects of that sacrament is its being the sacrament of continuing conversion, the sacrament that accompanies, celebrates and sanctifies the lifelong task of conversion.

It is a sacrament that has changed its form a number of times over the centuries and there is a change happening again today. Where the sacrament is most alive today is in its communal form, and in this form it can offer much – both in healing and in preaching – for the journey of continuing conversion. Most obviously there is the simple fact of our togetherness as what one person called 'a fellowship of failure'. The encouragement of such solidarity has the power to transform us into a fellowship of hope. As well as that, the communal celebration offers the possibility of proclaiming more adequately God's word and God's grace to all who seek strength in responding to the call to conversion.

An older theology spoke of grace as both healing and elevating. God's grace heals us and makes us whole; and it also lifts us up to share in God's own life. Perhaps the future of the sacrament of reconciliation lies in its being more deliberately the communication to God's people of a grace that is both healing and elevating. Experience tells us that the knowledge of being loved is one of the most powerful forces for healing that we know. If that knowledge can be communicated when people join together in this sacrament, then the 'I can't', that so many whisper, might find itself being eased gently into a new context of hope.

CHAPTER 10

Conscience and Community

When morality is viewed from the perspective of the person, conscience is a central consideration. In this chapter we reflect on the dynamics of how conscience emerges and operates, both in a general sense and within the Christian community in particular.

Creativity or Conformity?

Talk about conscience can quickly become caught up in a false polarisation. At one pole there is the view that tends to see conscience as 'doing what you want' or 'doing what you feel is right'; at the other pole is the view of conscience as 'doing what you're told'. In a sense, conscience is both of these and neither.

The understanding of conscience as 'doing what you want' is quite common. It would not be unusual to hear a young adult saying something like: 'It is very hard to know what is right and wrong anymore... If you do what you feel is right, then you are right.' The naïvety of this will be plain to those who have had the experience a week later of discovering that they were wrong! Yet, when there is no clear moral order, but only a confusing plurality of voices, such a stance is as much a cry of despair as anything.

If this sounds like a quite recent stance, we might recall Cardinal Newman's *Letter to the Duke of Norfolk,* written in 1875:

'When men advocate the rights of conscience, they [mean]... the right of thinking, speaking, writing, and acting, according to their judgment or their humour, without any thought of God at all. They do not even pretend to go by any moral rule, but they demand... for each to be his own master in all things, and to profess what he pleases, asking no one's leave...'

On the other hand, the understanding of conscience as meaning 'doing what you're told' is still quite widespread. For many, obedience is fundamental, and sometimes this sense is so strong as to leave the impression that conscience is almost redundant, the right answer being supplied by the moral authority. Even the language of informing conscience can seem to suggest that, 'if you inform your conscience you will come around to our way of thinking anyway'.

Conscience is neither doing what you want nor doing what you are told, though it includes elements of the creativity of the former and of the conformity of the latter. We might rather see conscience as the decision-making part of our 'internal moral system'. Much of that system, as we noted, is obscure, like deep waters or tangled undergrowth. But conscience is the sensitive part, near the surface. It is where our internal moral system emerges to act upon the world.

As we act, our actions form into patterns and form us into the people we are, each with our particular mix of virtue and vice. So conscience is not just about deciding what to do. It is also about deciding what to be. Thus it might be a more complete definition to speak of conscience as making the links between what we do and what we will be. It is where we become aware of the possible effects of our actions upon our character, so that in deciding what to do we are, in however dim or explicit a fashion, also deciding what to be. Deciding to go to work or to stay in bed; deciding whether or not to tell a lie; deciding what to do for Lent; each is also a decision about ourselves and the kind of person we would become.

There will be elements in this process both of conformity and of creativity. Conformity means that part of the working of conscience is the effort to see truthfully. If there is anywhere that obedience is absolute and unconditional it is here. The very nature of conscience is that it search for and conform to moral truth. If it discovers, for instance, that other people simply cannot be used, or that a certain item belongs to a certain person, then it must submit to this truth. The fundamental perversion of conscience is that it would be satisfied with anything else. In this sense conscience informs itself; it opens itself so as to be formed by the truth.

But there will be as much creativity as conformity. Many of the difficult moral situations we enter into are quite uncharted and we experience a gap between where our acquired wisdom stops and where the contours of this situation start. Other times our moral experience can be quite paradoxical, as we find ourselves making decisions so as to deceive in order to remain faithful, or to hurt in order to protect. But creativity is part of most moral decisions, not just unusual ones. For, unless we are automatons, in every situation we reflect and we deliberate and, given how difficult it can be to discern and decide, the more creative we can be, the better. As well as that, the moral rules that our tradition gives us cover only very few of the moral decisions we will make in life.

Given this element of creativity, we might even suggest some unusual metaphors for conscience. Might conscience be likened to a chef or to an artist or to a composer? Each of these starts off by learning the rules, whether it be using the oven or working with colours or learning an instrument. Some go no further and what they produce is plain and unexciting, but solid. Others become great and they achieve this because they play around with possibilities, going beyond the rules they learned. Certainly if they had done no more than keep to the rules they would never have known greatness.

Applying this to morality, we would not wish to say that conscience becomes better by occasionally disregarding the rules and doing wrong. Rather, we could put it the other way round: will conscience ever grow if it never does other than scrupulously observe what is laid out for it in advance? Creativity comes of internalising the core values underlying the rules, to such an extent that one is operating in a truly autonomous fashion. Morality has become second nature.

In the section of *Veritatis Splendor* on 'Conscience and Truth', John Paul II speaks critically of what he calls the 'creative' interpretation of conscience. By this he means a conscience that departs from moral norms in favour of deciding for itself in an autonomous and even arbitrary way.[1] Obviously creativity is distorted if it is set apart from, or in opposition to, the moral truth in this way. Equally, moral truth is distorted if the processes of individual deliberation are neglected.

Perhaps the problem is that the whole discussion is cast from the start in terms of law. In what follows, we will be thinking more in terms of personal growth and of the relationship between an individual and a community.

Conditioning

There is a *Garfield* cartoon that has the cat approaching the bowl of food. A voice comes from the bowl, 'Don't eat me. You're too fat already!' Garfield asks, 'Who are you?' 'This is your conscience speaking', comes the reply. 'I don't have a conscience', says Garfield. 'I know. I'm free-lancing'.

Does everybody have a conscience? The answer is yes, but we would be forgiven for forming the impression that many people do not have one. It is not just that some people have a more refined sense of right and wrong than others, but that there are people who do not even seem to think in terms of right and wrong. Some think purely pragmatically: 'If it works, do it'. Others think only: 'What's in it for me?'

There is, in other words, a moral kind of consciousness, and it may be relatively more or less sensitive. This is what we mean by conscience. We might add that this moral form of consciousness may be spoken of in terms of any of the five ways of looking at morality. Its sensitivity may be in terms of a sense of right and wrong, or of being true to oneself, or of what one is becoming, or of what is loving or not, or of what is just or unjust. Whichever way it thinks, conscience is consciousness in a moral mode. It might in fact be more helpful to think in terms of the person *being* a conscience than *having* a conscience, for conscience is less a thing the person *has* than a dimension of what the person *is*.

However, the variations of moral sensitivity between different people lead us to appreciate the significance of the way in which conscience emerges as a person grows. A useful analogy might be to compare conscience to the faculty of speech. The faculty of speech is there from the start, but it is unformed, a naked capacity. As we grow up we will learn to speak; but we do not just learn to speak, we learn to speak English or Irish or Italian or whatever. The capacity is formed according to the language of the culture to which we belong.

Conscience too is there at first as potentiality, as an orientation towards the good, but an orientation that is in need of formation. As we grow up we will become morally aware, but this will happen according to the pattern of values and priorities in the culture. If stealing is regarded as normal, we will tend to think likewise. If cruelty is abhorred we will tend to feel thus ourselves. We learn this particular language. What we are learning is, of course, one version of what counts as success and failure, one version of what it is to be a human being.

Thus far it could be said that conscience is little more than conditioning. What this means is not that we, as growing persons, are being manipulated in any way, but that we have not yet developed the capacity to be anything other than conditioned into a moral sense. Researchers into moral development would back this up. They talk, for instance, of the 'mirror conscience'. When we are still too young to think things out for ourselves, we find moral truth in the faces of the adults around, in their approving or disapproving looks. For quite a number of years, our conscience is made for us, be this for good or for bad.

Whence Wisdom?

But conscience does not remain as conditioning. There begins to develop what might be called an internal dialogue within each of us. It has to do with the developing psychological capacity to think abstractly as well as concretely, and it has to do with the emerging adolescent sense of identity. But it also reflects a new quality of interaction between ourselves and our environment, between the morality we have been initiated into and a stance of our own.

Perhaps this independent stance was there in a less differentiated form for quite a while. For instance, a child might suspect the wrongness of being treated in a certain way without being able to formulate why. But as we grow, we are becoming articulate in our own right. As we move towards adulthood, we become able to stand back and to be critically aware of the moral language that we have learned. We become aware, for instance, of hypocrisy in adults. Or we sense an inconsistency between God being good and so many innocent people suffering.

By virtue of our own internal dialogue, we are each becoming a

moral authority in our own right. We are learning to speak for ourselves. We might say that autonomy is emerging from community.
Where once there was a child who saw right and wrong in the face
of a parent, there is now an adult, morally conscious and articulate
in his or her own right. In this way we come to find out for ourselves that we have to decide for ourselves what to make of ourselves.

As this happens, our belonging to the community assumes a critical
quality, in the sense that the values that have been communicated
may now be personalised, internalised, made our own. Now it can
be said that conscience is made *by* us and no longer just *for* us. Of
course it may be the case that some of the value-orientations we
absorbed early on are never completely internalised, so that in
some cases we remain more conditioned than free. But this is not to
take away from the overall thrust towards self-appropriation.

But there is great variety in how people negotiate this crucial
process. It can go wrong in two ways in particular. On the one
hand, where people reject the morality they have been conditioned
into, the rejection can be quite vehement and irrational, and can
issue in a very false sense of what autonomy is, along the lines of
'I'll do what I want now, because I'm sick of being told what to
think.' In other cases the reaction will be less vehement but no less
real.

On the other hand, there are those who refuse the hurdle. Perhaps it
is fear. Perhaps they have been so conditioned to obey that they
cannot think for themselves. Perhaps they do not want to think for
themselves. It is, after all, insecure, much less secure than leaving
the responsibility to others. And so, some stay as children, declin-
ing the new freedom. Others may resemble this state, but with a
residual restlessness or with an anger seething underneath.

Both outcomes are to be lamented because, like the creativity and
conformity we spoke of earlier, each has only a piece of the truth.
And that truth is that conscience, when it matures, is neither blind
obedience nor splendid isolation. It is, rather, a synthesis of inner
and collective wisdom. Conscience must learn to rely on its own
inner wisdom, though it will take time before it can trust itself and
have confidence in itself. At the same time, it will know its need of

the collective wisdom, which nurtured it originally and with which it must remain in dialogue. We decide *for* ourselves but we do not decide *by* ourselves.

In that continuing dialogue between the inner and the collective wisdom, things are complicated by the fact that either may fall short of what it should be. We all know how inner wisdom can be lacking, but it can also happen that the collective wisdom cannot be relied upon. But if the latter is not reliable, and we innocently continue to trust in it, then we may end up both utterly genuine and yet completely at sea.

Being Affected

Let us look a little more at this dialectic of inner and collective wisdom. If we take each in turn, when we see how each can go so easily wrong, then we can appreciate better just how hard-won freedom of conscience is.

Conscience as inner wisdom is a rich notion that can at times be reduced to something quite glib. Frequently the demand is expressed that people be left free to follow their own consciences. As a rejection of authoritarian morality and an affirmation of personal responsibility, this is to be welcomed. But the demand sometimes has other aspects to it which deserve to be scrutinised.

One of these aspects is that it can imply that following conscience is easily done if we were just left alone. If only others would stop interfering there would be no problem. Such confidence is quite naïve. As Cardinal Newman observed, while conscience is the highest of all teachers it is also the least luminous, because the sense of right and wrong is 'so delicate, so fitful, so easily puzzled, obscured, perverted, so subtle in its argumentative methods, so impressible by education, so biassed by pride and passion, so unsteady in its course' (*A Letter to the Duke of Norfolk*).

It is also naïve in that the demand to be left alone can suggest too assertive an image of conscience – a picture of conscience in terms of people asserting their stance in a manner that is self-justifying. This may be understandable if conscience has previously been repressed, but that does not make it an accurate picture.

For conscience is more receptive than assertive. It is well described as a quality of being affected, for this quality captures a central truth about conscience. Here conscience is being likened to a moral sensorium. It is that inner place where all the moral messages are received, and where all depends on the quality of the receptivity. Those who are not affected receive little or nothing. They are little affected by whatever comes into their lives. They miss the moral significance of most of what goes on around them. Thus when they decide and act, they are deciding and acting on the basis of a meagre sensitivity and are likely to be out of tune with much of their situation.

Being affected means being open to what there may be that might inform and refine conscience. It is receptivity to the significant, to whatever may have meaning and value. It means that a thoughtful, sensitive listening is the first moment in the activity of conscience. It is a quality of the conscientious person to be open and sensitive in this way to all aspects of the situation.

Two great impediments to such an open spirit are ignorance and bias. Ignorance of moral values, or of morally significant aspects of a situation, may mean that we are doing no more than sincerely and even confidently making a mess of things. Bias means that our conscientious deliberations are blinkered from the start and that we will either fail to take into account all that should be taken into account or else distort what is there according to the particular bias.

Openness means that we can recognise these possibilities in ourselves. The open spirit knows that it may not understand, that it may have blindspots, that its horizon is limited. It knows that it may be prejudiced and that its motives will more than likely be mixed. Therefore it listens all the more attentively and hopes to be affected by all that there is to receive.

Sometimes this is called an attitude of docility, that is, an attitude of being willing to learn, because we do not presume to know or to be impartial. In the end, the best guarantee of attaining moral truth is this self-demanding, docile openness to being affected further and more fully by what is there. It is in this spirit that Bernard Häring has said:

> 'The most precious thing on earth is a healthy, alert and faithful conscience, free for others, free for all moral values, and able to discern the scale and urgency of values.'[2]

These themes of ignorance and bias also relate to our discussion above of freedom and of conversion. As we become free we are learning to see, both in terms of recognising the situation and its limitations and in terms of seeing more lovingly. Learning to see also means overcoming the distorted vision that comes of both self-righteousness and self-negation. Such self-transcendence, in turn, makes for a conscience that will be sensitive to, and affected by, whatever is truly of value.

Voices

The inner wisdom we are talking about is one aspect of the hard-won freedom to follow conscience. The other concerns the ongoing dialogue between inner wisdom and collective wisdom, between conscience and community. Emerging out of community as an autonomous individual is not a once-and-for-all achievement, in the sense of there being no need to refer to the community thereafter. The emergence is ongoing. Just as a new self is continually emerging out of our relationships, so a new moral consciousness comes of the deliberation that continuing dialogue with the larger community and tradition gives rise to.

It would, however, be more accurate to speak here of community in the plural. Even if the context of our early upbringing is relatively uniform, the context of adolescent and adult life is not. We find ourselves in interaction with a complex of communities, communities to which we belong with different degrees of attachment. These include our families, our friends, our companions at work or at school, fellow-members of different clubs or societies, our parish community, our town or village or neighbourhood. They also include more diffuse communities such as our society, the western world, the world of the media of books and magazines, television and radio, music and films.

A traditional image has pictured conscience as a voice within. *The Church in the Modern World* (paragraph 16) understands this as the voice of God echoing in our depths, calling us to do good and avoid evil. Others would be more sceptical and speak of the Freudian *superego*, of conscience as a guilt mechanism where the voices are internalised authority figures. We would place beside these (not to replace them) another interpretation of conscience as voice. It is that the different communities of which we are a part each functions as a voice, speaking to our moral consciousness or moral receptivity its own vision and values.

These are the voices by which conscience is being formed, so it is important to discern what conscience is being most affected by. We might imagine a series of concentric circles, with conscience at the centre. The inner voices come from those communities that speak most persuasively, the ones we are most receptive to or influenced by. The outer voices also speak, but less is received. And there is movement. Voices that were once dominant recede to the outer edges of moral consciousness, while others that were dim advance towards the centre. Who, then, is being heard?

Here, conscience begins to appear very much like 'doing what you're told'! As we said, talk of being free to follow conscience can sound as if this is an easy thing to do. But it is not, not only because of ignorance and bias, but also because the influence of these voices can be so powerful, both in telling us what to do and, more importantly, in telling us what to be. They can be very hard to ignore.

They are so powerful because they are voices that speak to the heart and not just the intellect. They speak especially to our need to belong and not to be left alone or isolated. Think of the voice of the peer group in the life of a young person who would rather not drink. Think of the voice of the rural community in the life of somebody who does not want to go to Mass. There is more involved than listening and then going our own way. It may be that the price of autonomy is that we no longer belong.

This raises the question of how free we are at all in following our consciences. The pressure to conform is so great, even (as young people will readily recognise) the pressure to conform to non-conformity. And perhaps in some respects the tables have been turned. It is said that, in the past, religion performed the function of a *superego*, creating the need for approval and the corresponding guilt mechanism. Now religion has receded into the outer circles for many, and other voices from the culture we live in have moved to the centre. It is they who now constitute the *superego*, who generate the pressure to gain approval, the fear of stepping out of line, the obsession to conform. We may not be any freer at all. Autonomy may be more often presumed than possessed.

This has implications for voices that are on the margins. Voices that are more insistent are those bound up with belonging and the fear of isolation or ostracisation. But voices on the margins tend to be little more than voices, like a message being blared out on some distant radio, but commanding little or no attention.

We might think here of the teaching style of the Church, with its penchant for pastoral letters and encyclicals. The general consensus is that these do not communicate; very few read or even notice them. A voice that is just a voice will not speak to moral consciousness. There is needed the deliberate effort to create belonging – not the uncritical belonging that characterises the mass-media culture, and to some extent also the religion of the past – but the critical belonging that can satisfy the need for both autonomy and community in a synthesis of inner and collective wisdom.

From the point of view of the individual, though, these reflections bring us back to the fundamental point about freedom, namely, that it begins in the recognition of its unfreedom. A free conscience begins to be born when moral consciousness becomes critically aware of the pressures and constraints being exerted upon it. When it can stand back, it is beginning to take possession of itself and to assert its own transcendence. In refusing to be told what to think, it leaves itself open and receptive to the truth.

Christian Conscience

The specific topic of Christian conscience brings up the issue of obedience and, indeed, the question whether obedience is a virtue. It is a complex question, given the problematic nature of obedience in contemporary society. No doubt people realise that society would become unworkable without some obedience: think for instance of an educational system without any obedience. But it is probably fair to say that people today would like to see obedience reduced to a minimum, and that our goal should be maximum possible self-determination. Such self-determination can only be attained if obedience is made superfluous.

This cult of self-determination seems diametrically opposed to what often seems to be the cult of obedience in the religious tradition. Whatever the answer, it is hardly either total self-determination or blind subservience. In the Church as elsewhere, one would expect a synthesis of inner and collective wisdom.

While conscience is an aspect of being human, it is nevertheless proper to speak also of the Christian conscience. What this means is simply the moral consciousness that is characteristic of Christians. Just as conscience generally makes links between actions and values, between what we do and what we are, between what we are and what we may become, so Christian conscience makes the further links between the person's concrete situation on the one hand, and on the other, the call to discipleship for the sake of the kingdom. Christian conscience is thus the sensorium of discipleship, the place where we are receptive to and responsive to all that speaks to us about the direction discipleship should take.

In its Christian sense, conscience is a relational term, involving both the disciple and Christ. Moral consciousness is about 'we' rather than just 'I'. It is our awareness of the relationship of discipleship, where we see living in terms of 'we' – as when Paul said that 'It is no longer I who live but it is Christ who lives in me' (Galatians 2:20). Christian conscience allows itself to be affected more and more by its relationship with Christ, so that what it decides may be expressive of, faithful to, and enhancing of, the relationship.

This is where obedience is primarily to be located. We said earlier that the only absolute obedience owed by conscience is to the truth. In a religious context, this would translate into saying that obedience to God is the only unconditional obedience. And in a specifically Christian context it would mean obedience to what has been called 'the law of Christ', in other words, to the demands of being a faithful disciple.

The Bible tells us that the basic tension or conflict involved in such obedience is between listening and rebelliousness. The key notion for the covenant people was the 'Hear O Israel' (Deuteronomy 6:4), the attitude and disposition of listening, even clinging to God's word. The Latin for obeying, *obedire*, also means to hear or to listen. Listening is a constant looking out for God's will and word.

The opposite is rebellion. Jeremiah's refrain is that the people will not listen; they have a hard, stubborn, rebellious heart (e.g. 5:23; 6:10; 7:25-26). Rebelliousness is the kind of self-assertion or wilfulness that pits itself against God. It refuses to think in terms of relationship; it would insist on 'I' rather than contemplate 'we'.

Obedience, in this sense of a listening heart living in covenantal fidelity, is quite different from blind subservience. It is not an option for self-abandonment in contrast to self-determination. It does not so much surrender autonomy as recognise the true source of its completion. The obedience of disciples is the obedience of those who have come to see where their true good lies.

But all this does not happen to the disciple in isolation; it happens in the Christian community. In this way, we can begin to think of the Church, not in terms of moral discipline, but as a conscientious community of disciples. The Church is the place where people together seek to grow in their conscientiousness as regards discipleship and its demands. Belonging to this community, we might expect, will increase awareness of the call of discipleship. It is this common commitment which informs conscience, not in the sense of information, but in the sense that it forms, moulds, shapes our sensitivity and our seeing, along Christian lines.

Belonging to this community, we find ourselves part of a bigger story than the story of our own lives. We are part of the story told over the centuries, of countless other disciples, of the harms and dangers that came their way, of the inner wisdom that grew cumulatively into the collective wisdom of the present. Because of this, we submit humbly in order to listen and learn what the larger story can teach. And because we are ourselves mature, responsible disciples, we hope thereby to continue this tradition in new ways for new times – what Jaroslav Pelikan called 'the living tradition of the dead' in contrast to 'the dead tradition of the living'.

Obedience may not be the best word with which to grasp this dynamic interaction of disciple, community and tradition, of inner wisdom and collective wisdom. A phrase such as creative fidelity might capture better the synthesis of love for the bigger story and responsibility for its further telling. But for all its creativity, fidelity will be shot through with humility regarding what we ourselves can contribute. This spirit of humility is well conveyed by Isaac Newton's self-description (Brewster's *Memoirs of Newton*, II, 27):

> 'I do not know what I may appear to the world, but to myself I seem to have been only like a boy playing on the sea-shore, and diverting myself in now and then finding a smoother pebble or a

prettier shell than ordinary, whilst the great ocean of truth lay all undiscovered before me.'

Conscientious Disagreement

The collective wisdom of the Christian tradition, is of course, articulated in creed and code, and its articulation embraces a range of formulations from the Apostles' Creed right down to regulations concerning fasting. There is, however, the possibility that disciples will not be at one about everything and, while united on the broader strokes, may disagree on some of the more detailed parts of the picture.

Perhaps this is more likely today than before. The sheer complexity of life in the contemporary world means that no moral authority can work out everything in advance, and that to an increasing degree people have to figure out creatively for themselves how to be true to their tradition in concrete situations. As well at that, in today's pluralist culture many voices speak to conscience, calling it in different directions, and some of them may be as impressive as that of the Church. People may wonder what voice to agree with and they will sometimes feel that it is not the Church that has got things right. The remaining reflections suggest a manner of dealing with disagreement that remains faithful both to conscience itself and to the community tradition.

First of all, being faithful is not the same as being blindly obedient. There might be a place for something resembling blind obedience if the case was one where a person felt quite incompetent about the arguments but quite confident about the competence of the authority. Perhaps blind is too strong a word, for this is a reasonable thing to do, an autonomous decision to be dependent.

The first point, then, is that we cannot hand over to anybody, even the Church, the responsibility for directing our own lives. 'For freedom Christ has set us free' (Galatians 5:1): we are called to be free, and that includes the responsibility for forming and following our own consciences. To quote again Newman's *Letter to the Duke of Norfolk:* 'Certainly, if I am obliged to bring religion into after-dinner toasts… I shall drink – to the Pope, if you please – still, to Conscience first, and to the Pope afterwards.' Conscience is so sacred that following it well must be our primary concern.

This is not the same as 'doing your own thing'. We decide for ourselves, not by ourselves. In following our inner wisdom we draw on the collective wisdom. But even then, we will have to work out most things for ourselves. *The Church in the Modern World* says that Church leaders will not always be so expert as to have a ready answer to every problem (even every grave problem) that arises and that it is up to lay people 'to shoulder their responsibilities under the guidance of Christian wisdom and with eager attention to the teaching authority of the Church' (paragraph 43).

Secondly, the conscience of the Christian would normally coincide with the vision and norms of the community. Even though it is also quite normal that an individual would not agree one hundred per cent with everything the Church says (that would be more like blind obedience), such an individual would presumably be inspired by the same values and concerns and would be at least largely in agreement with the way they are applied.

Given this context, the attitude we called docility is desirable. This attitude presumes in favour of the bigger story that is the tradition of the Christian community. Humbly recognising its own smallness, conscience submits for the moment. It makes a greater effort to appreciate the why and the wherefore of that which it cannot understand. This is particularly important because there can be so much ignorance of why the Church says what it says (an ignorance that is not necessarily the fault of the one who is ignorant). This listening is known as the informing of conscience.

Thirdly, while this listening may resolve many differences, it will not resolve them all. No matter how genuine the docility and how intent the listening, we may still find ourselves disagreeing. At this stage there is a number of questions we can ask ourselves.

We can ask: how serious is the matter of the disagreement? How central is it to faith? Is it something fairly fundamental or is it more in the way of a conclusion from, or an application of, what we believe? The more serious the matter, the stronger the reasons there would have to be for disagreeing. If the matter is very serious, it is hard to imagine any reasons being sufficient. This question recognises a hierarchy of moral truth: not everything is of the same order.

Further, we can ask whether the disagreement amounts to saying that a particular teaching is wrong or whether it amounts to saying that the fulfilling of it is not possible in this situation. The former is a more serious matter as it challenges the teaching itself. The latter does not, but only says that circumstances leave its fulfilment beyond reach.

Again we can ask: are there others who think likewise? This is not the same as reducing truth to statistics and surveys and majority views. But if there are others, and especially if there are many others who share the same difficulties, that is an indication that something is amiss. At the same time, it is not to be presumed that what is amiss is necessarily the teaching. It could a widespread bias, the internalisation of some cultural blindspot, that is the problem. For instance, the Church's teaching about sex belonging to marriage is clearly out of tune with today's culture, but it may be the culture's own trivialisation of sexual encounter that most needs to be questioned. Nevertheless, there may be instances where the extent of disagreement with what the Church says is inviting the Church as a whole to review its own position.

Finally, we can ask about the person's own state of belonging. Is he or she a serious, committed Christian, reluctantly but responsibly disagreeing? Or is it a case of nominal Christianity, where discipleship is being lived in rather lukewarm fashion? Where people lie on this spectrum will be an indication as to how seriously they should take their own disagreeing with the Church.

Fourthly, if people are still unhappy after these questions have been answered and these processes have been gone through – if in other words they have rigorously and openly searched themselves and their tradition, and end up unable to assent and perhaps feeling obliged to act otherwise – can we say that, while they cannot conform to the teaching, they have maintained fidelity?

Is there some recognition of this in what *The Church in the Modern World* says, that a conscience can go astray through ignorance 'without thereby losing its dignity' (paragraph 16)? Of course, in the case we are presenting, conscience does not think itself to have strayed. But the quotation does at least recognise the principle that a conscience in genuine disagreement is not a conscience to be condemned.

In his book *Magisterium*, Frank Sullivan discusses this matter in detail. He takes up the theme of the 'religious submission' *(obsequium religiosum)* that Vatican II called for *(The Church,* paragraph 25), understanding it to mean the docility that makes an honest and sustained effort to overcome any contrary opinion and to achieve a sincere assent of mind to the teaching in question. What then, he asks, if after such an effort, people find themselves unable to give their sincere assent to the teaching?

> '...if, in a particular instance, Catholics have offered their 'religious submission of mind and will' to the authority of the magisterium, by making an honest and sustained effort to achieve internal assent to its teaching, and still find that doubts about its truth remain so strong in their minds that they cannot actually give their sincere intellectual assent to it, I do not see how one could judge such non-assent, or internal dissent, to involve any lack of obedience to the magisterium. Having done all that they were capable of doing towards achieving assent, they actually fulfilled their obligation of obedience, whether they achieved internal assent or not.'[3]

What we have been outlining, and likewise Sullivan, is a quite stringent set of criteria that takes equally seriously the integrity of conscience and the respect owed to the larger tradition of which Christian conscience is a part. It may be, however, that the problem is more widespread, more systemic, and that the disagreement is on a large scale or across a number of issues. In this case something different is required, something more in the nature of dialogue. Dialogue conducted in an atmosphere of freedom and trust has the potential to bestow on conscience the affirmation it seeks and to restore to authority the credibility it deserves. But as this theme brings us beyond the individual to the social context, it will be taken up again in the final chapter.

CHAPTER 11

What is Justice?

The next three chapters reflect on morality from a social perspective. They will elaborate mainly on the fifth way of looking at morality, that of morality as social transformation. The present chapter reflects on what we mean by the idea of justice.

Privatisation

To say that morality is social may appear to be an unproblematic proposition, but it is not quite so obvious as it seems. This is because there have been and still are strong tendencies towards making morality a relatively private affair. To the extent that these tendencies hold sway, the social nature of morality is obscured.

Such privatising tendencies have existed within religious morality, though they are not so strong as they used to be. Phrases like 'saving my soul' present a very individualistic picture of morality, as if each of us were just out for himself or herself. Even when we do good to others, it is sometimes done from this self-centred motive of advancing our own salvation. This is not meant as a condemnation of all religious morality, but is simply pointing out one significant strain in it.

More generally, in our religious tradition we have tended to think of morality as a matter of individuals making moral decisions. Chapter headings in textbooks of moral theology confirm this. With titles such as 'The Human Act' and 'Conscience' and 'Sin' to the fore, morality was seen largely in terms of what an individual does. Much effort went into discussing tangled cases of conscience confronting the individual. Today it is seen that this focus on the individual, while real and valid, neglects the larger picture.

But while religious morality is correcting the excessively individualistic focus of the past, a new form of the privatisation of morality has been arising from our secular experience, from the free-market economy and from the culture of consumerism. We are familiar with the significance of the term 'privatisation' within the context of capitalism, but we may not be as familiar with how morality is being drawn into the privatising trend.

It has been argued that with the Reformation and the religious wars that followed, religion ceased to be the unifying basis in society, and that what replaced religion as the underpinning for all social relationships was the capitalist principle of exchange. All else was now subordinated to this principle. Other values receded into the private sphere. The real world was now the world of commerce. Religion and morality became privatised, for domestic use. We see the outcome of this in the distinction made today between the private (or moral, or religious) and the social (or economic) world.

This process was in some ways helped along by religion itself. The Reformation contained within itself a tendency towards a religion of inwardness, and this was subsequently consolidated. Religion came to be seen as a matter of the heart, between the individual and the Transcendent, in contrast to a more socially focused religion. Such an inward religion is easily left to one side in the new social, economic and political scene.

Putting it more bluntly, buying-and-selling has become the paradigmatic form of human relationship. Human encounter is being progressively reduced to commercial transactions. Such is the extent to which exchange has become the basic stuff of human society. Morality is very far from the logic of this world. Note how often people regard 'political ethics' or 'business ethics' or even 'journalistic ethics' as little more than an oxymoron. Indeed, one newspaper survey into the moral respectability of different professions and occupations showed members of parliament, business executives and journalists at the bottom of the list.

One might call this the 'de-moralisation' of society. The public sphere is the sphere of buying and selling, and its logic is the logic of growth, expansion, profit. Morality has, if anything, a minimal role. But not alone is morality removed from the public sphere; in the private sphere it has become a matter of individual discretion. This is the downside of what is meant by pluralism and a culture of tolerance. Morality comes to mean personal ethics, personal ethics comes to mean that right and wrong are a matter of subjective choice, and tolerance means not interfering except insofar as third parties are affected. We are left with a real question as to the social nature of morality and the moral nature of society.

Social by Nature

By way of background to the above, we might refer to some strands in the history of thought in recent centuries. One finds in philosophers of the seventeenth and eighteenth centuries what has become known as a 'social contract' theory of society. What this term means is that society is a later addition to human history. Originally there were individuals pursuing their own interests, until eventually it was seen that some form of social organisation was necessary in order to curb excessive self-interest. For this reason people gave up some of their rights to a government in order to secure their own protection – thus the contract.

In this way of understanding society, society is seen as a multiplicity of free individuals pursuing their own interests, with little or no obligation to others beyond respect for the rules of exchange. Property and the rights of property are prior to justice. In fact, justice is largely about enforcing property rights – the original motivation for the social contract. Justice serves the ends of property, and not the other way round.

It is perhaps no coincidence that this philosophy was being articulated in the same era as the industrial revolution was dawning and the capitalist economy was being born. What we are left with today is a conception of society as a place where individuals are free to pursue their own interests and where justice is a matter of the ground rules for this pursuit, focused particularly on the protection of property. In this view, there is relatively little feeling that economic freedom should be restrained because of the needs of others who are suffering deprivation.

Such is one thread feeding into our experience of society. Another, much older one is the very opposite. It says that society does not come after, but is there from the start because it is part of our human make-up. Belonging to society is more like the way we belong to our families than the way we might belong to a local

social club. In other words, society is part of people from the beginning, not something that they subsequently become part of by
choice.

To say we are social by nature, and not by contract, is to say that
prior to any individuality there is sociality. Prior to the 'I' is the 'we'
that is the symbiosis of life in the womb, out of which I emerge. And
ever after, life is the process of an 'I', with its own identity, emerging out of relatedness – and where often the quality of self depends
on the quality of relationships. Thus *The Church in the Modern World*
could say that 'by our innermost nature we are social beings and if
we do not enter into relationships with others we can neither live
nor develop our gifts' (paragraph 12).

Here we have a very different picture of exchange from that of commercial transactions in a world dominated by economics. It is a picture of personal exchange issuing in personal enhancement. The
underlying worldview is one that sees reality, especially human
reality, as an infinitely complex web or network of relationships, a
dynamic pattern of exchange where what is exchanged is best captured by words like *life* and *being* and *love*.

We are part of, and receive our identity from being part of, this infinitely complex web of relationship. But also, in this picture of society, the emphasis shifts away dramatically from individuals being
left to pursue their own interests. Instead, attention is concentrated
on the quality of interrelatedness. In this picture, something like
'everybody matters' is the fundamental principle, rather than simply 'everybody is free'.

In this context, the idea of 'the common good' makes sense. As
defined in *The Church in the Modern World*, the common good is the
'sum total of social conditions which allow people either as groups
or as individuals, to reach their fulfilment more fully and more easily' (paragraph 26). It concerns a set-up based on the understanding
that the good of each and the good of all fit together. It represents
the affirmation of all rather than the assertion of self.

However, it would be a different picture if we were to emphasise
the social to such an extent that the individual lost out. Such is the
collectivism that is associated with repressive communist regimes,
where the individual is reduced to being a cog in the machine.

Something similar can happen with the utilitarian principle of 'the greatest good of the greatest number'. Here, the individual may be forgotten or even sacrificed for the greater good. These are as much distortions of the truth about humanity as is the individualism of the free-market economy with its minimising of social obligations.

The phenomenon of competition provides an engaging illustration of the issues we are suggesting. If we were asked whether competition is something good or something bad, we would soon find ourselves having to qualify our answer. Competition is good in that it motivates and energises people and thereby maximises quality. Think, for instance, of sport, or of advertising, where competition pushes standards up. Obversely, we can think of instances of nationalisation where the lack of competition makes for complacent performance.

But competition brings out the worst in us as well as the best. It encourages excessive individualism. The desire to succeed or to profit, and the fear of losing or of losing out, can tempt people to resort to illegitimate means, so that anything may potentially be justified. This raises the question as to whether this excessive individualism can be confined, or humanised.

Once we accept the legitimacy of this concern, we accept that we are social by nature and not by contract. We sense that our sociality and solidarity must be protected against our individualism. There is something more important than the success and quality and achievement that competition brings, namely, the quality of how we get on together. So we may ask: Is our economic system designed to promote the common good, or is it designed for the acquisition of wealth? Could it include both? Can we have both economic success and justice for all? This may be the fundamental problem of the capitalist society. It is a moral and not an economic problem.

Solidarity

Different ideas of society yield different ideas of what justice is. In the social contract view, justice is no more than a minimal regulation of how people relate, so as to leave them free to pursue their own interests to the greatest extent possible. Much of the concern for justice revolves around the protection of the property people possess and acquire. Indeed, we can see this reflected in the extent to which the work of the police and the prison system in a capitalist society is concerned with enforcing property laws and protecting the propertied from the poor.

But when we understand the person as being social by nature, justice is the virtue of other-centredness, whereby we realise our nature as social beings. To the question, 'Why should we treat other people well?', the answer is, 'Because we are other people'. Our sense of justice is a sense of the other as other, one who is as valuable as ourselves. This is more than the enlightened self-interest that treats others well in order to be treated well in turn (one version of 'do unto others as you would have others do unto you'). Rather, it is a disposition towards others that is grounded in an appreciation of their uniqueness and dignity.

Many today would say that this experience of 'the other' is the fundamental 'moral' experience. Aquinas thought similarly in saying that justice is the greatest moral virtue because it regards the goodness of the other. We do not speak of being just to ourselves: with justice we go beyond ourselves. It is the virtue whereby we are rightly disposed towards the other, whereby we have a lively appreciation of the rights of others and hence are filled with the constant determination to give to others what is due to them as persons (*Summa Theologiae*, II-II, 58; 1, 2, 12).

The virtue of justice involves a reorganisation of our affections and priorities. It calls us to resist the temptation towards individualism. Our spontaneities are to be reordered with the other in mind. Justice here means *adjustment*, adjusting our living to what is required of us by the presence of the other and the call of the common good. As we respond to this call, we are becoming the social and sharing animals that we were created to be.

The word justice may not, however, be able to bear this weight of meaning. It is, after all, a legal word. The mentality behind the word is one of clear definition, so that all will know where they stand and what is required of them in relation to others. It is not that such thinking is dispensable, but that it may be an inadequate vehicle for communicating the depth of what justice means as a moral concept.

It is significant, therefore, how John Paul II has used the word 'solidarity' as a synonym for justice. In *Sollicitudo Rei Socialis* he speaks of our becoming 'personally affected' in our conscience by the sufferings of others, even those in far distant lands, and he goes on to speak of solidarity in the very terms traditionally used to define justice:

> 'When interdependence becomes recognised in this way, the correlative response as a moral and social attitude, as a 'virtue', is *solidarity*. This then is not a feeling of vague compassion or shallow distress at the misfortunes of so many people, both near and far. On the contrary, it is a firm and persevering determination to commit oneself to the common good; that is to say to the good of all and each individual, because we are all really responsible for all.'[1]

Solidarity may be a more promising term than justice. It is less suggestive of rules and more suggestive of relationship, of the infinitely complex web of relationships that is the stuff of human society. Solidarity means concern for those relationships, that they be sustained and strengthened rather than severed or harmed. Where justice could suggest obligations, solidarity suggests care.

It may also be the case that the language of solidarity is more in tune with feminine experience. Carol Gilligan's *In a Different Voice* asks whether thinking in terms of justice and rules and rights is not a predominantly male way of thinking, and whether thinking of care for networks of relationships is not more characteristic of women. She is not, however, arguing for one over and against the other, but that each completes and corrects the other.[2] In this vein the idea of solidarity can be seen as filling out and enriching our understanding of justice.

Rights and Needs

The contrast between justice and solidarity leads us into another contrast, that between rights and needs. The idea of rights is part of the harder, legal language of justice. While rights language seeks to articulate some of the basic demands made on us by the humanity of others, in the context of liberal capitalism its meaning shifts slightly. It tends to mean 'my rights'. When society is seen as separate individuals pursuing their interests, rights help define separateness in terms of what we may each demand for ourselves.

Rights language may in this way become highly individualistic. If there is any solidarity, it may be no more that than which says, 'I'll look after your interests if you look after mine.' This is justice language in the social contract mode.

On the other hand, the softer language of solidarity and care would speak of needs rather than rights as the fundamental category. If what is due to others is what they are entitled to by right, then they may get very little. If what is due is what they need, the picture is changed entirely. People may even sacrifice themselves for others who are in need.

The category of need refers far more strongly than that of rights to the humanity of the other. The experience of reverence and awe before the humanity of the other leads into a responsiveness to human need. There is the sense that if certain needs are neglected, then the humanity of the other is denied. Whereas if rights language becomes individualistic, it becomes part of the logic of pursuing self-interest which, as we have said and as all know, is quite compatible with the continuing presence of even extreme need.

At any rate, we are not suggesting that a choice has to be made between thinking in terms of rights and thinking in terms of need. Rather, the two terms complement one another. The category of need corrects the individualist bias in rights language and encourages us to think of rights in an other-centred mindset of solidarity. In this context, the language of rights helps in turn to define what is demanded of us by the needs of others.

We might refer here to a third contrast, that between love and justice. Regarding this, John Paul II has said that human experience teaches us that justice alone is not enough and that it can even destroy itself 'if *that deeper power, which is love,* is not allowed to shape human life in its various dimensions'.[3] Besides the justice that gives what is due, there must also be the love that thinks in terms of what people need and not only of what they deserve. Without this there will the letter without the spirit of justice in society. Without this there will be perhaps great injustice.

Both Personal and Structural

Traditionally, moral theology has distinguished a number of

aspects or dimensions of justice. These distinctions help us to appreciate the importance of thinking of justice in terms of social structures. What we have to say here will also develop our earlier discussion of sin as social or structural.

The distinction is between three kinds of justice. The first is justice on a one-to-one level – justice between two individuals or two groups. This would include such demands as honesty in dealings, respecting property, fulfilling contracts, paying fair wages. It breaks down when people are dishonest or exploitative or when they do not honour their commitments.

The second is the justice owed by the state towards individuals and groups. This would include equitable health care provision, education, access and participation, taxation – in other words, a fair distribution of both benefits and burdens. It breaks down when some individuals or groups receive preferential treatment and when others are the victims of prejudice or discrimination, be it economic or racist or sexist or whatever. Note that 'fair' is not always the same as 'equal': we would not expect the poor to pay the same taxes as the rich or to have to pay as much for their health care.

The third kind of justice is that owed by the individual to the state. It includes the duty to contribute and to participate, to vote and to pay taxes, to obey the laws and respect the institutions. It breaks down in the attitude of 'them and us' as expressed in such phrases as 'they won't miss it anyway' or 'what's the point of bothering?' The latter sentiment points to the failure of politics as the exercise of collective responsibility.

It can be seen from this that justice is a complex notion, involving a whole web of relationships between individual and individual, between group and group, between the individual or the group and the state. Earlier this century the idea of 'social justice' came into vogue. It is used in different ways, but it is significant mainly for referring to structural or institutional aspects of justice.

For instance, if there is unfair access to education or to the courts, the fault may not lie so much with any individual as with an inherited structure that is now embedded in society, part of 'the way we do things'. It may be the residue of some past prejudice. But also it may simply be in the nature of things. For human initiative and tal-ent are not equally apportioned. Inevitably, some do better than others and inequalities come about. It comes about that the way things are works to the benefit of those who are already quite content rather than to the advantage of those in greater need.

The fact that justice is a structural as well as a personal matter means that change for justice does not come from the heart only. It is not enough for individuals to be converted so as to become more just in their own dispositions and dealings. The problem is also in the set-up of things as they are. Structures have to be altered, or even dismantled and replaced, and this will not happen without a strong political consensus. In the absence of such consensus, people will tend to feel helpless, wondering what difference their own meagre efforts could make.

Let us now relate these distinctions both to the capitalist society and to the Church. The tendency of capitalism is to think of justice in one-to-one terms only. There is justice when individuals or groups fulfil their legal obligations to others. In the extreme, this has two implications. First, needs go unmet. People can say, 'I've given you what is due to you; that's all I'm required to do'. The mood is contractual and minimal.

Second, the larger, structural questions are ignored and inequality increases as the pretence continues that there is nothing wrong with the way things are. Whether naïvely or disingenuously, it is contended that problems can be solved from within the system as it stands.

There are parallel issues for the Church. Because of the tendency in the past to see morality in individual terms, one-to-one justice was the focus of attention in moral theology and much was written about contracts and property and restitution. Such issues of personal honesty remain important and, if anything, deserve more attention than they receive today. But there is much more attention being given today to issues to do with society as a whole.

Something of the shift is captured by the way people now talk less of 'charity' and more of 'justice'. When we study the documents comprising the Church's social teaching over the past century, we find that early on it is charity, the rich coming to the help of the poor, that is seen as the resolution of society's ills. This is because, with the fear of socialism being so great, no solution by way of changes in the *status quo* was even contemplated. Later the idea of social justice became prominent, as it was realised that change in society would require the reform of structures or institutions as well as the conversion of hearts.[4] Charity without structural change would be akin to binding up wounds without any attention to why they are being suffered in the first place.

A Divine Affair

If we look further into the Christian tradition, we shall find an even more radical statement of these perspectives on justice, but a statement which also sets them in a theological context. Indeed, when we look at the Bible we find that, in common with the ancient world generally, it associates the word justice first of all with the deity. Justice is something that God does. This is part of why the Bible speaks of God's 'righteousness' and God's 'justification'.

In the Old Testament, justice has two senses. The narrower one concerns justice in a specific instance of one person giving another what is due, or of a judgment between two people. The broader notion, often translated as 'righteousness', refers to God. By this justice, God through the covenant brings the people into right relationship with Godself. Righteousness on the part of the people will then involve fidelity to the demands of covenant relationship.

Thus, in the Bible justice is not primarily an individual trait or virtue. It is a quality of the whole society, which is present when God's righteousness is being faithfully represented, so that there is right relationship throughout the whole web of relationships between God and God's people and amongst God's people themselves.

An image used frequently in the Old Testament to express this is the image of water. Just as water flows through and permeates everything, so would God's justice be a quality characterising the whole life of God's people:

> 'Shower O heavens, from above, and let the skies rain down righteousness... O that you had paid attention to my commandments! Then your prosperity would have been like a river and your success like the waves of the sea... let justice roll down like

waters, and righteousness like an ever-flowing stream.' (Isaiah 45:8; 48:18; Amos 5:24)

Where the Old Testament speaks of righteousness, the word in the New Testament is 'justification'. God's justice is God's justifying God's people through the death and resurrection of Jesus Christ. This is often understood in individual and spiritual terms of the sinner being set right by God's grace. But its dimensions are much broader, in line with the Old Testament notion.

Justification means that right relationships are made possible through Christ between God and humanity as a whole. Thus, in Ephesians 2, Paul speaks of Christ breaking down the dividing walls between Jew and Greek and between humanity and God. Justification is thus a social reality. Again, Paul says: 'There is no longer Jew or Greek, there is no longer slave or free, there is no longer male and female; for all of you are one in Christ Jesus' (Galatians 3:28). Now humanity is called to make this justice the basis for right relationships throughout all society.

An indispensable aspect of this call is inclusiveness – indeed the idea is already there in the passage from Galatians. God's justice envisages right relationships among all humanity; its embrace excludes nobody. Whereas we regularly justify the exclusion of some or discrimination towards some, God justifies everybody. Just as Jesus imaged the kingdom of God as a banquet to which all are invited (Luke 14:15-24), so commitment to establishing right relationships omits nobody.

Compassion and Criticism

To see God's justice taking shape among God's people, we can look to the life of Jesus. The word that perhaps best gives us entry into this is the word 'compassion'.[5] It occurs in some important passages in the gospels. Seeing the people, Jesus 'had compassion for them', harassed and helpless and directionless as they were (Matthew 9: 36). He 'had compassion for' the widow burying her son at Nain (Luke 7:13). The good Samaritan was 'moved with pity' for the man who had been beaten up – again the same word in the Greek (Luke 10:33). And the father, on seeing his prodigal son returning home, 'was filled with compassion' (Luke 15:20).

The bible's word for compassion is quite direct. It means to be affected by the situation and plight of another right down in our bowels or innards. In our deepest self we feel the pain. One thinks of the fourth servant song, read each Good Friday: 'Surely he has borne our infirmities and carried our diseases' (Isaiah 53:4). This compassion is closely related to the beatitude, 'Blessed are those who mourn'. Jesus grieves and mourns over the pain he comes in contact with. Like the prophets before him, he is personally affected by the lack of God's justice in the land. It is out of this grieving and compassion that he acts.

While this compassion comes from the heart, it might be more accurate to say that it comes from the heart of God. For it is ultimately God's own grief that Jesus feels. We could say that he is feeling the feelings of God. He is the one who is absorbed by God and whose heart is filled with the experience of God's infinite compassion. In the advent of Jesus, the grief of God at human pain is penetrating the numbness or insensitivity of human society.

Compassion leads in turn to criticism. This is not quite what we call social analysis, nor is it our critique of structural injustice, but it is nonetheless the gospel basis for these. Compassion cannot accept human pain as in any way normal or natural, but demands that it be taken seriously and regarded as an abnormal and unacceptable condition. Therefore compassion cannot but make itself felt in a criticism of society's tolerance of the pain and in a criticism of what are perceived to be the sources of pain.

Thus, for example, Jesus criticises the systems of relationships that leave people out in the cold, in pain or in despair. In particular we recall his critique of the Pharisees' religious system whereby people were classified and ostracised. With such criticism, compassion becomes a risk, as it provokes the wrath of the powers that be. In the words of the Latin American bishop, Dom Helder Camara: 'When I help the poor I am called a saint; but when I ask why they are poor I am called a communist.'

Transformation

From the writings of the early Church Fathers down to the series of papal encyclicals on social morality over the past century, the Christian tradition has sought to respond to the implications of the

divine vision and practice of justice. Two ideas from that long tradition stand out today. These are not just ideas in an abstract or
notional sense. Rather, they are ideas that can motivate and inspire,
that can fashion attitudes and priorities. They are transformative
ideas, because they capture so much of the spirit of justice as a
divine affair.

One of these ideas concerns the meaning of possessions and their
use. As formulated in recent Church documents, it says that the
goods of the earth are originally meant for all, that they are destined
for everybody. This means that, while people have a right to private
property, that right is not absolute. It is secondary to the right of all
God's children to a share in the goods of the earth. Thus this principle represents the truth that God's justice is concerned with the
establishment of right relationships throughout the whole of society.

We already saw an application of this principle when we discussed
the legitimacy of a person stealing when threatened by starvation.
But apart from such exceptional cases, the principle makes the right
to property relative and prioritises instead the social obligations of
property. However honestly individual possessions may have been
earned, the priority is to bring about a situation that reflects God's
intentions for God's people.

By way of background, we might recall the considerable interest in
this theme in the gospel of Luke and in the early Church Fathers. We
can conclude from the sayings and stories in Luke – most of which
are found only in this gospel – that the teaching of Jesus, while not
rejecting property and wealth, represents a deep suspicion of them.
The story of the rich fool (Luke 12:13-21) is a lesson on how possessions come to dominate their possessor. The story of the rich man
and Lazarus (Luke 16:19-31) illustrates how riches deafen us to the
cries of others. But the story of Zacchaeus (Luke 19:1-10) speaks of
hope. Here one rich person gets through 'the eye of a needle' (Luke
18:25), not by renouncing all his possessions, but by being inspired
to share.

Among the Fathers of the Church there recurs the idea that possessions and possessiveness are something of an illusion. John Chrys-
ostom reflects: 'What is the meaning of 'mine' and 'not mine'? For
truly, the more accurately I weigh these words, the more they seem

to me but words.' Ambrose says: 'Not from your own do you bestow upon the poor man, but you make return from what is his. From what has been given in common for the use of all, you appropriate to yourself alone.' And Augustine: 'Those who offer something to the poor should not think that they are doing so from what is their own.'[6]

The second idea today goes by the name of the 'preferential option for the poor'. While this phrase comes from the Latin American Church, the idea goes right back to the Old Testament. There the thirst for God's righteousness is reflected in the people's legislation protecting the defenceless and vulnerable members of society – the widow and the fatherless child, the stranger, the casual worker, slaves, those in debt (e.g. Exodus 22:21-27; Deuteronomy 24:10-22). The passage from Deuteronomy ends: 'Remember that you were a slave in the land of Egypt...' To remember Egypt is to remember the experience of being poor; this in turn is meant to heighten the sense of scandal at the existence of poverty in the present, and it is this sense that makes for the people's particular regard for the defenceless.

In like spirit, Jesus brings hope to the poor and the vulnerable and the outcast. As his heart feels the feelings of God, these people become the particular object of his attention. They rediscover their humanity and find new hope for their lives. They find they are included whereas previously, like all who are poor, theirs was an experience of exclusion, not belonging, not participating, unable to influence their own destiny.

An option for the poor can sometimes sound like an option against the rich. But what it means is, in fact, an option for everyone. It is a further application of the ideas that the earth is meant for all and that everybody matters. An analogy would be to imagine a mother with five children. Though she cares for all of them, if one were to become sick that child would receive preferential treatment. This is not an option against anybody but rather, in the context of a commitment to all, it is a preferential attention to the need that is greatest.

We might picture a very different scene, where the same family was undergoing extreme hardship, unable to make ends meet and where the parents called the family together around the kitchen table to announce that, because things were so bad, 'We're going to have to let two of you go'. It might be worth reflecting on which of these two family scenes images more closely the spirit of our society today.

These ideas – of the social obligations of property and of the preferential option for the poor – are radical ideas. They have the power to transform society, were they to lodge themselves in our thinking. As it is, they contrast significantly with the spirit of the age. That spirit would say: 'Why should I have to share what I have earned?' Of course that question expresses a legitimate concern. It also brings to mind a question asked at the dawn of history: 'Am I my brother's keeper?' (Genesis 4:9).

Faith and Justice

There is phrase in the introduction to the document from the 1971 Synod of Bishops, *Justice in the World,* which has occasioned much debate. It stated that: 'Action on behalf of justice and participation in the transformation of the world fully appear to us as a constitutive dimension of the preaching of the gospel'. Some would have substituted 'important' for 'constitutive', which would have been a considerable watering down. But the text stands.

In one sense the debate was solved long before it started, in the Old Testament's insight into the bond between faith and justice. And today, for more and more people, justice is the face of faith and faith is being revitalised in the form of justice. The practice of justice is not simply an adjunct to faith. It is no less than a new form of mysticism and holiness. For many today, mysticism is the experience of being affected by the inequality, suffering and poverty in the world, and holiness is being experienced in the corresponding commitment. We could speak of a political form of holiness.

This brings to mind the words of Dom Helder Camara, that in our age the road to holiness necessarily passes through the world of action. This path to holiness begins in the loving vision of the Christian conscience. As it learns to see lovingly – to feel the feelings of God – this conscience is affected by the contrast between what is and what is yet to be. Being affected by all that is not right, or not yet right, in the world, becomes the wellspring of action.

Yet we can go too quickly to action. The very intensity of our love makes us fly to action when we might contribute far more by restraining ourselves for a while. There is a saying that 'you can't feed the world from an empty dish'. In order to have something to give to the world, we need to resource ourselves. Otherwise our action may be frantic and superficial. We might think of a cycle of 'Becoming informed – Becoming interested – Becoming involved.' Some may begin with being involved in God's work of justice, but then find that they need to inform themselves more. Others begin with wanting to find out more, as a result of which their interest grows.

For many of us, perhaps our best service initially may be simply to find out more about the world in which we live. Just as a critical conscience emerges out of the conditioning of childhood, we too are conditioned to think of the way things are in society as natural, and we need to stand back and inform ourselves more critically. As we do, we may begin to experience ourselves as guilty bystanders in need of conversion. We may have to contend with our own ingrained ideals of always having more, and to struggle against the permeation of the whole of life by exchange and competition. We may have to reconsider the fundamental ideas on which our life in society is based.

CHAPTER 12

Sex and Society

Another significant area of social morality is that of sexuality. The present chapter offers a way of thinking about sexuality as a social issue. It will go on to indicate how the Church is, and can be, a prophetic a voice with regard to sexuality, just as it is called to be in other areas of social morality.

Contrasting Styles

It may seem strange to find the theme of sexuality included as one of a set of chapters looking at morality from a social perspective. Many would more likely expect to see treated issues of injustice, violence or crime. Part of the reason for this is that there is a tendency to think of sexual morality as more a personal or private concern. Indeed, the privatising tendency we spoke of in the last chapter encourages the view that decisions to do with sexuality are private to the person and not to be interfered in except where harm to a third party is threatened.

Much of the concern of this chapter, however, is to show that matters of sexuality and sexual morality are of great social concern. We would almost go so far as to say that they are possibly better appreciated as being a social rather than a personal concern. Certainly, if they are relegated to the private realm, our understanding of them becomes quite confused and distorted. But common sense can tell us much of this. It is quite clear, on reflection, that the social ramifications of issues such as procreation or pornography take them far beyond the realm of the private.

If we turn to the teachings of the Church, the picture is not totally clear. It has been commented that there is a contrast of styles between the teaching on social and on sexual matters. Apart from anything else, this makes the sexual appear to be something quite distinct from the social.

For instance, as we remarked earlier, when Church documents consider social issues, the theme of conscience is often to the fore. Conscientious objection to war is admirable; the right of conscience to freedom of religious practice is asserted. Yet when we turn to documents on sexual morality, conscience seems to be downplayed in the concentration on the objective moral order. Again, the idea that some actions are intrinsically morally wrong appears quite a lot in the documents on sexual morality, while in the social teaching we find notable cases of exceptions to moral norms, such as the idea of a just war or a just revolution.

The dichotomy between the sexual and the social can also be observed in the work of moral theologians. There they are regularly regarded as two separate areas of morality. For instance, there are well-known books of moral theology which are divided into a section on 'social ethics', which includes topics such as economic and social reform, and a section on 'personal ethics', which considers themes such as contraception, abortion and divorce.

People have come to sense this contrast. Social teaching is widely perceived as radical, positive, dynamic, prophetic. But sexual teaching is even more widely perceived as authoritarian, negative, static, antiquated. The social teaching has even been referred to as 'the Church's best kept secret', while it has been suggested that the Church could do itself a service by not speaking about sexual ethics for the next twenty years.

A Social Concern

There have been quite a number of Church documents in recent decades on moral issues to do with sexuality. There was a document in 1968 on contraception (*Humanae Vitae*), in 1974 on abortion, in 1975 on sterilisation, in 1975 on various questions of sexual ethics, in 1981 on marriage and the family, in 1986 on homosexuality, in 1987 on techniques for alleviating infertility.

It is probably accurate to say that these documents have been largely received as being teachings on personal ethics. Further, they are widely seen as saying 'No', forbidding individuals or couples to engage in certain practices. The documents certainly have this dimension. It clearly is being said to couples not to use contraceptive means, or to other couples not to resort to *in vitro* fertilisation, or to others again not to have sex with others of the same gender. The point, though, is that this is not the only dimension of the documents.

In these documents, there is also a very important thread of social concern. For instance, the document about infertility is not just telling infertile couples to avoid certain artificial techniques of reproduction. It is also speaking to the medical profession and voicing a concern about where medical technology is headed. We can well understand this concern when we read in the papers stories such as that about whether an embryo that had been frozen after fertilisation would be entitled to the inheritance of the rich couple who were the genetic parents but had been killed in a plane crash. The possibilities open to medical technology today are dizzying and the human creativity is admirable; but it is only proper that the ethical questions be asked. Otherwise there is no difference between 'we can' and 'we may'.

Again, the document about homosexuality is probably best known for telling homosexual people what they should not do. What is less known is the social concern that motivated the publication. It had to do with the very strident gay rights movements that exist in the western world and which would want it recognised in society that heterosexuality and homosexuality are equal, one as normal as the other. There is no doubt that we have a distance to travel yet in our understanding of homosexuality, but it is not hard to see how this movement, and the implications of what it is proposing, would be of considerable concern to all in society.

The document about marriage and the family is most often referred to today for what it says about reception of communion by those living in second relationships when the original marriage, though irretrievable, has not been annulled. The stand taken is the source of great debate and the issue would seem far from resolved. But the document is about more than this. It is also about what is happening marriage in our world when half of all marriages in the United States and two-fifths of all marriages in Great Britain break up. There is something gone terribly wrong in society.

Lastly we might mention *Humanae Vitae*. It is very clearly about how married couples may go about regulating conception. Yet there is more. The document came in the same decade as the contraceptive pill became widely available. Even though other contraceptive methods had long been available, the advent of the pill was particularly symbolic of the separation of sex from conception. For so long seen as directed towards procreation, the meaning of sex was now free-floating. One thinks of a balloon that is released, no knowing where it might drift. In this sense, the question of contraception stands for the question of the very meaning of sex. And when we observe the culture's widespread trivialisation of sexual encounter, we cannot but be concerned about what is going on in society.

A New Balance

Nevertheless, the two concerns, the social and the personal, would not appear to be explicitly distinguished from each other. The result, as far as public perception is concerned, is that the social concern gets lost, and what is left is a feeling of condemnation on the part of many committed believers doing the best they can in sometimes quite trying circumstances. When we grasp the social concern, we see that there is a confrontation taking place between the Church and the world on these matters. Yet one feels that these many people have innocently got caught in the crossfire.

One place where things may be different is in John Paul II's 1995 Encyclical, *Evangelium Vitae*, which is mainly about abortion and euthanasia. For the concern of this document is very clearly focused on the social. It speaks of a 'structure of sin' in society; of a 'society excessively concerned with efficiency' where 'our cities risk becoming societies of people who are rejected'; of a 'culture of death'. It speaks not only of individual conscience but also of the moral conscience of society, as encouraging the culture of death and the structures of sin.[1]

Thus when the document comes to talk about abortion, while teaching that it cannot be justified, that it is against 'the objective moral order', it pays much more attention to subjective and social factors. It recognises (as we already saw in a previous chapter) that the blame may lie elsewhere than with the woman – not just with her partner or with her family, but also with legislators and others who promote abortion legislation, and those who encourage sexual permissiveness. It concludes: 'In this sense abortion goes beyond the responsibility of individuals and beyond the harm done to them, and takes on a distinctly social dimension.'[2]

We glimpse in this something of the balance between objective, subjective and social dimensions of morality. Perhaps it is only when all three can be seen together that any of the three can be properly appreciated. For a start, we can see from the above that a concentration on the social nature of the problem makes possible a better appreciation of the person's subjective situation, which is after all inseparable from its social context.

But also, the social focus makes for an effective re-assertion of the objective nature of morality. Rights and wrongs are no longer seen to come out of some abstract and inaccessible moral order, but are clearly the conclusions of a quite concrete analysis of what is going on in society. If this is so, then morality goes beyond simply telling people to obey the law, to become a matter also of addressing the social conditions that are influencing people's moral outlook and practices.

All this encourages us to think of sexual morality in a social context and to develop a social perspective on it. Accordingly, we will be suggesting that the roots of contemporary problems of sexual ethics are to be found in what is going on in society and not just in what is going on in individuals. This line of thought further suggests that if those roots can be exposed, we will gain both a better insight into what it means to speak of the objective truth about sex and sexuality, as well as a better appreciation of the subjective experience of sexual morality.

Sex and Society

So we proceed from the basis that sex and sexuality are not a private but a public and a political issue. Any tendency to see the individual as simply private is likely to miss the individual altogether. Existence is social and today the individual is perhaps more caught up than ever in the movements of society, so that more than ever our experience and our existence cannot be understood adequately without reference to the social context.

To say that sexual experience is public and political is to say that it too can only be understood with reference to what is going on in

society. In fact, our sexuality could be said to be socially constructed. By sexuality here is meant aspects of our sexual experience such
as our sexual desires and their objects, our fantasies, our sexual
pleasure and our thinking about sexual pleasure, our ideas about
sexual goodness, our sexual values and our sexual identity. These
aspects of our sexuality are not simply pre-given but are to a great
extent defined in and through our interaction with society.

Some people think that sex is for fun, others think that its purpose is
having babies. But where do such ideas come from? It is not enough
to say that these are points of view that different people happen to
have and that we are, after all, living in a pluralist society. It is probably more accurate to say that people *receive* such views than that
they generate the ideas themselves.

It may be the case that, having absorbed such views, people move
on from absorbing these views to a critical reception or rejection of
them. But we should not overestimate the amount of critical thinking that goes on. It is more likely to be the case that many people –
notably younger people in our culture – uncritically accept what
they are being told. Here as elsewhere, conscience and freedom do
not come that easily.

To say that sexuality is socially constructed means that we are being
told what to think about our sexuality and how to experience our
sexuality. 'Told by whom?' one might ask. Recalling what we said
about conscience and community, it is probably the case that there
are a number of voices telling us different things. Perhaps we are
being told at the same time that sex is for fun and that sex is for having babies, by the different voices of the different communities in
which we participate. Perhaps we are being told both good things
and misleading things about our sexuality. And amongst these
voices some presumably dominate the cultural scene and determine the general consensus among different groups.

Think for instance of the account of sex and sexuality that is to be
found in a wide variety of magazines and television programmes
and advertising and music. One group of young adults made the
following analysis. Promiscuity is in, except to be careful of sexually
transmitted diseases. Monogamy is out. Sex is something to be
good at. It is for your own pleasure rather than for the other; it is not

relational. It is casual. It is easy, the most natural thing in the world, to go to bed with somebody (anybody). There is very little about it that has to do with the person.

It is not just that this view is out there somewhere. It is much more insistent than that. We are being told what to think. Our understanding of sexual desire and sexual pleasure is being defined from outside of ourselves. Our sexual identity is being constructed by social forces. We could say that in a very real sense our sexual desire is society subjectively reproduced. To say the least, it is in our interests to become critically conscious of this social constitution of our sexuality. Being able to think for ourselves has rarely been so important, given the impoverished quality of much of what is being communicated to us.

We could say that there is now a huge question mark hanging over the very meaning of sex. This is perhaps the ultimate, though obscurely expressed, concern of the Church's documents. Sex does not have to be for having babies any longer. In fact, babies can be generated without any sex at all. If sex need not be for procreation, then what is it for? Is it for love, and if so, just what does that mean? Is it just for fun? Not alone that, but it seems it may be experienced with someone of the same gender as oneself. What does that imply for the meaning of what sex is?

Thus it could be argued that the society we live in is undergoing a profound trauma about the very meaning of sex and sexuality. And we are all part of the confusion and the searching. It is true that, in some ways, ours is an age of enlightenment and liberation in its appreciation of sexual freedom and sexual pleasure. But, in other ways, it is simply that we have lost our bearings.

Where does Christianity stand in all this? Some would say that it is the repressive sexual mores of religion that we have been liberated from. Nobody can deny the truth there is in that. But are there resources in Christianity for offering an alternative account to that which predominates today, particularly in the media? Are there resources for building on the positive aspects of the contemporary experience of sexuality? Some would think not, after all we have been through. But there is more to what Christianity has to say about sex than what many people have yet heard.

The Spiritual and the Sexual

It is difficult to sort out the sources of the negativity in the Christian view of sex and sexuality. But they would seem to go a long way back. For instance, there were theologians in the fourth and fifth centuries who thought that sexual desire was corrupted for ever by the fall, or that sexual intercourse came into the world as a result of original sin and that in paradise there would have been some more seemly way of generating offspring. We might be inclined to conclude that Christianity's understanding of the sexual is inherently distorted.

Things, however, are not quite so clear-cut. Apart from anything else, there is no reason to think that negativity about the sexual is a specifically Christian phenomenon. More positively, it would seem that the key factor governing early Christian thinking in this area was its sense of the relationship of this world to the next. This was the sense that the death and resurrection of Christ bring the present age to an end and usher in God's future. The fragility of this world is laid bare and Christians orient themselves to the age to come, already inaugurated in Christ.

This consciousness soon began to express itself in the practice of sexual renunciation. The movement towards virginity grew stronger and stronger, and it assumed the status previously held by martyrdom. In this process there was a shift away from seeing death as the measure of human frailty. Sex was now seen to be that measure, the weakpoint in our fallen humanity. Sexuality and procreation were seen to be what perpetuates the present age, so that sexual renunciation as it were 'throws the switch' and liberates the body for the new world.

The consciousness grew that sexuality clings to this world and coarsens the spirit, whereas abstinence lets go of time and makes the body a better vehicle for the divine. Much of this represents, not so much hatred of the body, as a desire for the transformation of the body. But it gradually becomes something negative. Ambrose is said to have viewed the body in its frailty as 'a perilous mudslick, on which the firm tread of the soul's resolve might slip and tumble at any moment.'[3] Soon after him, Augustine understood sexuality to speak of one thing only, the fall, leaving us with a permanent derangement of the sexual urge. The only sexual intercourse that was without fault was that engaged in for the purpose of procreation.

The subsequent reception of this heritage was one where sexuality and spirituality were sharply disjoined. Sexuality was not understood as part of the practice of Christianity, as a condition in which spiritual growth was possible. If marriage was valued, it was not because of its nature as a sexual relationship, but for its place in society. Sexual activity as such was not the focus of appreciation. Thus there has been an inability to imagine how sexual experience might contribute to the formation or cultivation of the spiritual self. For such cultivation celibacy was seen as much more appropriate.

The effects of this consciousness are evident in what was, until recent times, the definition of chastity. The following is from a moral theology textbook of the 1930s:

> 'Chastity is the moral virtue that controls in the married and altogether excludes in the unmarried all voluntary expression of the sensitive appetite for venereal pleasure... This virtue connotes a great victory over an imperious appetite.'[4]

This suggests that people must keep the lid on their sexuality at all times and only remove the lid for the sake of procreation. Sexuality is a danger, an 'imperious appetite'. Ideally it is altogether suppressed. There is no sense that it is a good or even ordinary part of human experience. This is far from the understanding of virtue as loving vision that we spoke of earlier.

Sexuality and Salvation

The negativity in all this must be acknowledged. Nevertheless, the original motivating experience was not itself negative. That motivation concerned the way in which the world was experienced as a result of faith in the resurrection of Christ. Everything was seen in the light of the glory to come and this led to the prizing of virginity. This in turn made for the gradual downgrading of the body.

But this is not to say that seeing life from the perspective of the world to come necessarily means a suspicion of the sexual. Indeed, when we look again at the Christian tradition we can find other, more positive threads, that lead us to think that it is not beyond the imagination of Christianity as such to see sexual experience as contributing to the cultivation of the Christian self, as a genuine experience of the spiritual.

There is, first of all, the Genesis story of the creation of man and woman. The context against which this account was composed was one where the surrounding Canaanite religions had sacralised sex. Sex and fertility were linked directly to the gods. Worship of the fertility gods, male and female, was seen as a magical means of gaining fertility for both land and wives. Part of this worship were the orgies of prostitution that took place in the temples.

The story of Genesis stands as a desacralisation or demystification of sex. Sex is not something divine, even though it is something created by the divinity. It simply part of creation, and a good part at that. 'God saw everything he had made, and indeed, it was very good.' Because they are part of God's good creation, sexuality and the togetherness of man and woman are simply good.

Next, the Song of Solomon is a book about the love between a man and a woman. It is romantic and it is erotic. 'Your rounded thighs are like jewels, the work of a master hand... Oh, may your breasts be like clusters of the vine, and the scent of your breath like apples, and your kisses like the best wine.' Again: 'I am my beloved's, and his desire is for me. Come, my beloved, let us go forth into the fields, and lodge in the villages; let us go out early to the vineyards... There I will give you my love' (Song 7:1, 8-9, 10-12).

Yet, the Song of Solomon never mentions God! Perhaps there is no need to mention God. Perhaps the very inclusion of this book in the Bible is testimony that the book is a celebration of sexuality and the sexual love between a man and a woman as a good gift of the Creator. Later times would interpret the book spiritually as standing for our relationship of love with the Lord, and that is quite valid and valuable. But it is not what the book is basically about.

Again, we can refer of the prophets' struggle to bring the people back to a sense of their covenant relationship to God and of their covenant obligations to one another. Among the many images that spoke to them of God, the one that spoke most deeply was that of man-woman. The nearest thing in all creation to what God is like, the created thing that speaks most eloquently of God, is the love between a man and a woman.

Turning to the New Testament, we find further resources for a Christian affirmation of sexuality and the body. There are, first of all, the accounts of Jesus' encounters with women. There is Mary Magdalen; there is his encounter with the woman of Samaria (John 4); there is his meeting with the woman who was a sinner (Luke 7: 36-50).

In the latter encounter, one is struck by the sensuous tone, as the woman 'stood behind him at his feet, weeping, and began to bathe his feet with her tears and to dry them with her hair. Then she continued kissing his feet and anointing them with the ointment' (Luke 7:38). In the encounter with the woman of Samaria, a significant part of the atmosphere is supplied by the awareness that in an isolated place a man and a woman encounter each other as man and woman.

These stories are stories of significant human encounters between man and woman. The texture of the stories tells us of something other than a disembodied experience. And at the same time they are stories of salvation. They are encounters where sexuality and salvation become part of one another. Salvation may be sensed, while sexuality can be saved and saving.

At a more general level there is the event itself of the crucifixion. Here the human body becomes the very medium of redemption. 'The Word became flesh.' God does not redeem just our souls but our whole selves. The Irish word for salvation, *slánú*, is indicative of the person being made whole. And God does so in and through the body itself. Through the body we are saved; not by fleeing the body, but through the body.

A friend of mine tells the story of the birth of her first child. There were five or six women in the ward and there was the same feeling among them, a feeling of 'do anything you must to me, as long as this child is alright'. Her subsequent experience bore out this willingness to give her body for this new life. She gave birth on a Saturday and on Sunday was well enough to go to the hospital chapel for Mass. At the Mass, the words of consecration affected her as never before and had almost a physical impact. 'This is my body, given up for you... this is my blood, poured out for you.' Her reaction was: 'Jesus! I know what you mean!' It was a feeling that she and Jesus were like-minded. We might add the comment that the core of this woman's sexuality and the core of God's identity fused together.

Celebrating the Body

These are just some of the grounds for a positive Christian theology of sexuality and the body. They suggest something quite different from the idea of chastity as suppressing our sexuality. Rather, they suggest a positive, appreciative attitude to sexuality as something to be grateful for – to be grateful for, as D.H. Lawrence said, like sunshine on a grey day. They suggest that our sexuality is meant to make us smile rather than cry, to bring us joy rather than fear.

In this spirit, Christianity at heart celebrates the body. It sees that sexuality is not to be sacralised and it knows that it is not dirty either. It is the way we are in the world as male and female, a cherished part of us rather than something to be afraid of. Though it can turn bad on us and though we can misuse it, it is given to us so that we may know both that we are lovable and that we are able to love.

We might list some of the words that could be used to describe sexual encounter when it is experienced at its best and deepest. They might include: celebration, intimacy, fun, promise, healing, togetherness, reconciliation, pleasure, trust, revelation, giving, vulnerability, hope, thanksgiving, and many more besides. If such words cannot be used in a given situation, the encounter is probably inappropriate.

But it is the significance of such language that led one prominent writer in this area to say that sex is the great act of prayer in married life.[5] This is not meant to spiritualise sex. Rather, it suggests that sex has the same kind of significance within married love as the eucharist has within the larger Christian community of love. We have only to look at how many of the above words can be used of both.

We can see how this kind of thinking could be the basis for a very stimulating dialogue between Christianity and contemporary culture, regarding today's fundamental question as to the very meaning of sex. At its heart, Christianity is saying that the body is good and that sexuality is wonderful. It does not condemn or distrust the body, though it has done so. And just as there are both positive and negative strands in the Christian tradition concerning sexuality, so too with the world. For all its celebration of the sexual, it may be the world which in the end does not understand.

Take, for example, the idea of being 'good at sex' and what it might mean. One meaning that is current has to do with physical perform-ance, bordering sometimes on the athletic. The account which Christianity offers would speak of pleasure, yes, but of insight as well as instinct, of the will as well as the urge. It would speak about sex being a good part of the person, serving the cause of love in the person's life, being a medium of love and salvation and not of abuse or sadness or fear. It would speak of integrity and integration. It would speak of sexual goodness.

The problem with the contemporary liberalisation of sex is not that sex and sexual desire are wrong. The problem is that they are good and that today's liberalisation does not fully appreciate their good-ness. It is right that sexual experience is being freed from repression and fear and guilt, but the widespread trivialisation of sexual encounter suggests that what has been freed is still not cherished or understood enough.

Solidarity with Suffering

We have been talking about sexuality as socially constructed, and about Christianity as itself a society or community that tells us how we might think about and experience our sexuality. All this has been part of seeing sexual morality as part of social ethics rather than some kind of private affair.

But if sexual morality is understood as social, then we should be able to apply to it the principles which theology draws upon in treating social questions generally. As we saw in the last chapter, one of the foremost principles in contemporary Christian social ethics is what is known as the preferential option for the poor. If sexual morality is social morality, then how does this principle apply to it?

A preferential option for the poor means a preferential attentive-ness to the greatest need. It means solidarity with victims. It means being with those who are suffering. Therefore the question is: who is suffering because of their sexuality? Where is there suffering that is bound up with sexual experience in some way?

There is quite a list. Think of those who suffer sexual violence, people who have been raped or otherwise sexually abused as children or as adults. The pain of this probably never goes away. Think of those who have had an abortion, who experienced the trauma of having to decide and now experience the pain of having decided. Think of the victims of pornography, particularly of the women and children drawn into its production, as well as the adults and children harmed by its consumption. Think of all who suffer because of society's trivialisation or casualisation of sex; perhaps it is the young who suffer most. Think of the painful confusion that attends the emergence of sexual identity and the achievement of sexual peace.

Then there are the many people whose marriages have broken up, many of whom would say that the trauma is comparable to that of a death in the family. There are many others whose marriages have not ended but continue as a living nightmare, whether because of violence or of years of almost total non-communication. And there are many others who, after undergoing the trauma of break-up, find another partner and perhaps their first experience of what marriage was meant to be like, only to find that their Church refuses them communion, and perhaps also that their own parents do not accept them.

The list goes on. There are many who suffer for reasons to do with fertility. Perhaps they have painfully discovered they cannot have children, and perhaps the pain is prolonged by knowing the Church's opposition to some of the new reproductive technologies. Or perhaps they are fertile and trying to regulate their fertility, but are pained by what the Church's teaching asks of them here. There are many who do not have the typical marriage, but are single-parents, or deserted, and often experience life as a great struggle. And there are those whose experience is even less typical because they are homosexual, and who have to deal with both confusion within and discrimination without.

Others are disabled, and that has its own complications and pain in the quest for sexual peace. Others suffer intense guilt, for instance if afflicted with a long-term habit of masturbation. And others, though we might find it harder to understand, suffer because they have abused their own sexuality or because they are victims of their own deviation.

It is quite disturbing to think just how much human suffering is bound up with sexuality and how often the experience of sexuality is an experience of pain. As a Church, our reaction must be to blush at our lack of awareness. But it is not just lack of awareness. It is that when there is an awareness of suffering, it does not always receive the priority that the option for the poor demands.

For instance, in the documents on homosexuality and on infertility mentioned above, there is reference to the suffering involved, but it comes late, after the moral issues have been worked out and couched in the language of 'carrying one's cross'. If there is to be preferential attention to suffering, then this should come first and not as what appears to be an afterthought. This in itself is a moral issue.

Again, we might note how few Church pronouncements there are on pornography, as compared to the amount of attention given to contraception. The imbalance is huge and certainly the proportions do not correspond to the relative harm being done. There would seem to be priorities and preoccupations at work other than the priority of suffering.

Solidarity with suffering would mean two things. First of all, it would mean listening, so that suffering may be voiced. Most suffering is silent and unheard; most of those who suffer do not have a voice in any case. So solidarity means attending, listening to the pain being expressed, accepting it as part of the life of the community. At the very least, those who suffer may come to feel that their pain matters, and matters more perhaps than some of our other concerns in this area of morality.

Secondly, solidarity means asking 'why?' Just as the compassion of Jesus signified that the hurt was not to be accepted as normal, and led him to criticise those who were the cause of it, so here also, solidarity leads to wanting to know why the pain is happening and what or who is causing it.

Certainly in the case of some of the suffering we have listed, solidarity will lead to a critique of society, along the lines of what was quoted above from John Paul II concerning society and abortion. Similar critique might be directed at society's intolerance of its homosexual members, or at its toleration of freely available pornography, or at its seeming lack of interest in searching out the causes of marriage breakdown. But the motivation of such critique would be a solidarity with the victims and the passionate desire that there be no more victims in the future.

A Prophetic Church

All of this would make for a prophetic style on the part of the Church, expressing its positive theology of sexuality in a solidarity with those who know little other than the pain of sexuality, and in a commitment to confronting those forces in society that make things thus. Like prophecy generally, it will not be easy. On the one hand, financial interests are making a lot of profit out of sexuality and those who are profiting will resist change. On the other hand, those who are victims are often unaware of the reality of their situation and will find it incomprehensible to be told that they might be victims.

This shift to a social context for thinking about sexual morality will help rather than hinder the so-called objective style of moral teaching in the Church. It roots questions of right and wrong concretely in what is going on in society and confronts this with a positive vision of what might be. This does not mean that people will respond, but they cannot say that what they are rejecting is some set of obsolete, worn-out, abstract principles that bear no relevance to reality as it is being experienced.

But there is a further challenge to the Church itself. Attending to suffering means listening, but listening has a price. To listen is to take the other seriously and to take on board what is heard. To listen is to be open to being influenced by what is heard. To listen to people's sexual experience includes accepting whatever implications that experience may have for our understanding of sexual goodness and of sexual right and wrong. This topic brings us beyond the theme of suffering and sexuality to the more general theme of a listening Church.

CHAPTER 13

The Church as Home

In the case of the Christian, morality as a social reality is lived out most deeply in the context of the Christian community or Church. This final chapter will be exploring how we might think about this and it will do so by elaborating on the image of the Church as 'home'.

Church

The word 'Church' may not sit too easily here as it can be suggestive of an enormous, world-wide organisational structure, far from our picture of what a home would be. So perhaps, when the word Church is used, we might also think of community and of the local parish community, rather than only of the global institution. Indeed, the parish is itself the universal Church in a particular place. It is, in the words of John Paul II's *Christifideles Laici:*

> 'the place where the very 'mystery' of the Church is present... not principally a structure, a territory, or a building, but rather 'the family of God'... the parish is the Church placed in the neighbourhoods of humanity.'[1]

We must be careful not to divorce the universal Church and the local Church from each other. What we will be saying in what follows is about the way moral living might be experienced in the local Christian community. But this will have substantial implications for the way the Church at the more global level goes about its moral teaching. Otherwise there is danger of an intolerable tension between what is experienced locally and what is promulgated globally.

Clubs and Rules

The association of the words 'Church' and 'morality' has a bad feel for many people. It will feel even worse if there lies behind the feeling a personal experience of hurt or condemnation. For very many,

Church morality is suggestive of all that is felt to be negative about morality. It is about fear and it is about guilt. It is about authoritarian teaching that seems to have little conception of what it is to be an autonomous adult human being. It is about obscure argumentation whose connection to the real world is hard to grasp. It is about teachings that lack credibility because of their failure to square with experience. It can even be about the scandal of discovering that not all who occupied the 'high moral ground' were all that they seemed.

That this is not the whole picture hardly needs to be stated. Hopefully, previous chapters will have communicated much of what is positive and prophetic in the Christian moral vision. Nevertheless, what we are describing is a significant strand and it deserves to be addressed as a matter of some importance, as it is the cause of both pain and alienation. Ultimately it harms the Church itself also, in that people cease to regard their Church as an authoritative interpreter of their moral experience.

In all of this there is, of course, the view that the problem does not lie with the Church at all, but with its members. One way in which this view is expressed is in the image of the '*à la carte* Catholic'. This image is meant to represent those who see conscience as itself the creator of right and wrong, and who believe and do as they themselves please. They see freedom as the power to do what they themselves want. Thus these people pick and choose from amongst the moral teachings of the Church according to personal preference.

This is quite a powerful image but one which, on reflection, is quite objectionable in what it implies both about individual disciples and about the Church itself. It implies, first of all, that anybody who disagrees with anything the Church teaches is a kind of casual Christian whose moral behaviour is a matter of following whims and who regards the teaching of the Church as being about as weighty as today's newspaper editorial.

This is a considerable injustice to the very many who find themselves in disagreement and who are far from casual in their discipleship. Their lives are characterised by a deep relationship with Christ and a strong attachment to the Christian community. Their being out of step with the Church on a particular moral issue is a source of great concern and agony, so much so that many would sooner cease the practice of their religion than feel themselves hypocrites by going to Church while still out of step. Meanwhile, if we were to take a larger view, we would sometimes find their discipleship to be a far more inspiring witness than that of many who have no particular disagreement with Church teaching at all.

Secondly, the image of the *à la carte* Catholic contains implicit within it an image of the Church which is woefully inadequate and which, because it remains implicit, is allowed to fester. It suggests that the Church is like a club or an organisation where, on joining, people are presented with the rules and told that if they do not like any of them they are free to approach any of the other clubs or organisations in the area. It is as simple as the whole package or nothing.

This is what the image implies and some would say that it captures something that is actually true of the Church. The image suggests a group that tends more to exclude than to include, a group more interested that people conform than that they belong. If it is true at all, what perhaps is most sad about it is that the image is so impersonal. It suggests no bond at all of intimacy between the person and the Church, no prior family affinity, but instead a cold, clinical transaction.

The Church itself might want to acknowledge that it has been guilty of this way of being. But what is deeply wrong with the image of the *à la carte* Catholic is that it implies that this is what the Church should be like all the time. It says that the Church should be hard and strict about rules and regulations, that it should treat people according to the law, and that it should keep its membership pure. The question then is: is this what the Church is meant to be and, if not, what it is meant to be like?

The Church as Home

In response to this question we would offer the alternative image of the Church as 'home', as one which provides a much richer context within which to consider these concerns about morality. The image is already implicit in the above quotation's description of the parish as 'the family of God'. Another way of looking at it would be to say that if the family is seen as 'the domestic Church', then the obverse of this is to see the Church as the home writ large.

The spirit in which the image of home is intended, is captured well in the dialogue of Robert Frost's poem, *The Death of the Hired Man:*

'Home,' he mocked gently.
'Yes, what else but home?
It all depends on what you mean by home.
Of course he's nothing to us, any more
Than was the hound that came a stranger to us
Out of the woods, worn out upon the trail.'
'Home is the place where, when you have to go there,
They have to take you in.'
'I should have called it
Something you somehow haven't to deserve.'

Home is where a person always belongs, where there is always a place at the table, where belonging does not have to be earned. This is true even for the black sheep of the family, though there may be a process of time involved. Gradually, eventually, while things may never be what they used to be, people will come to break bread together again.

It is unnatural, though understandable, if this does not come about. Imagine that a man, whose marriage has been a disaster and who, after the parting of ways, comes to love another, decides with her that they will live their lives together. Imagine that this man's mother cannot accept what he has decided and is so unable to accept it that she will not have anything to do with him again, even to the extent of eliminating his name from her conversations, so that it is almost as if he had ceased to exist. Imagine her going to the grave like this. We can appreciate the deep pain, while at the same time recognising that it would be so unnatural, so much the opposite of what home means.

To speak of the Church as home is to see the Church as always open to accommodate those who belong to the family. It is to see the community as called to be what *Christifideles Laici* described as 'a house of welcome to all and a place of service to all' – in a passage which goes on to quote Pope John XXIII's image of the parish as the village fountain to which all might have recourse in their thirst.[2]

This way of thinking may make for a messy rather than a tidy place. It will not be conducive to a membership consisting only of the pure and worthy. There will be a varied membership, including the wounded and the damaged, the imperfect and the inadequate, the sinner and the failure, as well as people with differing perspectives – because it will be open to all who in their thirst are drawn to the village fountain.

Such a home would be a place of hospitality. The emphasis would be on inclusiveness rather than exclusion, on ensuring that all would feel welcome, no matter what their situation, and that all would sense that they belong. An attitude of exclusion would want to check the credentials of all before they enter, to see where they have been. Hospitality would sit everybody down. Turning up at the door would of itself signal the disposition that gains entry. Hospitality would look to the future rather than the past.

If we refer this line of thought back to the gospels, a passage to consider might be that of the story of the prodigal son (Luke 15:11-32). Usually it is understood as a story of God's mercy which precedes and embraces our repentance. Perhaps, though, it may also be taken as an image of the Church. Hospitality, arms open in anticipation because, quite simply, this is a son coming home.

We might develop this imagery further by suggesting that the elder son represents another image of Church, one that is closer to that implied in the idea of the *à la carte* Catholic. Here hospitality, as well as the sense of family, fade into the background with the words: 'But when this son of yours came back, who has devoured your property with prostitutes...' Everything is defined by the past and a price will be exacted before there is any entry.

Thinking of the Church as home and as a place of hospitality also brings to mind Jesus' practice of table-fellowship. It is well known that association and table-fellowship with tax collectors and sinners was one of the most distinctive aspects of Jesus' ministry (e.g. Mark 2:13-17). But the gospels also present Jesus as eating on a number of occasions in the houses of the Pharisees (e.g. Luke 7:36; 11:37; 14:1). Hospitality as an attitude and practice of Jesus means an openness to everybody. It is in stark contrast to the hospitality of his Pharisee hosts, which makes a sharp division between those who are clean and those who are unclean.

One might object that this seems to imply that anything goes. What of those whose lives are a positive contradiction to the Christian vision? What of those who come casually, uncommitted, yet expecting the same access as anybody else, to the sacraments for instance? Obviously such cases make the implementation of the image difficult. The point, though, has to do with the fundamental attitude which the image of home conveys, that of thinking in terms of inclusiveness and belonging, thinking in terms of 'this is family'.

It should also be noted that the somewhat cynical disposition of the so-called *à la carte* Catholic does not at all represent the disposition of most of those we are talking about. Generally, those who are anywhere near the door and desirous of belonging are far from cynical or hypocritical, and are at least as single-minded in their commitment as others who sit comfortably inside by the fire.

Listening

Home is a place where parents are attentive to all that is going on in the lives of their children. Ideally there is time spent individually with each child, whereby each has a sense that his or her story is both known and cared for. There are places like the kitchen table where difficulties are worked through and where, when something has been messed up, the sense of threat is eased by the assurance of care.

If the Church is home for all its disciples, it likewise attends to what is going on in their lives. As with the kitchen table in the household, there is a forum for discussing things that come up. People have a sense that their experience counts and has authority and, complementing this and sometimes because of this, they have a deep respect and thirst for the common wisdom.

But if the approach is that everything is already worked out and all the lines are drawn, then experience does not matter. Worse still, if everything is worked out and people find that it conflicts with their experience, then there is a real impasse. On one side there is a feeling of dissent or at least of some of the faithful being blinded to the truth. On the other there is a suspicion that those in authority do not have the truth about what they are pronouncing upon and cannot therefore be trusted.

In such a situation the way forward is listening. Much as when there is an impasse at home, positions entrenched, and the lines of communication down, the only way forward is the kitchen table. People have to sit down and talk and everybody has to be listened to properly. In this spirit we would suggest that much could be put right and much could be transformed in the experience of morality in the Church, if listening were put at the top of the agenda.

An image that it may be helpful to keep in the background here is that of the potter and the clay, an image with which the Bible expresses something of our relationship with God. 'Just like the clay in the potter's hand, so are you in my hand, O house of Israel' (Jeremiah 18:6). There is something about this image that we resist. It makes it appear as if we are totally dependent, completely pliable, without self-determination. It contradicts our sense of ourselves as mature, responsible Christians.

It is good, then, to listen to what a potter would say about the imagery. If you and I were potters, we would know as potters to respect the clay in our hands. We would not just do as we wanted with the clay. But we would hold the clay in our hands and allow it to speak to us. We would listen to the clay and allow the form to emerge, to speak itself to us. While always able to mould and remould the clay, we would always respect the material that is under our hands.

If this is an image for God and ourselves, it means that God listens to us intently and respectfully. In the silence of God we are given space to speak and what we say matters to God. The form of our life emerges out of our conversation. But if this is an image for God and ourselves, it is also an image for the Church and ourselves. It means that listening to God's people is at the heart of what goes on in the Church. It means that in the Church, God's truth is to be found when God's people are 'heard into speech'.

Yet one suspects that the experience of Church and morality for many of God's people is an experience of being silent. Silence is of course appropriate where somebody is not qualified to speak, but this is different. There is something not quite right when, with regard to areas of moral experience that mature, adult Christians encounter daily and have reflected deeply upon and have struggled faithfully with, their only role is one of silence. With regard to these areas of experience, they find themselves having to listen while oth-

ers tell them what their experience means. Whether what these others say is right or wrong is not the point here; it is that it is only
these others who have a say.

A New Style of Teaching

One of the most celebrated passages in Vatican II's *The Church in the
Modern World* is one which gives a primacy to listening. 'At all times
the Church carries the responsibility of reading the signs of the time
and of interpreting them in the light of the gospel, if it is to carry out
its task' (paragraph 4). This is the direction in which our reflections
are moving, namely, that listening should be an intrinsic moment in
the moral teaching of the Church.

Since this is sometimes misinterpreted as meaning that moral truth
can be decided by taking a vote or that everything is up for review,
some illustrations will help clarify what is meant. In 1992 the Irish
Bishops published a major document on work and unemployment.
Perhaps the most significant aspect of its preparation was the exten-
sive consultation that went on, particularly in listening to the experience of unemployed people. The effects of this process on the final
document are palpable, and in the introduction the Bishops say:

> 'We earnestly hope that the process of consultation and dialogue
> which has marked the preparation of this Pastoral will intensify
> and deepen after its publication. We do not see publication as an
> end in itself but as contributing to the clarification of the root
> causes of our high unemployment and emigration, and to the
> fostering of the solidarity needed to combat them.'[3]

More elaborate examples come from the bishops of the United
States. During the 1980s they published two major pastoral letters,
one on war and peace and the other on the economy. In each case
there was widespread consultation before a draft letter was published, which was then revised in the light of feedback, and a second draft was presented before each document was finalised.
Introducing the letter on war and peace, the bishops say:

> 'The experience of preparing this letter has manifested to us the
> range of strongly held opinion in the Catholic community on
> questions of fact and judgement concerning issues of war and
> peace. We urge mutual respect among individuals and groups

in the Church... we believe that such differences should be expressed within the framework of Catholic moral teaching. We need in the Church not only conviction and commitment but also civility and charity.'[4]

And in introducing the letter on the economy the bishops say: 'The pastoral letter has been a work of careful inquiry, wide consultation and prayerful discernment. The letter has been greatly enriched by this process of listening and refinement.'[5]

These three documents represent a new style of teaching. What is new is that teaching is envisaged as a process where listening is an intrinsic moment. Presumably not everything in Christian faith and doctrine would be the subject-matter of this teaching process. Rather, what it concerns is the translation of the Christian vision into a response to specific issues and the discernment of what constitutes moral truth in particular contexts. What is new is the recognition that part of the process of translating and discerning is listening to the experience and reflection of God's people.

In such a view of teaching, the Spirit is present in the whole Church, and it is recognised that the Spirit may speak from anywhere within the Church. In this way listening embraces all God's people. While some are leaders, this does not mean that the Spirit speaks only through them. Rather, part of the charism of leadership is to listen to the signs of the times and to what the Spirit is saying to and through God's people.

All of these documents concern what would be called issues of social morality. We have seen, however, that issues of sexual morality are also to be regarded as issues of social morality. This means that, just as with the principle of the option for the poor, so too the principle of incorporating listening into the teaching process would apply to issues of sexual morality. Indeed, just as the moral experience of mature, committed disciples includes wrestling with questions of unemployment and questions of war and violence, even more so does that experience include the whole area of sexual morality.

This would mean that just as the experience of being unemployed has entered into the fabric of teaching about work, so too the experience of sexuality would enter into the fabric of teaching about sexuality. The experience and reflections of married people would contribute to teaching about sexuality and marriage and the regulation of conception. The experience of the infertile would contribute to teaching about the alleviation of infertility. The experience and reflections of homosexual Christians would be a moment in the teaching about homosexuality.

Possibly most significant, and crossing these different categories, the sexual experience of women might be heard and incorporated. This listening would touch on the whole range of sexual ethics, and would certainly feed into the teaching on the many moral issues to do with fertility and reproduction.

For, as is widely recognised, we cannot understate the extent to which teaching on sexual morality has up to now been formulated and defined exclusively by men. Some would claim that the problem with the Church's sexual teaching is that it is far too conservative. But it is probably far more significant that the teaching, be it conservative or anything else, has been the product of the thinking of men only. In other words, the voice of half the Church has not been heard, its experience and perspective not taken into account.

Trust in the Process

It is worth emphasising that the concern for listening is a concern more for the process than the content of moral teaching. If listening to the experience and reflection of God's people becomes an intrinsic moment in the process of formulating moral teaching, it may or may not modify the content of that teaching. But that is not the point. The point is that, on a matter of principle, such listening should constitute an intrinsic part of the teaching process. What comes up will then have to be acknowledged for whatever truth it possesses.

On this view, the teaching process is as much a matter of opening up questions as of closing them down, as much a matter of provoking thought as of ending it. There is a phrase that says: 'Rome has spoken, the matter is closed', but many would feel that often the matter never gets to be opened. Definition precedes discussion. To incorporate listening, on the model of the documents referred to, is to open up a process of provoking thought, stimulating debate, being enriched by what has been called 'the light of disagreement', so as gradually to come to the teaching as the culmination of a process that has been characterised throughout by its inclusiveness.

There is a theme of trust in all this and it manifests itself in a number of ways. There is, first of all, the trust placed in adult, mature Christians. We all know that being listened to is a dignifying experience and that to be ignored or unheard is humiliating. In this case, listening is a recognition that God's people are committed and responsible. It recognises that they have personal experience of many of the moral issues the Church has to speak about. It recognises that their reflection on their experience, as mature, adult Christians, has put them in touch with the moral truth in different areas of experience.

There is, secondly, the trust placed in the truth itself. Back in the thirteenth century, the theology of Thomas Aquinas represented an integration of the Christian tradition with the pre-Christian philosophy of Aristotle, a synthesis of faith and reason. A quality of this synthesis was Aquinas' conviction that the truth of reason could not contradict the truth of Christian faith (*Summa Contra Gentiles*, book one, chapter seven).

The conviction is a trust in the search for truth. Just as Aquinas trusted that the truth of Aristotle's philosophy would not and could not contradict the truth of Christian faith, so we may trust that listening for the truth in the moral experience and reflection of Christian people will not contradict, but will rather enrich our appreciation of the truth of the Christian faith.

In fact, one need not suppose that there is going to be large-scale opposition or contradiction. We are talking about a process that brings together inner wisdom and collective wisdom. We are talking about the collective wisdom of the Christian tradition on one hand, and the inner wisdom of adult, responsible disciples on the other. This would lead us to expect convergence rather than divergence, more consensus than conflict. It would lead us to expect that what conflict there is will not concern fundamental vision and values so much as their detailed specification.

Thirdly, the process of listening will make for a renewed trust in authority itself. Teachers and parents will both have had the experience that if they respectfully listen to the children in their care, rather than dogmatically dictate to them, the children will then be more likely to want to know the teacher's or parent's own view. Respectful listening begets respectful listening. The mentality of 'us-them' shifts into a mentality of 'we'. Listening becomes mutual, between the inner and the collective wisdom. Real love for authority, a seeming contradiction in terms today, becomes a real prospect.

Part of the significance of this is that one of the notable causes of disagreement or disaffection with Church teaching is a lack of appreciation of the grounds and rationale of that teaching. Most people know what the Church says about many prominent moral issues, but far fewer people know *why* the Church says what it says. When mutual listening develops, this situation can be changed.

Public Opinion

This last point brings us to a somewhat neglected thread in what the Church says relative to these matters. We refer to a series of statements in various contexts over recent decades concerning the desirability of an ethos in the Church that encourages public opin-ion and freedom of expression. We say 'neglected' because there seems to be little awareness of just how much is affirmed in these statements.

In 1950, Pope Pius XII spoke of public opinion as the natural portion of any human society. 'Whenever there is no manifest expression of public opinion at all, and above all whenever one must admit that public opinion does not at all exist, this lack must be regarded as a fault, a weakness and a disease in the life of that society.' This applies too to the Church concerning matters that are 'left to free discussion'; 'there would be something lacking in her life if there were no public opinion in the Church.'[6]

Vatican II's *The Church in the Modern World* encourages such a spirit in a number of passages. In the context of culture generally, it affirms the freedom to search for the truth and to express one's opinions (paragraph 59). Among Christians it recognises that they have to shoulder the responsibility for applying their faith to life in the world, and that the same Christian vision will often lead people to see a particular problem quite differently from each other; such situations should be informed by a spirit of sincere dialogue (para-graph 43). And as regards theological research, it recognises that 'all the faithful, both clerical and lay, possess a lawful freedom of inquiry, of thought, and the freedom to express their minds humbly and courageously about those matters in which they enjoy competence' (paragraph 62).

The 1971 Vatican document on communications speaks with striking confidence about public opinion within the Church:

> 'Since the Church is a living body, she needs public opinion... Catholics should be fully aware of the real freedom to speak their minds which stems from a 'feeling for the faith' and from love... Those who exercise authority in the Church will take care to ensure that there is responsible exchange of freely held and expressed opinion among the people of God... There is an enormous area where members of the Church can express their views... This free dialogue within the Church does no injury to her unity and solidarity.'[7]

Finally, twenty years later, a further publication on the same themes, after speaking of the need for the Church to 'maintain an active, listening presence in relation to the world', goes on to speak of the Church's own life:

> 'Along with all this, it is necessary constantly to recall the importance of the fundamental right of dialogue and information within the Church... Among the members of the community... there is a radical equality in dignity and mission... and this equality necessarily will express itself in an honest and respectful sharing of information and opinions.'[8]

The document sees this necessity as being both a matter of credibility and, more fundamentally, a matter of concretely expressing the nature of the Church as communion. It is also, of course, an eminently practical and pragmatic matter. Quite apart from listening as a theological principle, it is common sense that the leadership in the Church would want to know what its people are feeling and what is the actual situation among its members.

These documents do, of course, make the qualifications we would expect, such as that not every aspect of Christian life is a matter for open-ended discussion. But it is the spirit of these statements that is most striking. It is a spirit of confidence in God's Spirit working

among God's people. It is a spirit of conviction about the fundamental importance of allowing God's Spirit to speak through the
experiences and reflections of God's people.

Such a listening spirit makes real the image of the Church as home.
This picture of the Christian community as a listening family is well
expressed in a Lenten pastoral letter of the Archbishop of Dublin,
which sees listening as the way to bridge the gap that is there
between what the Church is saying and what its members are
experiencing:

> 'The parish itself of course is a pattern of family... And it is only
> when the parish actually functions as a family, reaching out to
> embrace all families, and listening to the needs of families in a
> genuine and open manner, that it can begin to bridge the gap
> which sadly exists between the teaching of the Church and the
> perceptions and lived experience of many of its members.'[9]

The image of bridging the gap suggests that all are suffering in the
current situation, both the teaching Church and the members of the
faithful. The listening dialogue that would bridge the gap would
therefore serve both, and make for a new harmony between the
moral teaching of the Church and the lived experience of the faithful.

Parish

It is notable that the above quotation envisages the parish as the
place where the gap is to be bridged. This suggests that the Church,
in the sense of the world-wide organisation, may simply be too big
and impersonal to be experienced as home, and that the parish is
the place where such an experience of the Church is possible. This
leads us to conclude with some reflections on the idea of a parish
and on the larger context in which it is home for Christians.

Our word 'parish' has its roots in the Greek word, *paroikia* (which
even sounds like our word, 'parochial'). The stem *oikos* means
dwelling and is the root of the further words, 'economy' and 'ecu-
menical'. The word has a strange story, for *paroikos* originally meant
a neighbour, but came to mean someone from elsewhere, a
stranger.

This contrast of meanings within the one word can be seen in the

New Testament usage. A good translation might be to say that Christians are resident aliens. The first letter of Peter, for example, offers advice on how to live during our time as 'exiles' (1 Peter 1:17; 2:11). It reminds us of the idea that we have here no lasting city but strive for one which is to come (Hebrews 13:14). In a sense, this was always the way with God's people. Abraham lived here as in a foreign city, looking forward to the city whose builder is God (Hebrews 11:9-10); while Abraham's people lived as resident aliens in the land of Egypt (Acts 7:6; 13:17).

There is the sense throughout that we are sojourners in this world, dwelling in this place as strangers. But to this Paul adds the thought that 'you are no longer strangers and aliens, but you are citizens with the saints and also members of the household of God'; in Christ we are 'built together spiritually into a dwelling place for God' (Ephesians 2:19-22).

So, Christians are at home and they are not at home. They are members of the household on the one hand, and they are resident aliens on the other. They are strangers but they have found their true home. This would suggest that Christians are quite different from anybody else in the world, at least in that this faith-perspective gives them a different way of being in the world. It is different because it is looking forward to its true home and seeking to live life on that basis.

This means that the very last thing that Christians can do is conform to this world and settle down, as it were. Therefore our image of the Church as home does not mean a configuring of Christian existence to the forms of the world. Rather, for Christians to experience the Church as home means to experience participation in a community that is living out of the future, living according to what will be. It means the creation of a community that encourages people to live in terms of their future home, that helps them and heals them to this end. Feeling at home in the Church means feeling at home in God's future.

It requires strength and courage to survive as a resident alien. We may not always be welcome in the world. The future is often unclear. It can be easy to lose sight of our identity. Because of all this, our companions are more important than ever, for keeping the vision in focus and for giving us new courage. In seeking to be faithful disciples with our hearts set on our true home, we nevertheless need to know the Church as a 'home from home'. We need the experience of homeliness that is a foreshadowing of the homely, heavenly banquet envisioned for us by Jesus. The last thing wanted is that any man or woman would lose touch with the community for any reason.

Endnotes

CHAPTER 1

1. Reference might be made here to some other schematisations of different perspectives on morality. H. Richard Niebuhr, *The Responsible Self: An Essay in Christian Moral Philosophy* (San Francisco: Harper and Row, 1978), pages 47-68, presents three 'symbols' with which to understand morality. Louis Monden, *Sin, Liberty and Law* (London: Chapman, 1969), pages 4-17, distinguishes three 'levels' of ethics.

2. For a similar classification, see A. Moser and B. Leers, *Moral Theology: Dead Ends and Ways Forward* (London: Burns and Oates, 1990), pages 2 and 16. The first three chapters are taken up with an analysis of the three approaches, the third approach being seen in terms of Latin American liberation theology.

CHAPTER 2

1. We will not be going into the technical discussion as to when the ten commandments were formulated and how they came to be seen as 'revealed'. For a brief and helpful presentation on this, see Andrew Mayes, 'The Decalogue of Moses: An Enduring Ethical Programme?' in Seán Freyne (editor), *Ethics and the Christian* (Dublin: Columba Press, 1991), pages 25-40. He suggests that the decalogue as we have it is 'a point of arrival rather than a point of departure' (34), a later distillation of material that was originally much more fluid.

2. Thomas Ogletree, *The Use of the Bible in Christian Ethics* (Oxford: Blackwell, 1984), page 51. The whole of chapter three is a helpful discussion of the link between covenant and commandment.

3. The text of Ezekiel 18:1-4 reads: 'The word of the Lord came to me: What do you mean by repeating this proverb concerning the people of Israel, "The parents have eaten sour grapes, and the

children's teeth are set on edge"? As I live, says the Lord God, this proverb shall no more be used by you in Israel. Know that all lives are mine; the life of the parent as well as the life of the child is mine; it is only the person who sins that shall die.' The text reflects the emerging sense of individual responsibility. Each person carries the consequences of his or her own deeds; personal guilt is not inherited.

CHAPTER 3

1. For an accessible presentation of Kohlberg's theory, see Ronald Duska and Mariellen Whelan, *Moral Development: A Guide to Piaget and Kohlberg* (New York: Paulist Press, 1975), pages 42-79 ('Kohlberg's Theory of Moral Development').

2. Pope John Paul II, *Sollicitudo Rei Socialis* – Encyclical Letter for the Twentieth Anniversary of *Populorum Progressio* (1987), paragraph 40.

3. Richard Atherton, *Summons to Serve: The Christian Call to Prison Ministry* (London: Geoffrey Chapman, 1987), page 100. For a discussion of the biblical theme of punishment, see Arthur Hoyles, *Punishment in the Bible* (London: Epworth Press, 1986).

CHAPTER 4

1. Joseph Cardinal Bernardin, *Consistent Ethic of Life* (Kansas: Sheed & Ward, 1988).

2. Quoted in Denis O'Callaghan, 'What is Mortal Sin?', *The Furrow* 25 (1974), page 74.

3. The category of grave or serious sin is recognised in Pope John Paul II's *Reconciliatio et Penitentia* – Apostolic Exhortation on Reconciliation and Penance in the Mission of the Church Today (1984), paragraph 17 – though the passage insists that the essential distinction remains that between sin that is mortal and sin that is not mortal.

4. For an example of this usage, see Pope John Paul II, *Evangelium Vitae* – Encyclical Letter on the Value and Inviolability of Human Life (1995), paragraph 12, which speaks of the many ways in which human life is held cheap and attacked in contemporary society, so as to make for 'a veritable *structure of sin*'.

CHAPTER 5

1. See for example Mark 7:1-4: 'Now when the Pharisees and some of the scribes who had come from Jerusalem gathered around him, they noticed that some of his disciples were eating with defiled hands, that is, without washing them. (For the Pharisees, and all the Jews, do not eat unless they thoroughly wash their hands, thus observing the tradition of the elders; and they do not eat anything from the market unless they wash it; and there are many other traditions that they observe, the washing of cups, pots, and bronze kettles.)'

2. A book which provides stimulating reflections on some of these themes is Dietrich Bonhoeffer's *The Cost of Discipleship* (London: SCM Press, 1959).

CHAPTER 6

1. An excellent reflection on this theme is to be found in John Macquarrie's essay, 'Freedom' in his *In Search of Humanity: A Theological and Philosophical Approach* (London: SCM Press, 1982), pages 10-24.

2. Here we are drawing on the thought of Bernard Lonergan: see his *Method in Theology* (London: Darton, Longman and Todd, 1972), chapter one. Also: 'The Transition from a Classicist World-View to Historical Mindedness' in *A Second Collection* (London: Darton, Longman and Todd, 1974), pages 1-9; and 'Natural Right and Historical Mindedness' in *A Third Collection* (New York: Paulist Press, 1985), pages 169-183.

3. Hans Küng and Karl-Josef Kuschel, *A Global Ethic: The Declaration of the Parliament of the World's Religions* (London: SCM Press, 1993).

CHAPTER 7

1. Pope John Paul II, *Evangelium Vitae*, paragraphs 58-59. See also paragraph 99, which speaks in a spirit of reconciliation to those who have had an abortion.

2. Pope John Paul II, *Veritatis Splendor* – Encyclical Letter on Certain Fundamental Questions of the Church's Moral Teaching (1993), paragraphs 71-83.

3. From a letter which appeared in *The Tablet*, 13th October 1984, page 1017.

4. For a presentation of this theory, see James Gaffney, *Newness of Life: A Modern Introduction to Catholic Ethics* (New York: Paulist Press, 1979), pages 127-136.

5. Pope John Paul II, *Familiaris Consortio* – Apostolic Exhortation on the Role of the Christian Family in the Modern World (1981), paragraph 34.

6. Pope Paul VI, *Humanae Vitae* – Encyclical Letter on the Right Ordering of the Procreation of Children (1968) paragraphs 18, 20, 25.

CHAPTER 8

1. Pope John Paul II, *Sollicitudo Rei Socialis*, paragraph 9 (though there is repeated reference to this idea throughout: cf. paragraphs 8, 17, 19, 23, 28, 33, 34).

2. Vincent MacNamara, *The Truth in Love: Reflections on Christian Morality* (Dublin: Gill and Macmillan, 1988), pages 115, 123, 128. The whole of chapter six ('The Moral Agent: Understanding Ourselves') is an excellent reflection on the themes we are discussing.

3. Iris Murdoch, *The Sovereignty of Good* (London: Routledge and Kegan Paul, 1970), page 54. Murdoch's book elaborates well on many of the themes of the present chapter.

4. Bernard Häring, *Free and Faithful in Christ*, volume one (Slough: St Paul, 1978), pages 201-208. Further New Testament perspectives can be found in Vincent MacNamara, *The Truth in Love*, pages 56-58.

CHAPTER 9

1. Pope John Paul II, *Familiaris Consortio*, paragraph 9.

2. An excellent example of this kind of thinking about conversion is Rosemary Haughton's *The Passionate God* (London: Darton, Longman and Todd, 1981), particularly chapter one.

3. Valerie Saiving, 'The Human Situation: A Feminine View' in Carol Christ and Judith Plaskow (editors), *Womanspirit Rising: A Feminist Reader in Religion* (San Francisco: Harper and Row, 1979), page 37.

4. Eamonn Bredin, 'Discipleship', *The Furrow* 32 (1981), pages 415-427.

CHAPTER 10

1. Pope John Paul II, *Veritatis Splendor*, paragraphs 54-64.

2. Bernard Häring, *Free and Faithful in Christ*, volume three, (Slough: St Paul, 1981) page 214.

3. Frank Sullivan, *Magisterium: Teaching Authority in the Catholic Church* (New York: Paulist Press, 1983), pages 164-166.

CHAPTER 11

1. Pope John Paul, *Sollicitudo Rei Socialis*, paragraph 38.

2. Carol Gilligan, *In a Different Voice: Psychological Theory and Women's Development* (Harvard University Press, 1982), for instance page 100.

3. Pope John Paul II, *Dives in Misercordia* – Encyclical Letter on the Mercy of God (1980), paragraph 12.

4. Most of these documents are collected in Michael Walsh and Brian Davies (editors), *Proclaiming Justice and Peace: One Hundred Years of Catholic Social Teaching* (London: Cafod/Collins, 1991). The collection does not include Pope John Paul's *Centesimus Annus* (1991). For a commentary on some of the major themes of this tradition, see Donal Dorr, *Option for the Poor: A Hundred Years of Vatican Social Teaching* (Dublin: Gill and Macmillan, 1992).

5. Walter Brueggemann's *The Prophetic Imagination* (Philadelphia: Fortress Press, 1978) is an excellent reflection on the themes we are discussing. See also Albert Nolan, *Jesus Before Christianity: The Gospel of Liberation* (London: Darton, Longman and Todd, 1977),

6. For a collection of such texts, see Charles Avila, *Ownership: Early Christian Teaching* (Maryknoll: Orbis Books, 1983).

CHAPTER 12

1. Pope John Paul II, *Evangelium Vitae*, paragraphs 12, 18, 24.

2. Pope John Paul II, *Evangelium Vitae*, paragraph 59.

3. Peter Brown, *The Body in Society: Men, Women and Sexual Renunciation in Early Christianity* (London: Faber and Faber, 1988), page 349. Much of the present discussion is based on this study. See also Margaret Miles, *The Image and Practice of Holiness: A Critique of the Classic Manuals of Devotion* (London: SCM Press, 1989).

4. Henry Davis, *Moral and Pastoral Theology* (London: Sheed and Ward, 1935), volume two, pages 172-173.

5. The comment was made by Jack Dominian, whose writings pre-

sent a very positive Christian theology of sexuality. See for instance his *Sexual Integrity: The Answer to Aids* (London: Darton, Longman and Todd, 1987).

CHAPTER 13

1. Pope John Paul II, *Christifideles Laici* – Apostolic Exhortation on the Vocation and Mission of the Laity (1988), paragraphs 26, 27.

2. Pope John Paul II, *Christifideles Laici*, paragraph 27.

3. The Irish Episcopal Conference, *Work is the Key: Towards an Economy that needs Everyone* (Dublin: Veritas, 1992), paragraph 10. See also the preparatory document from the Council for Social Welfare (a committee of the Bishops' conference), *Unemployment, Jobs and the 1990s* (Dublin: The Council for Social Welfare, 1989), chapter one.

4. National Conference of Catholic Bishops, *The Challenge of Peace: God's Promise and our Response: Pastoral Letter on War and Peace in the Nuclear Age* (Washington D.C.: United States Catholic Conference, 1983), introductory summary.

5. National Conference of Catholic Bishops, *Economic Justice for All: Pastoral Letter on Catholic Social Teaching and the U.S. Economy* (Washington D.C.: United States Catholic Conference, 1986), paragraph 3.

6. Pope Pius XII, Address to International Press Congress. *Osservatore Romano*, 18th February, 1950, quoted in Karl Rahner, *Theological Investigations*, volume 2 (London: Darton, Longman and Todd, 1963), page 261.

7. Pontifical Council for the Instruments of Social Communication, *Communio et Progressio* – Pastoral Instruction on the Means of Social Communication (1971), paragraphs 115-117.

8. Pontifical Council for Social Communications, *Aetatis Novae* – Pastoral Instruction on Social Communications (1992), paragraph 10.

9 Archbishop Desmond Connell, Pastoral Letter on *Catholic Family Life* (Dublin, 1994).

Index